the BINGE WATCHER'S guide to

THE
WEST WING

SEASONS ONE AND TWO

AN UNOFFICIAL COMPANION

Joshua Stein, Ph.D.

For more information contact:
Riverdale Avenue Books
5676 Riverdale Avenue
Riverdale, NY 10471.

www.riverdaleavebooks.com
Design by www.formatting4U.com
Cover by Scott Carpenter

Digital ISBN: 9781626016941

Trade Paperback ISBN: 9781626016958
First Edition, August 2024

Table of Contents

Foreword

The West Wing is a cultural monolith. For many, the show informs how people understand and think about politics, how they imagine what politics should be; for many others, it displays a naivete out of place in the 21st century. *The West Wing* is a show about political characters trying to do their best, morally. The show is formative and strange, because the idea of political actors trying to do the right thing is tantalizing and unfamiliar. There's no space for optimism about politics anymore; some 25 years on from the start of the series, it describes unrecognizable American politics.

I wanted to write this book because *The West Wing* is an opportunity to explore what politics should be, and what it isn't. I want to believe politics can be a space for civil service, for doing what is moral and good, while recognizing that politics is usually a game of power. I turned 18 during the 2008 financial crisis; I watched the spike in homelessness as the mortgage industry collapsed and the increase in unemployment as the auto-industry fell apart. I saw the backlash in the protests and election results, people angry at political and private sector institutions indifferent to the havoc wrought on the lives of so many by the greed and incompetence of a few. The inability of American politics to address clear cases of moral bankruptcy and corruption, leaving the wealthy unaccountable and the vulnerable suffering, made cynicism the political mood. I started writing this book in 2015, as a reflection on the cynicism around what would become the 2016 election; then that election happened, and I struggled to finish the project until 2021 (though I was also working on my Ph.D. at the time, so that should have been my focus anyway).

There have been optimistic moments in the 21st century, moments when it seemed like political leaders were committed to and capable of instituting meaningful change (the most prominent being a Senator from

Illinois elected to the Presidency), only to run headlong into the brick wall of institutional structures, political gridlock, and cynicism that made any change difficult. There have been meaningful moments in the progress of American politics in the last few decades; broad expansion of health care access for millions[1] marriage equality and expanded civil rights protection for LGBTQ+ people,[2] and accountability for sexual predators in various industries.[3] These steps came slowly and painfully. In most cases, they didn't through our political discourse, but in spite of it.

The West Wing is a major marker in American popular culture. As I discuss in the introduction, the show has a message that moral commitments matter in the face of brutal gridlock and amoral political tactics. The show receives criticism, often correctly, for being too optimistic. The public sees American politics as cynical, absurd, vitriolic, and inhumane.[4] Large parts of the series no longer seem plausible, even if there was a window when the show first aired where they might have been.

The West Wing feels outside of our political moment, especially compared to the pettiness of *Veep* or the manipulative evil of *House of Cards*. But those shows are easy to square with our attitudes towards politics; we see the worst of politics all the time. It is easy to talk about the silly and corrupt and cruel because it's visible. Those shows don't "expose" anything; they confirm what we know. It's harder to find optimism.

The West Wing is worthwhile because it is far removed from our present reality. It forces us to ask whether we can be optimistic and morally committed in politics. It forces us to ask whether core ideas about how politics ought to be done are right, or if we need to jettison them. The messages in the show are important because they are aspirational, because they strain our sense of possibility.

* * *

In 1977, my dad was an intern for a young congressman from Tennessee named Al Gore. My dad has been politically active since high school. I experienced *The West Wing* through bonding with my dad. Gore's 2000 presidential campaign was my first political memory, staying up late to watch the returns on that long election night and following the recounts and appeals during the next week before George W. Bush was eventually declared the winner. I was 10 years old.

The West Wing, then in its second season, was the way my dad taught me about politics and values. The show was optimistic that politics could improve the lives of the most vulnerable in our society, provide for common good, and engage publicly with the moral issues of our time. There is a difference between what politics and government are and what they should be; just because politics can improve people's lives doesn't mean it will; people in power have the ability and obligation to serve the most vulnerable.

Ensuring people have access to housing, health care, utilities, information, and safety is part of the goal. Kids should have access to food and education; adults should have access to opportunities and safety nets in the event of catastrophe. Communities should be protected from violence and have public utilities that work. We might disagree about how to achieve those things, but the basic moral obligations matter.

My dad ran for city council in 2002. I walked precincts with him and attended meetings with people around Oakland, California. He ultimately lost after a long runoff campaign; those long hours of walking, having conversations with strangers in the community, and wrestling with problems in education taught me a key political lesson: Cynicism is easy and convenient, especially in the internet age. It's also self-fulfilling. What matters is putting in the work, even knowing that doesn't guarantee success.

* * *

My dad's parents were Czech Jews. My grandmother was in Theresienstadt and most of her family died in the Holocaust; my grandfather fled through Morocco to Haiti and couldn't get into the United States until after the war, much of his family also died in the Holocaust. Genocide is among the darkest faces of political reality, entirely too common after decades spent repeating "never again." Bosnia, Rwanda, Darfur, Myanmar, Xinjiang, and many other places saw genocides in my lifetime. The worst face politics is no secret.

The West Wing is often criticized for its unrealistic sense of optimism about politics, that politics can be a space where we provide for the common good.

The reason the show matters today and continues to resonate with so many viewers is that the moral dimensions of politics are clearer now.[5]

The moral failure to care for those in search of safety, fleeing their homes and countries, is a constant problem in American politics. It took my grandfather years to get into the United States; that situation has hardly improved for those fleeing persecution and death.

Child poverty remains; people have to choose between bankruptcy or foregoing cancer treatment. Some people treat these issues as apolitical; other people treat them as political and economic problems, but not moral problems. The problems are moral and political; *The West Wing* tries to wrestle with both. Even when it fails, that effort means something.

A central moral commitment to many political views, including the liberalism of *The West Wing*, is that government is obligated to help those who are the worst off.

One philosophical expression of this, one I've taught for years in introductory courses, is John Rawls' argument from the original position. We try to consider impartially the range of potential life circumstances within our community. We could have been born into poverty or wealth, into a white, Black, Latino, or Asian family. The fact we were born into a particular life is not something we can control. When we consider public policy, we must remember individuals are not responsible for much of their circumstances. Rawls leverages this into an argument that a just and fair society should ensure the best outcome for the worst-off members of our society, because that might have been us, but for accidents of our birth and the course of our life.[6]

Aaron Sorkin focuses on child poverty as a major theme in *The West Wing*. President Bartlet comes back to it again and again in his speeches and introspective moments. Some children are born into crushing poverty, not afforded opportunity and have limited (if any) access to social services, food, shelter, education, and personal safety. These children are among the worst off in our society.

. Children aren't at fault for their suffering and can't help themselves; people who are struggling to subsist, to find somewhere to sleep or something to eat are not in a position to engage in the political process or advocate for their own well-being in the public square. We have an obligation to help because they are not able to advocate for themselves.

Sorkin's focus on reasonable disagreement is contentious. Reasonable disagreement is the idea that (for some questions) there are a range of defensible positions individuals may adopt. These are not matters of taste; one person can like vanilla ice cream, and another can like chocolate. Reasonable disagreement involves substance; in these cases, there are substantial answers to a question, like what we (as a community) should do. In a democratic society, we accept reasonable disagreement as part of political life.

Suppose that two people disagree about whether it is appropriate to use churches as polling places: Smith believes it is inappropriate for religious institutions to be used for civic duties like voting. Jones believes there are lots of communities where local churches are the best logistical option; those communities should focus on logistics to make voting easier. Smith and Jones disagree about what to do. Only one of the two can have their position implemented, but both are reasonable. We can understand and empathize with either, even if we disagree.

For some public policies, there are a range of views reasonable people might have, but not all views are reasonable. Someone who believes, for example, that only Catholic churches should be allowed to hold polling places is being unreasonable, because we don't privilege denominations.

My own academic work wrestles with this, especially in a world where extremist voices are louder, where unreasonable (even violent) disagreement seems the norm. Reasonable disagreement is a core democratic value, but there are limits.

The view that homosexuality should be criminalized, for example, is outside the boundaries of reasonable disagreement. Sometimes locating the boundaries of reasonable disagreement is difficult.[7] Sorkin's discussion of hate crimes laws, including positions taken by some members of the White House staff (some of our heroes) fall outside of the range of reasonable disagreement. One thing I develop throughout the book is how disagreements have shaped up, where the boundaries of reasonableness lie, and why.

In a political moment when much (even most) political discussion is unreasonable, from conspiracy theories to bigotry, it can sometimes be difficult to acknowledge reasonable disagreement. So many disagreements seem unreasonable that our default attitude is to regard everyone we disagree with as unreasonable. This is one thing *The West Wing* gets right.

* * *

This book, like the series itself, occupies a strange place between popular and political discussions. The series brings the expertise and conscience of its writing staff to stories at the heart of American politics at the turn of the millennium. Sometimes it tells those stories well; sometimes it doesn't. Some of those issues have changed; some remain 20 years later.

    The West Wing is still relevant because the major themes are relevant. Can we be optimistic about politics? Should we? What do our political leaders owe us? When are the dirty hands of political actors unforgiveable and unacceptable? In this book, I try to draw out, develop, and comment on those themes, updating them and discussing the problems in their presentation. I also provide historical, political, and literary context for the show.

    Interesting works of art are imperfect. Their imperfections make them better. *The West Wing* brings into sharp relief our present, inescapable political cynicism. That is part of what makes it worthwhile.

Joshua Stein
August 2024

Dedication

This book is dedicated to my dad, David Stein.
This book wouldn't exist without him; I wouldn't exist without him.

My dad lives by a central motto,
one I learned on backpacking trips with him:
Leave things better than you found them.

Introduction to Season One

"Government is not the solution to the problem; government is the problem."

—Ronald Reagan, Inaugural Address, January 20, 1981

Reagan's view of government wasn't just a political slogan or economic strategy. The view that "government is the problem" was widely adopted through the 1980s and persists today. The proliferation of anti-government sentiment, even among elected leaders, has been a part of American politics for the last four decades. Bill Clinton, in his 1996 State of the Union, announced "the era of big government is over."

The first two seasons of *The West Wing* are an explicit reaction to that cynicism. *The West Wing* tries to grapple with the problems of government without losing sight of the good government can do. Governments can wage war; government can incarcerate and prosecute and segregate. Governments can harm the people they're supposed to serve

But governments can also provide for vulnerable people, provide housing and food and medicine for those in poverty. Government can build and maintain the infrastructure we all use, the roads and bridges we drive, the subways and buses we ride, the shipping lanes that move goods around the world. Government can pursue justice for those harmed by violence or economic exploitation. *The West Wing* tries to grapple with cynicism about what government can be and do.

In "He Shall From Time to Time" (1.12), our heroes consider including "the era of big government is over," the Clinton line, in the state of the union. Toby fights against the line, despite the acceptance among the senior staff that it polls well and builds support from moderate, independent voters. In his rejoinder, at the end of the episode, Toby expresses his optimism about government:

I want to change the sentiment… that government no matter what its failures in the past and in times to come… government can be a place where people come together and where no one gets left behind. No one gets left behind. An instrument of good.

In 2008, there was an attempt to revitalize that optimism, political messaging focused on hope and change in the campaign of then-Senator Barack Obama. The 2008 Obama campaign was a direct appeal to the desire for optimism about what government can be.

The years following the Obama administration tested that optimism, with mixed results. The administration expanded health care coverage but created political backlash. The administration worked to address the rights of LGBTQ+ people, but with pushback from politicians and large segments of the American public.

Director and producer Schlamme notes in an interview[8] the vision of *The West Wing* was a "Frank Capra movie about government," that we can be optimistic about government while acknowledging failures. Mr. Willis of Ohio (1.06) evokes Capra's *Mr. Smith Goes to Washington* (1939) and its belief in the decency of people, including people in government. "He Shall, From Time to Time" (1.12) pushes back on the view that "government is the problem." In other moments, our staff falls into vindictive postures and transactional approaches that don't serve people; they fall short.

* * *

While the show wrestles with a hardline, cynical, transactional approach to politics, some of our main characters exemplify it. Josh applies political pressure to members of Congress, using a carrot-and-stick rather than arguments for policy. In "Five Votes Down" (1.04), Josh browbeats members of Congress into supporting a bill; in "Mr. Willis of Ohio" (1.06) Toby observes, "the merits of a particular argument generally take a back seat to political tactics."

"Mr. Willis of Ohio" is optimistic, but the episode itself falls prey to its own premise. From Capra's view, the moral decency of the "average man" is a superpower in Washington, because it is something politicians lack. The myth of the morally superior outsider is built on cynicism, that the people in Washington are incapable of serving the moral good. If something good comes out of Washington, it is a happy accident.

The West Wing ended before the financial crises of 2008, the collapse of the automotive and housing industries, which reinforced cynicism that the government had been serving corporate interests at the expense of those who needed and deserved support.[9] Billionaires got tax cuts while the rest of us got predatory loan debt; corporations got liability protection while the rest of us got saddled with the bill for their carelessness. Sorkin wrote about the '08 crash and the Occupy movement in *The Newsroom*, but more cynically than *The West Wing*.

In *The West Wing*, our heroes are civil servants, people working in government because they believe the government can serve the public. This message runs through the entire show, but is especially prominent in the first season, as the show develops its major themes. The show is sometimes criticized for unrealistic optimism; this criticism is fair. The show chases some moral principles beyond plausibility.

The show isn't always optimistic. Often, Sorkin's political world of the show directly criticizes real political actors. The first season includes direct critiques of the Clinton administration on major issues, including gun control ("Five Votes Down", 1.04), LGBTQ+ rights ("Take Out the Trash Day", 1.13), and child labor ("The White House Pro-Am", 1.17). The show is sharp in criticizing Clinton and Reagan, and eventually George W. Bush in the later seasons.

The show wrestles with moral conflict between Democratic protagonists and Republican opposition but argues for setting aside partisan bickering to work for the common good. The first season develops an antagonistic relationship with the Republican opposition, but then brings in figures within the political opposition who share commitments to public service. "Lies, Damn Lies, and Statistics" (1.21) shows the President working with a Republican Senator otherwise in complete opposition, trying to address campaign finance reform and political corruption. In "This White House" (2.04) introduces a principled, engaged, service-minded Republican attorney named Ainsley Hayes.

* * *

This book discusses the first two seasons of *The West Wing*, which aired September 22, 1999, to May 16, 2001. These two seasons occupy the space between the end of the Cold War (1991) and the terrorist attacks of

September 11, 2001. The start of the third season addresses American politics in a world after 9/11/2001. The foreign and military policy discussion in the first two seasons is jarring to watch in a post-9/11 world, especially how it talks about US military power.

Leo says to Bartlet in "A Proportional Response" (1.03). "You could conquer the world, like Charlemagne," giving a monologue about the President's desire to engage in a brutal retaliatory campaign against Syria after an American aircraft was shot down. The moral position of the United States and its role in global political, economic, and military matters are characteristic of the Clinton years. But we don't feel invincible anymore, like America is Andre the Giant in a room full of ordinary men.

The Russian invasion of Ukraine (in 2014, then with a renewed offensive in 2022) and the decision by NATO to fund but not engage; the expansion of Chinese military power and discussion of whether the United States would defend Taiwan during a Chinese invasion. The wars in Iraq and Afghanistan, their costs in the lives of young Americans and the lack of results after the US withdrawal, followed by the rise of ISIS/ISIL and the Taliban have changed the way the meaning of "superpower." American military power and a willingness to use it in the service of justice is a part of *The West Wing* from the first few episodes.[10]

I started writing this book during the last months of the Obama administration and am finishing it during the Biden administration. The book straddles three Presidencies, with radically different visions of the American role in the world, from the soft-power of President Obama to the isolationism of Trump to the more involved military policy of Biden. All of these differ from Presidents Clinton and Bush, during which the show was written.

* * *

A subtle critique in the first season, starting with "20 Hours in LA" (1.16) through "Lies, Damn Lies, and Statistics" (1.21) is the role of polling data in messaging and policy positions. The Clinton administration was obsessed with detailed polling data, which some critics argued resulted in the administration substantially changing messaging and policy when according to the polling cycles.

"20 Hours in LA" includes a storyline about a constitutional amendment banning flag burning. Sorkin's view (and the view of our heroes) is flag burning, while bad and offensive, shouldn't be prohibited; it's a form of political protest. Pollster Al Kiefer tries to convince the staff they should support a ban on flag burning, while the staff points out that they don't, and it would violate the free speech protections in the First Amendment. Will the staff stand by their convictions in the face of overwhelming polling data?

Sorkin sidesteps this issue. Joey Lucas provides polling data that the public may support a constitutional amendment banning flag burning but don't care much about the issue. The position isn't a deal breaker for the public.

Another criticism of the Clinton administration in the first season is their track record on LGBTQ+ rights. While the Clinton administration was certainly better than Reagan or the Bushes, the pursuit of LGBTQ+ rights was marred by insistence on appeasing parts of the American public that were homophobic. Clinton signed the Defense of Marriage Act; while this is sometimes defended as prudent, it exposes a lack of moral commitment. The development of Don't Ask, Don't Tell policies on LGBTQ+ service members and of restrictions on gay adoption, blood donation, and other policies were all transparent nods to the homophobic vitriol of the American public. *The West Wing* criticizes these moral failures across several episodes, especially "20 Hours in LA" and "Take Out the Trash Day" (1.13).

Sometimes the right thing is unpopular. A major criticism of the Clinton administration is that it failed when there was a moral imperative. Protecting the rights of minority groups is often unpopular; the Civil Rights movement of the '50s and '60s wasn't politically popular with white Americans, but there was a moral imperative for politicians. Lyndon Johnson used political tactics in service of that moral imperative to advance the Civil Rights Act, despite public opposition among white Americans.

The show wrestles with the complicated relationship between politicians' desire for power and the imperative to do what is right. Without power, a politician can't do what is right or be of service to those who need it, but if a politician just accumulates power without doing what is right, then there is no moral value.

Chapter One
Basic Elements of Season One

Sorkin works with many of the same actors and crew across projects. Season 1 of *The West Wing* was shot simultaneously with Season 2 of *Sports Night*. However, I have provided notes here on points where "Sorkin players" (those who appear in multiple Sorkin projects) recur.

Major Characters

Josh Lyman (Bradley Whitford) is the Assistant Chief of Staff, making him third-in-command in the White House senior staff below Leo McGarry. He previously worked for the Democratic Whip and former Senator (and now Vice President) John Hoynes. He is a brilliant legislative strategist; he is also egotistical and combative. He is from Connecticut. Whitford appeared on Broadway in the play of *A Few Good Men* (1990) in multiple roles and starred in *Studio 60 on the Sunset Strip* (2006-2007). Whitford won an Emmy for playing Josh in 2001.

Toby Ziegler (Richard Schiff) is the Communications Director. He is the highest-ranking member of the communications staff, making him C.J. and Sam's boss. Toby is also a direct counselor to the President. He is abrasive and misanthropic. He is from Brooklyn, New York, and a diehard Yankees fan. Toby and Josh are both Jewish; Toby is observant, regularly attending services. Schiff is an accomplished character actor and director. He won an Emmy for his role as Toby in 2000.

C.J. Cregg (Alison Janney) is the White House Press Secretary. She worked in public relations before joining the Bartlet campaign and eventually the White House staff. She is from Dayton, Ohio. Like President Bartlet and Leo, she is Catholic. She has a good working relationship with the press and her comfort with reporters often makes other members of the staff uncomfortable. Janney is an acting legend, with an Oscar (*I, Tonya*; 2018) and seven Emmys (four for *The West Wing*; 2000-2002, 2004).

Sam Seaborn (Rob Lowe) is the Deputy Communications Director and works directly with Toby in crafting most of the President's speeches. He was an accomplished attorney in private practice before joining the Bartlet campaign and eventually the White House. He is from Orange County, California. Seaborn is deeply optimistic, often acting as a foil for his cynical boss (Toby) and his Machiavellian best friend (Josh). Lowe is an accomplished actor who has worked primarily in television.

Leo McGarry (John Spencer) is the Chief of Staff, answering directly and exclusively to the President. He previously served as Secretary of Labor before managing the Bartlet campaign. Leo convinced Bartlet to run, and is Bartlet's closest friend. He served as a pilot in the Vietnam War. Leo is a recovering alcoholic and drug addict. While he is referred to at some points as "Boston Irish-Catholic," he is from Chicago. Spencer was an accomplished character actor, iconic for his work as McGarry (for which he won an Emmy in 2002) and incorporating much of his personal experience into the character.

President Josiah "Jed" Bartlet (Martin Sheen) is the former Governor of New Hampshire and previously served as member of the United States House of Representatives for New Hampshire's 1st District. He graduated summa cum laude from the University of Notre Dame with a B.A. in American Studies and a minor in Theology and an MSc and Ph.D. in economics from the London School of Economics. He was awarded a Nobel Prize in Economics. He has three daughters and several grandchildren (from his eldest daughter). Sheen appears in *The American President* (1995), Sorkin's predecessor to *The West Wing*. Sheen is an iconic actor, with three Emmy wins; he was nominated six times for *The West Wing*, but never won for the series).

Mandy Hampton (Moira Kelly) is the White House Media Director. She has a Ph.D. in political science. She worked on the Bartlet presidential campaign and dated Josh Lyman.

Donna Moss (Janel Maloney) is the assistant to Josh Lyman. She is curious and engages in debate with Josh on a range of issues, as well as providing a foil for explanations of how particular issues operate. Donna frequently takes moral issue with administration policy and argues with Josh about them. She is from Wisconsin. Maloney appears in *Sports Night* (1998-2000).

Charlie Young (Dulé Hill) was raised by a single mother, a D.C. police officer who was killed in the line of duty. He becomes Personal Aide to the President. Charlie raises his younger sister Deanna. He continues to work as the Personal Aide while studying at Georgetown University. Charlie is brilliant and driven, as well as self-conscious about his background in contrast to the privilege of the White House staff. Hill has an extensive acting resume and is an accomplished dancer, especially tap dancing.

Mrs. Dolores Landingham (Kathryn Joosten) is the personal assistant to the President and her time working with President Bartlet goes back to when Bartlet was a high school student. She is a widow and her two sons were killed in Vietnam. Mrs. Landingham acts as a big sister to Bartlet, regularly bantering with him but ultimately providing support. She also acts as a big sister to the community of assistants (all women) to other staffers. Joosten had an extensive acting resume, especially as a comedic actress.

Margaret (NiCole Robinson) is the assistant to Leo McGarry. She is eccentric and frequently engages with staff as they wait to talk to Leo. She cares for Leo and looks out for him during his divorce.

Ginger (Kim Webster) is an assistant to Toby Ziegler.

Bonnie (Devika Parikh) is an assistant to Toby Ziegler.

Carol (Melissa Fitzgerald) is an assistant to C.J. Cregg.

Cathy (Suzy Nakamura) is an assistant to Sam Seaborn.

Ed (Peter James Smith) and **Larry** (William Duffy) are "congressional liaisons" to the White House, though largely occupy a utility role, representing many jobs that might be done by various parts of the White House staff.[11]

Recurring Characters

Laurie (Lisa Edelstein) is a law student at Georgetown and an escort. She sleeps with Sam Seaborn and smokes marijuana in the pilot. After the appearance in the pilot, she and Sam become friends. Her friendship with Sam becomes a potential scandal. Edelstein also appears in *Sports Night*.

Admiral Percy Fitzwallace (John Amos) is the Chairman of the Joint Chiefs of Staff. His medals indicate that he served in both the Vietnam and Gulf wars. Fitzwallace is the senior advisor to the President on military issues; in addition to providing advice to President Bartlet and Leo, he regularly expresses concern about their well-being. Amos is an iconic actor, whose career spans *Roots* and *Good Times*.

Vice President John Hoynes (Tim Matheson) is a former Senator from Texas and was Bartlet's major opponent during the Democratic presidential primary. Hoynes has an antagonistic relationship with the White House staff (especially Leo) but is friends with Josh following their long relationship. Matheson is an accomplished television actor and director.

Danny Concannon (Tim Busfield) is a journalist in the White House Press Corps. He has written for *The New York Times, The Washington Post, TIME Magazine*, and the *Dallas Morning News*. Danny is a graduate of Notre Dame. He regularly flirts with C.J., while also investigating the administration. Tim Busfield has appeared in other Sorkin work including the Broadway run of *A Few Good Men, Sports Night*, and *Studio 60 on the Sunset Strip*.

Zoey Bartlet (Elizabeth Moss) is the youngest daughter of Jed and Abbey Bartlet. She is preparing to start college at Georgetown. Zoey is close with her father and develops relationships with the White House staff, including a romantic relationship with Charlie. Elizabeth Moss is an iconic actress, with credits including the lead in *The Handmaid's Tale*.

First Lady Abigail Bartlet (Stockard Channing) is a medical doctor and the wife of President Bartlet. She prescribed medication to Jed when he was diagnosed with multiple sclerosis. Dr. Bartlet is independent accomplished but is routinely used by the White House in more traditional ceremonial roles. Channing is an iconic actress with three Emmy wins (including a 2002 win for *The West Wing*).

Agent Ron Butterfield (Michael O'Neill) is the senior Secret Service agent in charge of the President's security.[12] Like Fitzwallace, Ron's experience in the White House extends long before the current administration, and so he is more confident in his job than many of our staff. O'Neill is an accomplished character actor.

Lord John Marbury (Roger Rees) is a former United Kingdom Ambassador to both India and Pakistan. He is regarded as an expert in foreign affairs. He is "eccentric," a polite word for a lush who flirts with most of the women around the White House (especially C.J.). Rees was an accomplished television actor who specialized in comedic roles; he also had an extensive theater career.

4

Joey Lucas (Marlee Matlin) is a pollster from California. She has managed congressional campaigns. She has a relationship with Al Kiefer, but they break up before she begins working in the White House. She has a regular flirtation with Josh Lyman. Matlin is an iconic actress who has won an Oscar and received numerous humanitarian awards.

Roberto Mendoza (Edward James Olmos) is a former New York City police officer who became an attorney by taking night school classes after he was shot in the line of duty. He eventually became an Assistant District Attorney in Brooklyn and then Assistant U.S. Attorney for the Eastern District of New York, before being appointed as a District Judge in the Eastern District. Olmos is an iconic actor who won an Emmy award.

Agent Gina Toscano (Jorja Fox) is the Secret Service agent in charge of protection for Zoey Bartlet, as Zoey faces increased threats in Washington, D.C., and later as she draws attention (from white supremacist groups) for dating Charlie. Fox has an extensive television acting career.

Al Kiefer (John de Lancie) is a pollster who has a combative relationship with the White House staff. He is briefly in a romantic relationship with Joey Lucas.

Production Staff Players

Aaron Sorkin is the creator and writer of *The West Wing*. He created the majority of the scripts (under the "teleplay by" credit) in the first four seasons of the series. Sorkin's work in theater, film, and television is extensive. In addition to *The West Wing*, he wrote Sports Night, Studio 60 on the Sunset Strip, and Newsroom for television. He wrote *A Few Good Men* (first as a play, then the film), *The American President, The Social Network*, and *Moneyball*, among others. Sorkin has a distinctive voice, with an aggressive and dense dialogue style, linguistic quirks, and a commitment to certain rules of dramatic storytelling.

Thomas "Tommy" Schlamme is a director and executive producer of *The West Wing*, widely credited with the visual style of *The West Wing*. Schlamme directed many of the major episodes through the early seasons. He was also director and executive producer on *Sports Night* (1998-2000) *and Studio 60 on the Sunset Strip* (2006-2007).

John Wells is an executive producer of *The West Wing*. He took over as showrunner from Sorkin for the final three seasons (5-7) of the series.

W.G. Snuffy Walden is a musician and composer who did the scoring for much of *The West Wing*, including its theme (for which he won an Emmy).

Dave Chameides is a steadycam operator and director, responsible for operating many of *The West Wing*'s defining shots, including the most notable walk-and-talk sequences throughout the series.

Alex Graves is a director and eventual executive producer on *The West Wing*. He directed 34 episodes of *The West Wing*, winning two Emmys and a Humanitas prize. He would go on to direct six episodes of *Game of Thrones*.

Christopher Misiano is a director and executive producer of *The West Wing*. He directed 35 episodes of *The West Wing* and won an Emmy. He also worked with Sorkin on *Studio 60 on the Sunset Strip*.

Recurring Plotlines through Season One:

- **Sam sleeps with Laurie**, causing a potential scandal for the White House because she works as a call girl. Episodes 1.01-1.03, 1.07
- **The President considers a proportional response to Syrian military action**, as a U.S. aircraft is shot down. President Bartlet has personal stakes as a friend is killed in the attack. Episodes 1.02-1.03, building on themes from *The American President*.
- **The Supreme Court Nomination of Roberto Mendoza**, following a Supreme Court Justice's sudden death. Bartlet appoints a Mendoza (rejecting an easier nomination fight), and the nomination is coordinated by Toby. Episodes 1.09, 1.15, 1.18
- **The collapse of Leo's marriage**, as he works long hours. Leo alienates his wife and she eventually leaves him. Episodes 1.04, 1.06, 1.08
- **Leo's history of drug abuse** is exposed. Leo is well-known as an alcoholic, but also has a history of substance abuse including prescription drugs. The prescription drugs are considered more scandalous. Episodes 1.09-1.11
- **Hate crimes and gay rights** take center stage after a gay high school student is beaten to death. The administration considers

adopting hate crime legislation. The storyline closely (and intentionally) parallels the murder of Matthew Shepherd. Episodes 1.10, 1.13

- **India-Pakistan enter military conflict**, with incursions into the neutral region. India and Pakistan threaten to escalate into a full military conflict. Episodes 1.11-1.12
- **Campaign finance reform** becomes a major issue, at the urging of the White House. President Bartlet and others in the administration consider appointing new members to the Federal Election Commission. Those new members' oppose soft money in campaign spending. This draws the ire of congressional Democrats, who use soft money in their campaigns. Episodes 1.19-1.21
- **Drug Policy** becomes a significant issue, as the administration considers a proposal to reform drug sentencing guidelines. The administration wants to focus on rehabilitation, rather than incarceration, bringing Leo's history of drug use up as a potential source of scandal. Episodes 1.20-1.21

Sorkinisms

Sorkin likes to borrow from himself. In some cases, this is probably accidental and includes figures of speech or examples Sorkin likes. In other cases, it seems intentional.

Regarding the dialogue, there is a "Sorkinisms supercut"[13] circulating on YouTube, a video of lines and phrases Sorkin recycles. I highlight some of these as they come up throughout the series, where they appear across Sorkin's other projects. I probably won't catch all of them but I'll do my best.

Sorkin also observes a set of dramatic conventions which cause similar plot loops. Hubris must be punished; this becomes a feature for our White House staff. There are other illustrations of dramatic rules, including Sorkin's use of motifs and foreshadowing (including Chekhov's gun). These aren't "Sorkinisms," but rules of classical drama Sorkin follows closely. I note both Sorkin's adherence to literary convention and his idiosyncrasies.

There are also framing devices Sorkin uses over and over. Some devices, like the weekly poker game bookending the episode[14] or the interview with flashbacks[15] are structural devices Sorkin uses across his television work; he isn't the only writer who uses them. Along with Sorkin's peculiar dialogue style, I try to give an account of what the "Sorkin style" is (both for those who want to imitate it and for those who mock it).

Chapter Two
Episodes 1.01-1.03

The pilot introduces the cast of characters, provides background, and illustrates their interactions and dynamics. This exposition uses Sorkin's signature fast-paced style of dialogue. The audience comes into interactions in the middle of a conversation (as in the opening scene with Sam in the bar) rather than seeing them from the beginning. Episodes 1.02 and 1.03 rehash central ideas from Sorkin's first drama set in the White House, his film *The American President* (1995).

Pilot (1.01)

Air Date: September 22, 1999
Director: Thomas Schlamme
Teleplay By: Aaron Sorkin
Writer: Aaron Sorkin
Plotlines:
   a) Josh offends evangelical Christians with a flippant remark.
   b) The President crashes his bike into a tree.
   c) Sam sleeps with Laurie (a call girl).
   d) Leo yells at *The New York Times* crossword editor.

   The episode opens in a bar, in the middle of a conversation between Sam (Rob Lowe)[16] and a reporter (Marc Grapey); the reporter asks, "Is Josh on the way out?" Sam avoids the question, distracted by a beautiful woman at the bar (Lisa Edelstein).[17]
   Cut to Leo (John Spencer) doing *The New York Times* crossword over breakfast, interrupted by a call "about POTUS." There is a sequence of characters whose mornings are interrupted by calls about POTUS. They are our central cast. C.J. (Alison Janney) falls off a treadmill. Josh

(Bradley Whitford) is asleep at his desk. Toby (Richard Schiff) berates a flight attendant.[18] Sam is in bed with Laurie, the woman from the night before. Laurie apologetically smokes a joint.

The staff responds to a call about "POTUS" running his bicycle into a tree. As Josh Malina later noted, "We're clearly supposed to be going, as viewers, who is POTUS?"[19] POTUS is an abbreviation for President of the United States; this is now common knowledge and the official handle on social media platforms, but that was not well-known in 1999.

Trivia:

President Bartlet crashing into a tree is likely a joke about presidential clumsiness harkening back to *Saturday Night Live* portrayals of President Gerald Ford. Ford was an excellent athlete who got an image for clumsiness during his time in office. In 2004, five years after this episode, then-President George W. Bush suffered a bruised ankle after falling off his bike while at his ranch.[20]

Synopsis, cont'd

Josh and Leo discuss refugees from Cuba and providing support for those refugees, before transitioning to the President being "pissed as hell" at Josh. Schlamme provides us with the show's first "walk-and-talk," as the two move through the building.[21] The opening sequence references religious leaders Al Caldwell, Mary Marsh, and John Van Dyke, who will visit the White House to try and smooth things over. Leo concedes at the end of the exchange that Josh was right, even though he shouldn't have insulted Marsh.

We are introduced to Mrs. Landingham (Kathryn Joosten), the President's personal secretary, and get a view of the Oval Office for the first time. The walk-and-talk shot continues. Leo tells his secretary Margaret (NiCole Robinson) to call *The New York Times* crossword editor about the spelling of the name of Libyan dictator Col. Muammar Gaddafi.[22]

C.J. asks Leo how she can spin the President running his bicycle into a tree. The conversation turns to the Cuban refugees. The show establishes a dynamic between the characters in the senior staff. Sam is the enthusiastic junior member of the group; Josh is an established senior figure who is anxious about being fired; Toby is ornery; Leo as the head honcho and father figure.[23]

C.J. briefs the press, competent and authoritative, gracefully handling the silliness of the President riding his bike into a tree with a joke: "By all means, enjoy yourselves."

The episode cuts to Josh, in his office, watching a clip of his gaffe during a talk show with evangelical leader Mary Marsh (Annie Corley). The flippant remark plays over and over. "The God you pray to is too busy being indicted for tax fraud."[24]

We are more comprehensively introduced to Josh's assistant Donna (Janel Maloney),[25] who gives us more exposition, "You [Josh] won that election for him. You and Leo and C.J. and Sam. And him [Toby]." Josh and Toby start talking about concessions to the religious right and "family values," again mentioning Al Caldwell and Mary Marsh, reminding us the religious right figures are coming for a meeting and setting up the climax of the episode.

We cut to Mandy (Moira Kelly), yelling into a brick of a cell phone and wearing a beret before being pulled over by a cop. She blows off the cop until he uses a sterner voice.

Leo, Sam, and Josh then meet discussing the Cuban refugees and pivot to talking about Mandy, who is helping Senator Lloyd Russell prepare for a primary challenge against the President. They joke about firing Josh. Josh and Mandy meet and talk about Russell before Mandy expresses concern about Josh being fired; the two used to be in a relationship. We also find out that Mandy is dating Senator Russell.

Cut back to Leo arguing with *The New York Times* crossword editor about the spelling of Gaddafi. C.J. and Leo discuss whether the President is going to fire Josh. Leo admits that he doesn't know.

Cathy (Suzy Nakamura) tells Sam that Leo's wife has called. Leo's wife asked Sam to give a tour to Leo's daughter's fourth grade class. Sam gets a page;[26] Sam calls the number on the pager. It is an escort service. Both Sam and the escort service are confused. Sam realizes he has Laurie's pager, Laurie has his pager, and Laurie is an escort. He calls Laurie to arrange to switch their pagers back.

We are introduced to Al Caldwell (F. William Parker),[27] who is talking to Leo. Leo talks about how religious the President is (an observant Catholic) and candidly points out Caldwell is associating with Mary Marsh and John Van Dyke, and Marsh and Van Dyke are bigots.[28] We also discover Leo is trying to convince the President not to fire Josh.

Sam meets with Laurie at her home. Sam asks and clarifies that Laurie is an escort. He cannot associate with her because it would be a serious scandal.

Donna convinces Josh to change the suit that he has been wearing for several days. Sam gives a tour of the White House to Leo's daughter's class, pressured into it by Leo. Sam does not know who Leo's daughter is, but quickly has a breakdown in front of the group because he doesn't know about the building. He then tells the teacher that he "accidentally slept with a prostitute last night." We then find out the teacher (Allison Smith) is Leo's daughter Mallory.

Trivia:

Leo's daughter Mallory points out (correctly) the Roosevelt room is named for Theodore Roosevelt, not (as Sam says) Franklin. As Sam makes the mistake, there is a large portrait of Theodore over his shoulder.

Synopsis, cont'd

The climax of the episode is a meeting between Toby, Josh, and C.J. and the leaders of the religious right: Al Caldwell, Mary Marsh, and John Van Dyke (David Sage). Caldwell starts by trying to address the remarks. Josh apologizes for the remarks. The tone quickly shifts, as Mary Marsh looks for a "deal." Things spiral when, during the exchange, Marsh comments and refers to Josh's "New York sense of humor."

JOSH: I'm from Connecticut, but that's neither here nor—
TOBY: She meant Jewish.
[pause]
TOBY: When she said, "New York sense of humor," she was talking about you and me.

Caldwell quickly tries to calm things down, but can't. Marsh doesn't like what she's "been accused of," and Toby continues to raise his voice at the antisemitism.[29]

The conversation continues to escalate, Toby's voice rising even over Caldwell, until they are interrupted by a limping President Bartlet (Martin Sheen). The President disarms the escalating temper with a joke and his authority. He then pivots to directing a straightforward question at Caldwell about "the Lambs of God."[30]

Bartlet gives a long monologue. Bartlet tells Caldwell that he crashed into the tree because he was angry and out of control. He was angry because the Lambs of God sent his granddaughter a Raggedy Anne doll with a knife through its throat. He then dismisses the representatives of the religious right, suggesting they denounce the group and confirming he won't fire Josh.

The staff moves to the Oval Office. The President says many of the Cuban refugees drowned while trying to make it to Florida. Those who survived are seeking asylum. This is the reason for good government, to work hard for those people. The staff should get back to work. The episode ends with the perennial tag, "What's next?"

Note on Real and Fake Names

The pilot includes two curiosities in tension: The Lambs of God (a made-up religious extremist organization) and Col. Gaddafi (the real leader of Libya). The tension between bringing up real people, states, organizations, and the like runs through the show. I have done my best to catch these in the notes. Sorkin often combines several countries or organizations together, rather than naming someone specific, but this isn't always possible. The show uses Syria (a real country) in episodes 1.02 and 1.03, but uses "Kumar" (the fictionalized middle eastern country) in other arcs later in the show.

The Arc of Sam and Laurie, and D.C. Sex Scandals

In the contemporary context, the notion of a White House staffer being friends with a sex worker seems quaint. The show comes out of the late-'90s, following scandals of then-President Bill Clinton having sex with a White House intern and then-Speaker of the House Newt Gingrich's affair. Even in the context of the late-'90s, the relationship between Sam and Laurie seems relatively mild. There was no coercion or conflict of interest; neither is married; she is an escort but doesn't Sam pay for sex.

13

In the context of American political history, there are a lot of political sex scandals. Sorkin develops the friendship between Sam and Laurie as a potential scandal throughout the first season; in the modern context, moralizing over the life of an unmarried White House staffer having consensual sex seems nonsensical. It was weak even at the time the episode aired.

Through the '00s, what constituted a political scandal (especially a scandal involving sex) changed radically. The so-called "D.C. Madam" scandal (resulting in the conviction and subsequent suicide of Deborah Jeane Palfrey)[31] exposed several high-profile political figures, including Senator David Vitter (R-LA). The investigation into Representative Mark Foley (R-FL) sending elicit messages to pages[32] and Governor Eliot Spitzer (D-NY) using an escort service[33] were both significant political scandals.

In those cases, there were additional layers of ethical impropriety. Gingrich and Vitter were moralizing hypocrites. Clinton and Foley targeted young people over whom they had power. It is hard to say whether there are more scandals today than in years past or if the public is more aware of them; there were lots of instances of sexual assault and harassment in Washington D.C. prior to the Clinton trial. Presidents Franklin Roosevelt, John F. Kennedy, and Lyndon Johnson all had extramarital affairs. Clarence Thomas was confirmed to the Supreme Court despite sexual harassment allegations. Representatives Dan Crane (R-IL) and Gerry Studds (D-MA) were censured for having affairs with 17-year-old congressional pages decades before Foley's scandal resulted in the end of the page program.[34] It seems most likely that what changed was the extent of media coverage and the increased appetite for salacious news.

Political figures have power. Given the number of political figures, some portion will abuse that power to pursue sex, money, and whatever else they crave. Sometimes these moral failures are only of public interest because the politicians are public figures; sometimes these moral failures involve abuses of public trust, like using public funds for personal gain.

Sorkin wrestles with this in a toothless way. Unlike the scandals mentioned above, Sam isn't near a moral wrong in this case. The idea that being friends with someone in sex work would constitute a scandal in the modern era illustrates a major shift. A consensual relationship involving no criminal activity seems unlikely to generate public outrage, especially compared to Bill Clinton. Bill Clinton had an affair with an intern[35] and he was married; he had a long history of such affairs and allegations of sexual assault. He also lied to investigators, itself a felony. Unlike Sam Seaborn, Bill Clinton arguably committed crimes and certainly acted immorally.

Having affairs sometimes prompts political resignations, as in the case of Governor Mark Sanford (R-SC), but Sanford's case also included duplicity and misuse of public funds.[36] One of the things that makes us sympathetic to Sam also makes the entire arc feel pointless. As Sam and everyone else in the White House acknowledges, Sam didn't do anything wrong. While we might swallow the premise that public perception makes this a scandal, it's pretty weak compared to the scandals in the real world.

Post Hoc, Ergo Propter Hoc (1.02)

Air Date: September 29, 1999
Director: Thomas (Tommy) Schlamme
Teleplay By: Aaron Sorkin
Writer: Aaron Sorkin
Plotlines:
 a) Hoynes issues a strange statement, creates friction with the White House.
 b) Bartlet struggles with use of military force (a proportional response).
 c) Mandy is fired and hired.
 d) More people find out about Sam and Laurie.

Mandy is driving recklessly. She pulls up onto the curb and berates her boss and boyfriend Senator Lloyd Russell (John Bedford Lloyd);[37] neither their professional nor romantic relationships survive the conversation. Russell cuts a deal with the White House not to launch a primary campaign against the President. There's a reference to nessun dorma.[38]

Josh gloats, establishing that he is pompous.[39]

Toby and C.J. start with a reference to "the joke," before Toby banters with Mrs. Landingham. The core of the staff (Josh, C.J., Toby, Sam, and Leo) enter the Oval Office to meet with the President. The joke upset the Ryder Cup team; the President blows it off to focus on other meetings.

C.J.: USA Today asks why you don't spend more time campaigning in Texas, and you say it's because you don't look good in funny hats.

SAM: It was "big hats."

The joke is nothing. It should be blown off.

Bartlet gives the title of the episode, "after it, therefore because of it."[40] The purpose is to highlight Bartlet's Latinizing.[41]

"We did not lose Texas because of the hat joke," he notes. He lost Texas because he is a New England Democrat and this is the '90s, when even affable southerner Bill Clinton lost Texas by five points.

Leo meets a man in military uniform in the hallway, Morris Tolliver (Ruben Santiago-Hudson).[42] The two men talk about Tolliver's newborn daughter, making Tolliver dangerously likeable. We find Tolliver has been acting as the President's doctor. The President likes him and wants him to stay in that role. Tolliver is working at a teaching hospital in Jordan for a while but will resume as the President's physician when he returns.

Mandy and her coworker Daisy (Merrin Dungey)[43] discuss losing Russell as a client, leaving them without income.

Josh and Toby talk about hiring a new media director, and Josh insists they will not hire Mandy. C.J. is taken off-guard by a reporter asking about a comment from the Vice President, and immediately pivots to "the joke" about the Ryder Cup team. The comment from the Vice President is another indication the White House needs a new media director. Sam tells Josh that he (Sam) slept with a call girl, Laurie.

C.J. walks angrily, fuming about the Vice President's statement, and goes to confront Vice President Hoynes (Tim Matheson).[44] C.J. tries to explain the White House's position and his statement; the Vice President blows her off.

Tolliver gives the President a physical in the Oval Office. The two banter briefly, with Tolliver landing jokes at the President's expense. The President confides in Tolliver that he feels uncomfortable with the Joint Chiefs of Staff, the military leadership. Tolliver gives him a flu shot and reassures the President about the Joint Chiefs. Their exchange provides insight into Bartlet's mind and presidency, especially his struggle with the military elements of the job.

BARTLET: I'm not comfortable with violence. I know this country has enemies, but I don't feel violent towards any of them. I don't know whether that's a weakness or not, but I think I know how the Joint Chiefs would answer that question.

It is a human moment between Tolliver and the President. Tolliver reassures the President that the Joint Chiefs will respect him, but that in the meantime, "you outrank them, so don't worry about it so much."
Note: This is the first appearance of Martin Sheen's idiosyncratic over-the-top-of-the-head way of putting on a jacket. The strange flip of the jacket is the result of an injury to Sheen's shoulder and becomes a regular feature of the character.

Synopsis, cont'd

Josh and Donna banter. C.J. tells Leo that she talked to Hoynes; she doesn't mention that Hoynes blew her off. Mandy and Daisy drink wine out of paper cups and commiserate. Mandy has a Ph.D. Sam is neurotic. This is all expository until Sam acknowledges to Toby (Sam's immediate supervisor) that he slept with a call girl. He met Laurie while he was at the bar with a journalist.

Our team meets in Leo's office to discuss a new media consultant and immediately decides to hire Mandy. Josh slowly figures out that he is being ambushed with this news. On the way out of the door, C.J. lies to Leo by saying the meeting with Hoynes was fine.

Mrs. Landingham withholds steaks from the President because the President has high cholesterol. Josh visits Mandy and Daisy to tell them that they are being hired by the White House. Mandy and Josh banter.

The Vice President visits Leo's office. Leo asks if the Vice President blew her off. C.J. didn't mention it; she was willing to take the humiliation to avoid conflict.[45] The conflict between Leo and Hoynes is clear, Hoynes resents being forced into a minor role. Hoynes does not respect the President, but Leo is clearly the more powerful figure.

Sam goes out looking for Laurie, who is with a client. Sam suggests he might call the Assistant Attorney General (an implied threat, since solicitation is illegal) and she storms out of the restaurant. Sam follows her into the street, the Capitol in the background. Sam tries to banter as Laurie panics about the threat. Sam appears to be stalking Laurie, as he called her four times and is explicitly trying to "save" her. The two descend into banter, because apparently this is an effective strategy to wooing.[46]

The staff is called in and we see military personnel.

We are informed Morris Tolliver is dead. He was killed by a missile attack while flying to Jordan. Leo gives the President this information; Bartlet is frazzled, but quickly starts working through the logistics. The first order of business is calling Morris' wife, who is caring for their newborn daughter.

BARTLET: I am not frightened. I am going to blow them off the face of the earth with the fury of God's own thunder. Get the commanders.

A Proportional Response (1.03)

Air Date: October 6, 1999
Director: Marc Buckland[47]
Teleplay By: Aaron Sorkin
Writer: Aaron Sorkin
Plotlines:
   a) Bartlet prepares for a retaliatory strike against Syria (a proportional response).
   b) Josh hires Charlie as the new bodyman to the President.
   c) The rest of the staff finds out about Sam and Laurie.

We open with banter between Josh and Donna. Donna wants a raise. Donna says C.J. is being denied information about Sam. Josh goes into his office, where C.J. is waiting to yell at him. Cut to opening credits.

C.J. is furious because she didn't know about Sam and Laurie, despite being the person who interacts with the press. Josh tries to disarm her with humor; he is unsuccessful. Josh says that Sam did not "witness anything illegal." It isn't brought up again, but this isn't true. The audience knows that: Sam interrupted Laurie on a "date" and Laurie was smoking weed in bed the morning after she and Sam had sex. In the '90s, both of those things were illegal. Laurie acknowledged as much when Sam interrupted her on a "date."

The argument between C.J. and Josh escalates into insults, Josh calling C.J. a "sheeksa,"[48] We learn Josh went to Harvard and C.J. went to Berkeley.

Toby is nervous about President Bartlet's temper following Tolliver's death. The President's anger makes the Joint Chiefs nervous. Bartlet is furious about the slow response. Leo leaves the President and joins the senior staff. They have a laugh at a congressman saying his constituents are "so patriotic" they might kill the sitting President;[49] this is taken as a joke (except by Toby). The major focus is retaliation against Syria.

C.J. expresses her anger at Sam over his seeing Laurie. They dispute what matters, what the press cares about, and Sam being patronizing to C.J. The story somehow spirals into C.J. being hurt she was left out of the loop. C.J. has a legitimate concern; she needs to be prepared for questions from the press.[50]

We see the inside of the situation room, with the Joint Chiefs in full military regalia. Chairman Fitzwallace (John Amos)[51] offers options to the President for a retaliatory strike, a proportional response.

BARTLET: What is the virtue of a proportional response?
FITZWALLACE: I'm sorry?
BARTLET: What is the virtue of a proportional response? Why is it good? They hit an airplane so we hit a transmitter, right? That's a proportional response…
FITZWALLACE: Sir, in the case of Pericles 1—
BARTLET: They hit a barracks, we hit two transmitters.
FITZWALLACE: That's roughly it, sir.
BARTLET: This is what we do. I mean, this is what we do… If it's what we do, if it's what we've always done, don't they know we're going to do it?

The President demands devastating options.

Sorkinism:

The scene develops from Sorkin's film *The American President*, where President Shepherd (Michael Douglas) says, "Someday someone's going to have to explain to me the virtue of a proportional response."

Synopsis, cont'd

The scene with the Joint Chiefs illustrates a disconnect. Bartlet wants a cataclysmic response; the Joint Chiefs want a restrained response.

Charlie Young (Dulé Hill)[52] is introduced; he has an interview with Josh for a position. Charlie thinks the interview is for a bike messenger job, but the job is for bodyman to the President, "personal aide to the President." Mrs. De La Guardia[53] recommended Charlie for the job. Josh is trying to vet Charlie to make sure there's nothing embarrassing in Charlie's personal life. Charlie is taking care of his sister after his mother, a police officer, was killed in the line of duty. We find out Charlie wants the job to support his sister. He is foregoing college despite having good grades.

We return to the President, who is presented with military options that would kill civilians and cripple the entire country. Fitzwallace warns him against the action. The President agrees to the proportional responses proposed earlier but does so with disappointment and frustration. We also learn Bartlet smokes.[54] He lights up in the situation room.

Josh continues to interview Charlie, explaining the personal aide job is better. Sam interrupts the interview to vent his frustration.[55]

Leo and the staff try to figure out how they are going to handle going public with the retaliatory attack on Syria; the President is still angry. The staff is worried about him making the announcement and taking questions, given his volatility. Josh is concerned about hiring Charlie because Charlie is Black.

JOSH: I really like him, Leo. I want to hire him.
LEO: So, what's the problem?
JOSH: He's Black.
LEO: So is the Attorney General and the Chairman of the Joint Chiefs.
JOSH: They don't hold the door open for the President. I'm not wild
    about the visual. A young Black man holding his overnight bag.
LEO: Josh, I hold the door open for him. It's an honor.

Fitzwallace enters the room. Fitzwallace intimidates and flusters Josh. As the highest ranking Black man in the military, Fitzwallace assures Josh that hiring a Black bodyman is fine. Fitzwallace advises Leo to reassure the President that the President is doing fine. Leo is not so sure, but Fitzwallace is certain, clarion.

Sam apologizes to C.J. She then goes on to brief the press. We are introduced to smart journalist Danny Concannon (Timothy Busfield). C.J. thinks Danny has questions about the impending attack, which she cannot yet discuss, and tries to blow him off. Danny clarifies he knows about Sam and "a $3,000 a night call girl."

Mandy is in Josh's office and starts giving him a hard time. Their banter is painful and awkward. C.J. intimidates Danny into dropping the story about Sam and Laurie; C.J. rewards him by giving him a heads up about the attack on Syria. Bartlet is yelling at everyone as he prepares to go on television; Josh tries to introduce Charlie to the President, and the President snaps at Charlie, being a jerk.

Leo takes the President into a side room and tells the President to stop being a jerk. This highlights the close personal dynamic between Leo and the President. Bartlet cools down, venting his frustration to Leo, before the conversation descends into friendly laughter. Leo tells Bartlet they were hoping to hire Charlie.

Toby responds to the comments from the congressman about "patriotic" supporters killing the President by suggesting to the press the member might be investigated by the Secret Service for making threats against the President.

The President reintroduces himself to Charlie by expressing his condolences about the death of Charlie's mother and trying to engage Charlie on gun control. It is an attempt at a human moment.[56] The President prepares to appear on television, announcing the military strike against Syria.

What is the virtue of a proportional response?

Episodes 1.02 and 1.03 discuss the role of the American military and overwhelming force. Seasons One and Two of *The West Wing* are situated at a strange time in American political history, when the United States was the only remaining super-power, after the collapse of the Soviet Union, and was not yet involved in the so-called "global war on terror." During and after WWII, the United States built one of the most devastating military forces of the modern era, comparable only to the USSR at the height of the Cold War and continuing long after the collapse of the USSR. The United States can reduce cities, even entire countries, to radioactive rubble. Bartlet wrestles with the instinct to do that when a country attacks Americans.

Mutually assured destruction and the use of devastating military force isn't a serious possibility in the modern era.[57] After the end of the Cold War, an American President could theoretically engage in military action without serious threat of retaliation, because of the United States' overwhelming military power. This was more-or-less what happened in Iraq during the first Gulf War (1990-1991), and what informs Sorkin's view of American military power.

After 9/11, some political actors considered the use of catastrophic force. Why not just obliterate entire countries as a reflexive response to terrorist attacks on 9/11? With a few arguable exceptions, the US has maintained a posture of proportional response. Starting with the conventional invasions of Afghanistan and Iraq, and later engaging in targeted drone actions.[58] These strikes haven't always been appropriate or within the laws of engagement; the US has killed civilians and arguably violated international law and American military policy. That's different than nuking Baghdad, Kabul, and Karachi.

Bartlet asks, "why not?" Why not rain radioactive ash on two million citizens of Damascus, or destroy their water supply? Bartlet asks why we bother with proportional responses when we are capable of total disaster. Fitzwallace responds, "it's all there is." Bartlet points out they have the capacity to rain down total disaster, but Fitzwallace is right. What Bartlet is proposing is illegal, and it is a moral disaster yet unseen since 1945, a disaster that our species will hopefully never see again.

Under international law, what Bartlet proposes would be illegal. Protocol I, Article 51 of the Geneva Convention includes the following:

4. Indiscriminate attacks are prohibited. Indiscriminate attacks are:
  (a) those which are not directed at a specific military objective;
  (b) those which employ a method or means of combat which cannot be directed at a specific military objective; or
  (c) those which employ a method or means of combat the effects of which cannot be limited as required by this Protocol.

Fitzwallace could point out that such a military action would kill civilians indiscriminately and would violate international law, this passage in the Geneva Convention in particular. He could also appeal to the President's basic moral decency; killing thousands of civilians by destroying water distribution centers would be monstrous. He instead appeals to the political repercussions, that it would be universally condemned and viewed as a massive overreaction by a President unfamiliar with military force.

Later in the series (3.21-3.22), Leo and Fitzwallace wrestle with the challenges of modern warfare, where enemy combatants no longer abide by the Geneva Convention.[59] The conversation in Season Three is grounded in a post-9/11 political world considering the assassination of Bin Laden (then still at large) and other leaders. The discussion in these episodes is rougher, when the combatants were still states (in this case, Syria) and not yet non-state actors. That shift is one change following 9/11. The United States can unleash catastrophe. Why not?

At the end of 1.03, Leo makes the practical point:

And you think ratcheting up the body count is going to act as a deterrent? Then you are just as stupid as these guys who think capital punishment is going to be a deterrent for drug kingpins, as if drug kingpins didn't live their day to day lives under the possibility of execution, and their executions are a lot less dainty than ours and tend to take place without the bother and expense of due process.

So, my friend, if you want to start using American military strength as the arm of the Lord, you can do that. We're the only superpower left. You can conquer the world like Charlemagne. Well, you better be prepared to kill everyone, and you better start with me, because I will raise up an army against you and I will beat you.

Leo is an Air Force veteran. Like Fitzwallace, he takes rules of engagement seriously because he knows how easy it would be to ratchet up the body count and kill enormous numbers of civilians. He fought in Vietnam, a war that had a catastrophic civilian body count, including the use of weapons and tactics which violate the Geneva Convention.

In "War and Massacre,"[60] Tom Nagel discusses the ethical considerations involved in military actions taken by the allied forces during WWII. In particular, he writes about killing civilians to induce an enemy to surrender, as the US did at Hiroshima and Nagasaki. He considers and rejects the position that "… such measures are sometimes said to be regrettable, but they are generally defended by reference to military necessity and the importance of the long-term consequences of success or failure in the war."[61]

Nagel pushes on the nuance of humanitarian necessity of such actions, considering the potential consequences of long-term engagement.

Even if certain types of dirty tactics become acceptable when the stakes are high enough, the most serious of the prohibited acts, like murder and torture, are not just supposed to require unusually strong justification. They are supposed *never* to be done, because no quantity of resulting benefit is thought capable of *justifying* such treatment of a person.[62]

The wanton killing of civilians may induce surrender; torture may support a military campaign. Nagel argues this is irrelevant. No practical value can justify them; no ends justify those means. Those acts are just prohibited. There is no excuse; there is no justification.[63]

The purpose of the rules governing a proportional response, including restrictions on catastrophic tactics causing mass civilian death, is to provide a clear line to prevent sliding into moral catastrophe. That is the virtue of a proportional response.

Chapter Three
Episodes 1.04-1.06

Five Votes Down (1.04)

Air Date: October 13, 1999
Director: Michael Lehman
Teleplay By: Aaron Sorkin
Writer: Lawrence O'Donnell and Patrick Caddell[64]
Plotlines:
 a) Josh whips votes on a crucial gun control bill, avoiding talking to Hoynes.
 b) Leo and his wife separate.
 c) The White House staff makes financial disclosures to the press.
 d) The President is stoned on Oxycodone.

Bartlet opens with an aggressive speech to an activist group. "Kids are dead! Kids are dead!" The speech is on gun control legislation.[65] Leo tells Josh they lost five votes. We later find out the votes are on a gun control bill.[66] Toby is unhappy with the delivery of the speech; this helps us to establish Toby as the speechwriter and internal critic of the President's speaking style.

Historical note:

This episode aired about five months after the mass shooting at Columbine High School (April 20, 1999). "Kids are dead" and the focus on kids alongside gun control is a direct response to Columbine. School shootings did happen prior to Columbine, but Columbine (15 killed) was the first shooting by a minor to result in more than five deaths. Up to this point, the deadliest school shootings had all been conducted by adults:

UT Austin in '66 (18 killed), CSU Fullerton in '76 (7), the Stockton elementary school shooting (6), and Iowa City in '91 (6). Columbine changed that, and marked an increase in the frequency and mortality rate through the '00s. At the time, Columbine was the second deadliest school shooting in American history (besides Austin); since this episode aired, there have been four deadlier school shootings: Virginia Tech (2007, 33 dead), Sandy Hook Elementary in Newtown, CT (2012, 28 dead), Robb Elementary School in Uvalde, TX (2022, 22 dead), and Marjorie Stoneman Douglass High School in Parkland, FL (2018, 17 dead).

Synopsis, cont'd

The show features a long walk-and-talk through a hotel after the President's speech.[67] Toby is critical of the speech while everyone else praises it. We hear "five votes" and the whip count. Toby and the President banter; it is friendlier than the previously formal relationship between the President and his staff.

BARTLET: You know what, Toby? You're what my mother calls a pain in the ass.
TOBY: That's what my mother calls it too, sir.

The President was prescribed Oxycodone for his back, but he says it makes him loopy.[68]

The staff eats Chinese food, still dressed up from the speech. They strategize about the bill, trying to get the votes back. You don't ever want people to see how you make "laws and sausages," as Leo puts it.

They start to talk about who the votes are; Sam suggests the Vice President can help, but Leo refuses and leaves the strategy session. Leo arrives home to find his wife Jenny (Sara Botsford)[69] upset. Leo forgot their anniversary. Maintaining personal lives is difficult (perhaps impossible) for White House staffers.[70]

Toby finds out he made $125,000 from a stock trade, creating a concern about profiting from his position.[71] The profit is related to Internet stocks and the testimony of one of Toby's friends before Congress. Toby doesn't understand the technology.[72]

They are looking at how to buy off the five votes with subsidies; Josh proposes threatening congressmen. People congratulate Josh on a bizarre set of financial disclosures regarding gifts from people who have crushes on him.[73]

Leo plans champagne for his wife to make up for missing the anniversary. "I don't drink champagne." We later find out Leo is a recovering alcoholic. We also find out Leo is independently wealthy from the lecture circuit.[74]

Leo gives Josh permission to strongarm members of Congress who jump ship on the bill. Leo says, "I should sell tickets to this meeting." Josh threatens to wage a primary challenge against one of the defectors, citing President Bartlet's political capital and popularity. These scenes display politics as sport, and polling and fundraising as tools for political pressure. This is a cynical moment, in contrast to the broader optimism of the show. Josh doesn't try to convince anyone; he just threatens and insults them.

Toby and Sam talk about the financial disclosure and how to blunt Toby's potential scandal. Sam talks about his friendship with Laurie; perception matters. C.J. makes financial disclosures to the press; Presidential property values increase because of Secret Service improvements, as well as being a "Presidential residence."

Josh is concerned that one of the five holdouts will not join back in without the help of the Vice President. Josh goes to meet with one of the defectors (Jay Underwood), who greets Josh with "dude." Josh asks the congressman's staff to leave and then dresses him down privately. The Congressman wanted a soft photo-op with the President in exchange for his vote.

Leo and Toby vent their personal issues. Josh tries to direct attention to the vote. Leo suggests, instead of going to the Vice President, he could meet with Rep. Mark Richardson (Thom Barry),[75] a leader in the Black community. Leo meets with Richardson. Richardson reads Leo's tactics immediately. Richardson will vote "no" because he believes the bill won't protect people. Leo gives a lecture on how it is Black kids being killed, enraging Richardson.

LEO: An entire generation of African American men are being eaten alive by drugs and poverty.
RICHARDSON: Well, I'm encouraged to hear that the White House has discovered there's a drug problem in this country. Your penetrating insight is matched only by the courage displayed in the authorship

27

of this bill… I want the guns. You write a law that can save some lives, I'll sign it. In the meantime, Leo, don't tell me how to be a leader of Black men. You look like an idiot.

This is striking awareness of the politics of anti-crime legislation in the '90s from Sorkin. Leaders representing Black communities were dictated to by white Democrats who presume a pragmatic view but just passed ineffectual law.

Notes on Rep. Richardson and gun control

We find out much later in the series (4.19, Angel Maintenance) that Rep. Richardson represents the neighborhood Toby Ziegler is from in Brooklyn. Toby is one of his constituents. In 1.05, Toby expresses similar concerns about the gun bill to those Rep. Richardson voices, as the bill carves out which weapons it bans.

Synopsis, cont'd

Offending Richardson leaves Leo with no other options but the Vice President. Leo comes home late again. Leo and his wife fight; "this is the most important thing I'll ever do" is not a good thing to say to your wife after missing your anniversary. Leo's wife leaves him.

Leo and Hoynes meet; Leo asks for a favor. Leo is frustrated and humbled by screwing up the meeting with Richardson. Hoynes gives no resistance and agrees to meet with Tillinghouse, the remaining outstanding vote. Hoynes and Leo have a personal relationship; Leo tells Hoynes that he and his wife are separating. Both Leo and Hoynes are recovering alcoholics, and that they have both kept it private; Hoynes hosts his own private Alcoholics Anonymous meeting and offers Leo an invitation.

Leo lies to the staff that his dinner with his wife went well.

Bartlet comes downstairs in jeans and a sweatshirt, stoned out of his mind on his "back medication." He greets Sam as Toby while rambling. We find out that he is on both Vicodin and Percocet, though he should not have taken both.[76]

Hoynes meets with Tillinghouse (Michael McGuire),[77] who is much more competent than the figures Josh bodied earlier. Hoynes suggests

Tillinghouse should do Hoynes a favor, because "I'm going to be President of the United States some day and you're not." Hoynes gets the credit for winning the votes in the media, which Leo hoped to avoid. Leo grudgingly accepts it.

The Crackpots and These Women (1.05)

Air Date: October 20, 1999
Director: Anthony Drazan
Writer: Aaron Sorkin
Teleplay By: Aaron Sorkin
Plotlines:
   a) Josh is issued a National Security Council card with instructions for the event of nuclear attack.
   b) Sam hears about a UFO over Maui.
   c) Toby has a crisis of confidence.
   d) C.J. hears about wildlife conservation issues.

Production Note

A centerpiece of this episode is the National Security Council cards for instructions in the event of a nuclear attack. In an infamous story, the idea developed when George Stephanopoulos showed Sorkin his [Stephanopoulos'] card; White House Press Secretary Dee Dee Myers denied the existence of such cards.[78] In Sorkin's version of the story, C.J. (the Press Secretary) doesn't know there are NSC cards, because she doesn't have one.

The idea of a "Big Block of Cheese Day" where the White House meets to discuss issues normally regarded as fringe was adopted by the Obama administration. The Obama administration explicitly credited *The West Wing* for the idea.[79] This episode is the first time the fully orchestrated opening theme is used; the show previously used an electronically supplemented version.[80]

Synopsis

The episode opens with the President and staff playing basketball. Toby and the President talk trash. Neither are athletic, but the President substitutes in a new member of the President's Council on Physical Fitness, Rodney Grant (Juwan Howard),[81] a Duke basketball star.

The episode introduces "big block of cheese day," where staffers meet with people with eccentric policy proposals. Josh is a jerk to Donna; Donna tells him that he has a meeting with someone from the National Security Council. C.J. wants to talk to Josh about smallpox and infectious disease terrorism. Leo says that Andrew Jackson had a big block of cheese; it was available to those who wanted it.[82] Given Jackson's views, perhaps one might better say that it was available to the white men who wanted it. It is "in this spirit" that Leo invites the "crackpots" into the White House.

Leo introduces Josh to the man from the NSC. The NSC representative gives him a card with instructions in the event of a nuclear attack. It is a jarring shift from the levity of "total crackpot day."

The team practices for a press conference on the economy with the President. They are nervous that the President gets too technical on economic issues. We find out the President is "an economics professor with a big ol' stick up his butt." President Bartlet doesn't want to talk about guns; Toby does. They fight. This is a shift from their playful dynamic playing basketball. The two are yelling at each other.

Sam and C.J. try to get out of their meetings with the "total crackpots." Leo insists they attend. Sam meets with Bob (Sam Lloyd);[83] Bob is from United States Space Command and wants to talk about UFOs and extraterrestrial life.

Mandy wants the President to attend a Hollywood fundraiser.[84] The President gets wonky on the economics of the budget; unfortunately, this is an area that can be frustrating, because it presents these issues as opaque to anyone except experts.[85] We learn the President was making numbers up about the economy.[86]

The President's youngest daughter is coming down to visit and the President wants to make chili. The President invites the staff, who cannot refuse. The staff fights over the Hollywood fundraiser. Toby doesn't want to align with a filmmaker whose work depicts sex and violence. Toby loses the argument, "Because it's Hollywood, who gives a damn?"

Josh asks Sam about the nuclear attack card, and Sam has no idea what Josh is talking about. Josh realizes most of the staff doesn't have a card.

C.J. meets with conservationists who want to construct a "wolves only roadway." The conservationists (Rachel Singer, Nicholas Cascone, and Nick Offerman) want money to protect wolves. It speaks to absurd, untenable proposals in early wildlife conservation, as well as the federal government's general indifference to acting beyond the Endangered Species Act.[87]

Mandy tells Toby she's glad "David Rosen passed on the Communications job."[88] Toby is self-conscious after discovering he was the second choice.

Josh talks to his therapist (Guy Boyd),[89] panicking about the new card and the smallpox virus being weaponized. This is a pre-9/11 world, where nuclear war still dominated the social consciousness. There is a worry about chemical and biological weapons. Josh's dead sister liked Schubert, especially the Ave Maria. Josh still wrestles with survivor's guilt after the death of his sister.

Sorkinism:

Freudian slips with therapists are a regular feature for Sorkin. We get them in two later episodes of *The West Wing*, Noel (2.10) and *Night Five* (3.14), as well as other Sorkin work.

Synopsis, cont'd

We return to Josh listening to the Ave Maria in his office. C.J. comes in, as they talk about smallpox. Josh admits he has the card to C.J., though he's not supposed to tell anyone. The NSC doesn't need communications staffers like her in the bunker. Josh asks if she knows the Ave Maria. "I'm Catholic," she scoffs.[90] Josh is worried about smallpox, a biological attack.

The President confirms Toby was the second choice. Toby's smack talk from the basketball game got inside the President's head. They apologize to each other.

We're introduced to Zoey, the President's youngest daughter (Elisabeth Moss)[91] and she has an awkward exchange with Charlie. Charlie is polite. Josh insists that he be less formal with Zoey. Charlie is working (and works for Zoey's father).

Josh tells Leo and the President, privately, that he doesn't want the card. The President praises "these women." The President says Mrs. Landingham lost two sons in Vietnam;[92] he praises C.J. and Mandy for their exceptional work. The President also addresses the room and notes that the descending object Sam heard about, the UFO over Hawaii, was a Soviet satellite falling out of orbit.[93] The attitude towards women is arguably patronizing.

Public Health as National Defense

Biological weapons, especially infectious diseases, were studied extensively throughout the 20th century. The Biological Weapons Convention of 1972 (of which both the US and USSR were signatories) prohibited the development, retention, and transfer of biological weapons. Nineteen seventy-five may seem late; strictly, the use of biological weapons is prohibited by the Geneva Convention, but the United States conducted research programs on biological weapons from before World War II until at least the late 1960s.[94] Anthony Rimmington writes that some Soviet biological warfare programs continued until 1992, meaning they outlasted the Soviet Union itself.[95]

All major powers have worked on defensive capabilities regarding biological weapons, because it seemed plausible that an infectious disease could be acquired and weaponized by a non-state actor more easily than a nuclear weapon. There have been a handful of incidents, but they have been low-casualty events. The Japanese cult Aum Shinrikyo attempted an anthrax attack in 1993, but failed to cause any infections.

In May of 2001, the Center for Disease Control and other organizations got together to run a simulation of a biological attack, focusing on anthrax.[96] The exercise was called Operation Dark Winter. The operation was a war game to map out a biological terrorist attack using anthrax. The exercise identified major weaknesses in the American health care and public health communication system.

On September 18, 2001, envelopes containing anthrax spores were mailed to politicians and public figures, the so-called "Americathrax" attack killed five and injured 17. Fortunately, there was no wide spread of anthrax. The major challenge in developing biological weapons is that it is difficult to develop something both contagious and fatal, because a disease that efficiently kills people it infects is less likely to be transmitted. Anthrax is dangerous because it can be transmitted through skin contact and inhalation, but once contracted, it's hard to transmit. The Amerithrax attack was overshadowed, largely lost in public consciousness as a result of timing. It came one week after the most consequential terrorist attack in American history.

September 11, 2001.

Despite the concern about biological and chemical weapons, despite focus of policy makers and defense experts (including the Bush administration, who overhauled efforts to combat biological weapons), biological terrorism took a significant backseat. September 11, 2001, changed how we think about terrorism.

One finding of Operation Dark Winter was that American public health infrastructure was not adequate to address either a biological attack or a naturally occurring pandemic. The hospital beds, staff, contact tracing, and so on were all underfunded. This has not changed much in the intervening years, as the coronavirus pandemic illustrated.[97] The discussion of bioweapons developed by Sorkin in this episode is consistent with the pre-9/11 understanding of the future of terrorism. Non-state actors were the threat; they used planes and guns instead of petri dishes.

Mr. Willis of Ohio (1.06)

Air Date: November 3, 1999
Director: Chris Misiano[98]
Teleplay by: Aaron Sorkin
Writer: Aaron Sorkin
Plotlines:
  a) A vote is planned on the Appropriations Bill, including a ban on sampling in the census. This motivates the meeting with Mr. Willis.
  b) There is a break-in on the White House grounds.
  c) Leo tells President Bartlet about his separation from his wife.

The episode opens with a poker game.[99] C.J. is dealing. The whole staff and the President are at the table, and we hear them check (opt not to bet) before we come to the President, who spouts trivia about strawberries as the staff moans in frustration. The President says the strawberry is the only fruit with seeds on the outside.[100] This illustrates Bartlet's inane knowledge, which is often a staple of the show.[101]

The tension at the poker table is between Toby and Bartlet. Bartlet poses trivia about punctuation and Toby answers. The tension drives a long arc in their relationship. "This is a pretty good illustration of why we get nothing done," Toby says.

Bartlet wins the hand. The game closes. Mandy made money and C.J. lost money. The Secret Service shuts down the Oval Office because someone has breached the building. This is the White House and there are intruders and threats, even when the characters are silly.

Toby asks for a copy of the Constitution, and no one has a copy.

C.J. meets with Sam, to ask if he can teach her about the census. C.J. butters Sam up with compliments so that he will help.

Production Note

The show often requires a lot of exposition to give the viewer context, whether background on characters, American history, or policy issues. Often this involves what Hrishi Hirway and Josh Malina call the "Tell-a-Donna," where Josh explains some function of government or issue driving the episode to Donnatella.[102] In this episode, Sam provides exposition, explaining the census to C.J.

Synopsis, cont'd

C.J. talks about the census from the podium; she's the White House Press Secretary and her job is to explain things to the press. Sam says, "OK, let's forget that you're coming a little late to the party and embrace the fact that you came at all."

Donna asks Josh about the budget surplus. Now we get a tell-a-Donna. She wants her money back from the surplus and supports the Republican plan for tax relief.[103]

Josh, Leo, Toby, and Mandy meet about the appropriations bill. The appropriations bill is legislation that designates how money is budgeted for the federal government, organized by department. There are other ways of allocating money, but the appropriations bill is the major vehicle. The Commerce Committee is holding up the bill; they suggest funding projects for congressmen they plan to meet.[104] One thing we learn is "Janis Willis' husband" is one of the swing votes on the committee.

Secret Service Agent Ron Butterfield (Michael O'Neill) briefs the President on the break-in the night before. The system worked the way it was supposed to work. "It was a mentally unbalanced woman in her 40s... You weren't the target." The target was his daughter Zoey. The woman was armed. Zoey is about to start college at Georgetown.

Josh, Mandy, and Toby meet with the three congressmen, including Mr. Willis (Al Fann)[105] whose wife was in Congress and whose seat he occupies after her death; Mr. Willis is Black and the other two are white.

Fact Check on Widow's (or Widower's) Succession and Mr. Willis

Historically, "Widow's succession" is when the spouse takes over the position of their partner. There is extensive international historical precedent for it. It does happen in American politics, but this is a bit complicated because of the differences in Senate and House rules. When a Senator dies, there is an appointment made by the Governor of that state until a special election can be held. In the House, there isn't an appointment mechanism; the seat just stays vacant. If Mrs. Willis were a Senator, then Mr. Willis could be appointed to her seat by the governor; this happened when Jean Carnahan (of Missouri) was appointed to fill her late husband's Senate seat.

In the House, the seat is left vacant, but there have been cases of "widow's succession" where the wife of the deceased politician won the special election. Most recently, Representative Julie Letlow (R-LA) won the special election for her late husband's seat; Luke Letlow died of coronavirus in 2020, after winning, but before being sworn into office. This form of "widow's succession" isn't what happened with Mr. Willis, since the episode is clear that Willis didn't win an election; Mr. Willis' case isn't possible, as the rules would just leave Rep. Willis' seat vacant on her death.

Synopsis, cont'd

The appropriations bill is massive; it funds the entire government.[106]

The issue is an amendment banning sampling in the census. This is not explained in the meeting. Instead, we return to Sam and C.J.

Sam explains the census to C.J. The census is necessary because the size of government representation in the House and distribution of funds and services is determined by population. The traditional approach to the census is a door-to-door headcount; the problem is some people don't answer the door when the government knock, some don't have stable homes. Some groups are systematically undercounted.

Leo and Mallory have breakfast; she encourages him to look for a place. He tells her the separation will blow over; Mallory says Leo's marriage is over.

Mandy argues with congressmen about sampling. Sampling is partisan because it would increase Democratic representation in the House; Democratic areas like cities are undercounted, because of the racial and urban-rural dynamics of the major parties.

Donna wants her money back from the budget surplus. Josh wants to pay down the debt and put some of the money into social security. Donna gives the "buying a DVD-player supports the people who make DVD players" argument.[107] The President asks Josh to take Charlie out for a drink. There is some veiled homophobia in Josh's response, that going out for a drink with Charlie is a homophobic suggestion.[108] Zoe and Mallory insert themselves into Josh and Charlie going out, and Mallory insists Josh also invite Sam.

Sam continues to explain the census to C.J. The congressmen insist sampling is unconstitutional. The Constitution requires that we count "the whole number of persons."[109] Toby argues the Constitutional passage in question is "arcane." Mandy reads Article 1, Section 2, Clause 5 of the Constitution, "Representatives and direct Taxes shall be apportioned among the several States which may be included within this Union, according to their respective Numbers, which shall be determined by adding to the whole Number of free Persons, including those bound to Service for a Term of Years…" Mandy omits the end. Toby asks Mr. Willis (a social studies teacher) about the end of the passage: "… and excluding Indians not taxed, three fifths of all other Persons." The three-fifths clause illustrates the passage is arcane and racist.[110]

The other congressmen prepare to leave; Mr. Willis says he will vote to drop the amendment in committee, paving the way for the bill to pass. His colleagues leave without him. Toby asks what changed his mind; Mr. Willis was moved by the argument.

TOBY: I'm smiling because around here the merits of a particular argument usually take a back seat to political tactics.
[…]
MR. WILLIS: I think the problems that we're going to face in the new century are far beyond the wisdom of Solomon, let alone me. But I think the right place to start is to say fair is fair, this is who we are, these are our numbers.

Mr. Willis is mourning the death of his wife, but he is doing the right thing for the right reasons.

36

Critical Note

This scene is cited by critics as evidence *The West Wing* is "liberal porn." Liberal fantasies are a big part of Sorkin's series, but this scene isn't good evidence. Toby is partly politically motivated, not expecting a victory from his argument, and is cynical about the political process. This episode is a direct nod to Frank Capra, not a post-Cold War liberal fantasy; Capra is cynical about the political process. Mr. Willis is exceptional because he's an outsider. His is exceptional because the political actors are selfishly motivated, including Toby.

Synopsis, cont'd

Leo tells Bartlet about his separation. Bartlet insists Leo and his wife could get back together. Leo is upset and wanted support; Bartlet isn't supportive.

Josh, Charlie, Sam, Mallory, Zoey, and C.J. are at a bar. They talk about Sam's friend the call girl, C.J. is shocked that both Mallory and Zoey know. Zoe goes to get drinks at the bar, where an aggressive young man (Eric Balfour) hits on her; Charlie comes over and they get racist with Charlie and call Sam a "faggot." Zoey users her panic button to call the Secret Service when the belligerents try to start a fight. They are arrested and the White House staff leaving the bar.

Bartlet talks to Zoey about her protection, how uncomfortable he is, and how his greatest fear is her being kidnapped or killed by people who want to get to him. It is fatherly and thoughtful, albeit unpleasant for a kid about to start college. He gives an account of "the nightmare scenario," that she is kidnapped and ransomed, and he is completely lost as a panicked father who cannot engage in the ransom, much less run the military when it is necessary.[111]

Bartlet apologizes to Leo for being a jerk about Leo's collapsing marriage and offers support. Bartlet chews out the staff for taking his underage daughter to a bar. Donna keeps Josh's change from his sandwiches as a protest for not getting her money from the budget surplus. They sit down to play poker and recap the day. Toby watches Mr. Willis of Ohio cast a vote.

Production Note

Representative Skinner (Charley Lang) reappears for a longer exchange with Josh in "The Portland Trip " (episode 2.07).

Mr. Willis Goes to Washington, and Aaron Sorkin's Capra

Mr. Willis of Ohio is a direct homage to Capra's *Mr. Smith Goes to Washington*. One of the core messages of *The West Wing* is that government service can do good, but Sorkin is aware that the audience is cynical about Washington. What defeats the evil entrenched politicians is the decency of the "common man," Mr. Willis,[112] someone who is self-effacing about his intelligence and displays moral decency. Moral decency is the purview of the common man, not the politician. This makes Mr. Smith exceptional, too.

The West Wing can't go full Frank Capra, because our heroes are civil servants. Sorkin doesn't really write "the common man" like Mr. Smith as his protagonist. In *The West Wing*, our heroes are from elite universities; Josh went to Harvard and Sam went to Princeton. The President is a Nobel laureate economics professor. Our heroes deliver extended monologues with careful metaphors. Most of the heroes and villains of *The West Wing* are career political operatives, denizens of the District of Columbia.

Michael Walzer wrote about "the problem of dirty hands."[113] Sometimes, politicians may need to violate certain moral obligations for the public good. For example, a politician might be required to break a promise or tell a lie to best represent their constituents. Bartlet wrestles with this in *Take This Sabbath Day* (1.14). He must abide by a death penalty ruling despite his own moral commitments. He has to put the law above his own conscience.

Al Fann's Mr. Willis and Jimmy Stewart's Mr. Smith are political superheroes, because their moral decency allows them to make clear choices. Mr. Willis can act his conscience; he doesn't have to think about his political party or his constituents' interests. There are cases where the problem of dirty hands pushes back. These create moral dilemmas for our heroes throughout *The West Wing*, who aren't superheroes.

Chapter Four
Episodes 1.07-1.08

The State Dinner (1.07)

Air date: November 10, 1999
Director: Thomas Schlamme
Teleplay by: Aaron Sorkin
Writers: Aaron Sorkin and Paul Redford
Plotlines:
  a) The White House hosts a state dinner for the President of Indonesia.
  b) A hurricane heads towards South Carolina.
  c) A militia gets into a standoff with the FBI in Idaho.
  d) Laurie attends a White House function as an escort.

C.J. describes the First Lady's outfit for an upcoming state function to the press.[114] The event is a state dinner to honor the President of Indonesia.

There is a hurricane on course for South Carolina and Georgia. The teamsters and trucking company executives are in a standoff about a new contract, which may result in a strike. The FBI plans to take a militia compound in Idaho. C.J. dislikes focusing on the First Lady's shoes, rather than substance.

Josh is preparing for the hurricane by calling the Red Cross. Josh wants Donna to set up a meeting with an assistant to the President of Indonesia, during the state dinner. Donna has issues with Indonesia's human rights record, including the extrajudicial killing of alleged sorcerers.[115] Josh blows this off. Leo is preparing to meet with the teamsters, who are upset companies are using part-time labor to circumvent union membership and benefits.

President Bartlet and the President of Indonesia pose for photos. The President of Indonesia is brief in his interactions, as President Bartlet tries to make small talk. Bartlet says, "YoYo Ma is going to play."[116]

Sam is working on the toast for the State Dinner. Toby wants language in the speech less attached to Indonesia, because of Indonesia's human rights issues and corruption.

Leo meets with the trucking companies and the teamsters; the strike is the result of a failed mediation process. Both parties are hostile; Leo tries mediating, stressing the importance of trucking and shipping to the American economy.

Mandy meets with Josh about the FBI raid in Idaho. The FBI sold the militia guns the FBI knew to be illegal.[117]

The President tries to get the President of Indonesia to say more to the press; journalist Danny Concannon (Tim Busfield)[118] mentions protesters of vermeil, which we learn later is silver plated with gold, being used as centerpieces at the state dinner. Vermeil is controversial because of its history with the French aristocracy.[119]

Leo tells the President that they're moving ships to avoid the hurricane.

Toby writes a more combative speech for the state dinner; the speech attacks Indonesia for inadequate freedoms, including freedoms the press and the exercise of religion. Sam protests, because it is not a good idea to insult people after inviting them to dinner.

C.J. gives a briefing on vermeil. After she leaves the podium, C.J. is angry that Danny made this a story when the protest was small and silly. "You rouse rabble" They flirt badly.

Laurie and Sam eat in a diner. Laurie is concerned about the optics of being out with Sam, if someone recognizes them. Laurie has a client and doesn't know where he's taking her. Laurie returns to studying for law school.

The FBI is concerned about the militia in Idaho[120] as Mandy argues the FBI engaged in entrapment. Mandy suggests they send a negotiator. President Bartlet agrees to Mandy's plan. Josh and Mandy flirt badly. Sam asks Josh if there is anything from the President of Indonesia's past to illustrate a relationship with the United States. "He was once almost pushed out of an airplane by a CIA-trained operative."[121]

An exchange between Josh and Donna sets up a long gag where they cannot find an interpreter, so they use two guys to translate with the

Indonesian government official, who we find out (in the punchline) speaks English.

C.J. and First Lady Abigail Bartlet (Stockard Channing)[122] talk about the vermeil.[123] We get the impression the First Lady, in her first appearance, is smart and grounded. The First Lady jokes with Leo. The President is trying to help with the teamsters, the hurricane, and the raid in Idaho.[124]

Leo introduces Sam, Toby, and Josh to a major donor. The donor is Laurie's date. Sam pretends he doesn't know Laurie.[125]

Charlie's grandparents were in the path of the hurricane. They are safe. The hurricane turns back out to sea. Unfortunately, there are ships in its path.

Josh tells Mandy the standoff in Idaho is over. The militia shot the negotiator. She panics over the consequences of her decision.

Sorkinism

Sorkin reuses the trope over a senior official listening to a suggestion and losing confidence (a "crisis of confidence") again in "The Lame Duck Congress" (2.06). The idea is borrowed by *Parks and Recreation's West Wing* homage episode, "Live Ammo" (4.19).[126]

Synopsis, cont'd

The President calls the carrier group about to be hit by the hurricane. The President returns to the party. We get the conclusion of the translator gag with the Indonesian official, and we learn Josh and Toby want him to get a man released from Indonesian jail. The man is a political protester and teacher. The Indonesian government is not inclined to help. The Indonesian official says no, and cites the insulting speech Toby wrote.[127]

C.J. and Danny continue to banter and flirt.

The President breaks up the negotiation between the teamsters and executives by threatening to draft the truckers into military service,[128] taking federal control of the businesses in a dramatic (probably illegal) fashion.

The First Lady interrupts a conversation between Sam and Laurie. Laurie introduces herself under her name assumed for the date.

The President and First Lady talk about the hurricane, the FBI raid, and the limits of the President's power. He can't stop a hurricane.[129] The First Lady both humbles the President by acknowledging the limits of his power and encourages him to do what he can; the moment is a tender reminder of the limits of President Bartlet, and shows a healthy relationship.

The episode ends with the President speaking to the communications officer (Jeff Lewis, voice only) on a ship stuck in the hurricane. There is panic, against the visual of the President and staff safe and well-dressed. There's a fire in the engine room. The President is going to stay on the call. Credits.

The Patronizing Defense against human rights obligations

Societies may have different views about taxation and trade. Those disagreements may be reasonable. Societies may also have different views about human rights, with some countries refusing to recognize the dignity of women, LGBTQ+ people, or ethnic and religious minorities. How do we engage with societies when their values don't respect human rights?

How do we approach differences in culture, social attitudes, and ethics? It is popular to adopt a live-and-let-live approach. The United States, for example, should not dictate to Indonesia that Indonesia be a secular state, rather than an officially Muslim one. That approach works for government structure and economic policy; it doesn't work for human rights.

Unfortunately, contemporary foreign policy often runs these two things together. For example, persecution of ethnic minorities is sometimes treated a matter of "internal affairs," like Chinese government's persecution of Uighurs in Xinjiang.[130]

Sorkin wrestles with this explicitly in "The Women of Qumar" (3.08), in addition to raising critiques of how the United States treats many of our fellow Americans, including LGBTQ+, Black and Latino Americans, Muslim and Arab Americans, and Native Americans.

Enemies (1.08)

Air Date: November 17, 1999
Writer: Aaron Sorkin
Teleplay by: Ron Osborn and Jeff Reno
Director: Alan Taylor

Plotlines
   a) Congressional Republicans sabotage a banking bill.
   b) The President humiliates Vice President Hoynes in a cabinet meeting.
   c) Mallory and Leo fight about Leo's separation from his wife.
   d) Sam and Mallory have a date.

Production Note

This is the first episode in the series where the teleplay is not written by Aaron Sorkin.

Synopsis

The episode opens with the President giving a lecture on national parks to Josh. "You're quite a nerd, Mr. President." Josh responds.

Fact Check:

Bartlet says, "There are 54 national parks in this country." That was likely true at the time of writing, but Black Canyon in Colorado was made a national park on October 21, 1999, before airing of the episode.

Synopsis, cont'd

Leo and Mallory have breakfast. Mallory is a public-school teacher; Leo is independently wealthy. Leo is congratulated by a congressman over the "banking bill." Leo has opera tickets; he gives the tickets to Mallory.

The President is excited about the banking bill. "This is *the* story." Mrs. Landingham distracts the President to help C.J. is avoid a conversation about national parks. The Vice President leads the cabinet meeting, as the President arrives late. The President enters the room and immediately humiliates the Vice President.

Sam and Toby talk about speech writing. Josh is nervous about the banking bill.

Danny ask C.J. for comment about the President humiliating Vice President Hoynes. She denies it on the record; she confirms it off the record. Danny asks C.J. out. She cannot date a member of the press, as this would be a massive conflict of interest. Dee Dee Myers, Press Secretary to Bill Clinton, was a consultant on the show; it's unclear whether this comes out of her experience.[131]

Danny asks Hoynes about the cabinet meeting. Hoynes denies anything happened.

Mallory asks Sam out to the opera. Mallory knows Sam slept with a call girl and she has a crush on him.

Sam and C.J. wait for Leo. Sam wants Leo's permission to date Mallory. C.J. wants to talk about the leak of the cabinet meeting.[132] Sam thinks Hoynes leaked the humiliating incident, though we know that isn't true from seeing the exchange between Hoynes and Danny.

Hoynes speaks to the press on the transformative role of the internet.[133] C.J. asks him about the leak; the Vice President denies he is the leak. We know he's not the leak, as we saw him deny it to Danny.

Two congressmen attached a land-use rider to the banking bill. "They want to strip mine the length and breadth of Montana." C.J. gets a question about the land use rider, but is unprepared. Danny follows C.J. back into the office, which he shouldn't do. Sam wants to pass the banking bill anyway; Josh wants to veto the bill.

The President and Leo make small talk and pivot to Leo's marriage. Mallory is furious at Leo, and the President points out being Chief of Staff is grueling.

Mandy wants to pass the bill. Josh makes it clear that the issue with the land use rider isn't the rider itself.[134] This is the cynicism about political process creeping in through our heroes. Legislation is about winning and losing, and not helping people or doing right by their constituents.

The President must send a birthday congratulation to a lower-level cabinet official. Leo sends the task to Sam. Leo is disrupting Sam's date with Mallory.

C.J. and Mandy discuss the banking bill; Toby and Josh want to fight back. Mandy suggests C.J. offer Danny facetime with the President in exchange for not running the story about the cabinet meeting.

The President asks Sam to continue with the birthday message; Sam will miss his date.

C.J. meets with Danny. Danny confirms the stenographer was the leak. C.J. offers him the interview; Danny will not run the story if the stenographer is not fired.

Mallory berates Sam for missing the date. Mallory realizes her father and the President made Sam miss the date.

Josh and Toby discover the land use rider came from one of Toby's friends.

C.J. brings the deal with Danny to the President. The President agrees. The President blames Hoynes for the leak. C.J. tells him the leak was the stenographer, not Hoynes.

Mallory storms into her father's office. The President interrupts. He reads Leo's schedule to Mallory, which illustrates the difficulty of the job. Leo and Mallory go out for dinner, leaving Sam to work on the birthday message.

The President and Vice President meet. The Vice President is a southern Democrat who helped Bartlet win the election,[135] despite losing in the primary and feeling entitled to greater success. Bartlet is angry, "you shouldn't have made me beg." Their conflict is petty.

Josh and Mandy argue about the banking bill. Mandy pushes him. "You're fighting the wrong fights and you're doing it for the wrong reasons."[136]

Josh proposes using the Antiquities Act[137] to make Big Sky (the land impacted by the land use rider) a national park, bringing us back to the lecture at the beginning. The President is excited about creating a new park.

Short Aside on Big Sky

The cast refers to Big Sky as a "pile of rocks" throughout the episode. Some[138] cringe at this. Presumably, having been to all United States national parks, President Bartlet would have seen this beautiful area. It's near Yellowstone and Grand Tetons.

Chapter Five
Episodes 1.09-1.11

This chapter and the next cover 1.09 to 1.15. These are among the strongest episodes in the series. The writers and cast find the human and moral center of the show. Richard Schiff won an Emmy for Best Supporting Actor in a Drama for "In Excelsis Deo" (1.10); Alison Janney won Best Supporting Actress for "Celestial Navigation" (1.15). "Take This Sabbath Day" (1.14) grapples with Bartlet's morality, religion, and the death penalty. "Take Out the Trash Day" (1.13) deeply impacted me as an LGBTQ+ kid following the murder of Matthew Shepherd, during public debates about hate crimes legislation.

These episodes also feature terrific guest actors. Edward James Olmos bookends this run, in "The Short List" (1.09) and" Celestial Navigation" (1.15). Roger Rees plays the manic Lord John Marbury, a recurring character. Academy Award winner Karl Malden gives his final acting performance as President Bartlet's priest and confessor. CCH Pounder gives a brief, powerful performance as Housing and Urban Development Secretary Deborah O'Leary.

These episodes develop the major tension of the first season: The staff gives up on doing the right thing for political reasons. This sets up the transition at the end of the season.

The Short List (1.09)

Aired on: November 24, 1999
Director: Bill D'Elia
Story By: Dee Dee Myers
Teleplay By: Aaron Sorkin and Patrick Caddell
Plotlines:
    a)   The President selects a Supreme Court nominee.

b) Rep. Lillienfield baselessly alleges that 1-in-3 White House staffers are on drugs.

c) Danny tries to get a date with C.J.

In the opening, the staff celebrates Judge Peyton Cabot Harrison III (Ken Howard)[139] agreeing to meet with the White House to discuss a nomination to the Supreme Court. The staff celebrates. The staff discusses the rollout and confirmation schedule.

The President meets with outgoing Justice Crouch (Mason Adams).[140] The Justice prefers "Mendoza" as his successor and dislikes President Bartlet, who he regards as weak.

CROUCH: Mendoza was on the short list so you could say you had a Hispanic on the short list… You ran great guns during the campaign. It was an insurgency, boy, a sight to see. And then you drove to the middle of the road the moment after you took the oath, nothing but a long line painted yellow. I wanted to retire five years ago, but I waited for a Democrat. I wanted a Democrat and instead I got you.

Danny knows the President plans to nominate Harrison, but C.J. will not confirm it. The President and Crouch continue to argue.[141]

Josh and Donna banter. Mandy asks Josh why Congressman Lillienfield (Holmes Osborne) is holding a press conference.[142] Lillienfield makes the unsubstantiated claim that 1-in-3 White House staffers use illegal drugs. The staff recognizes this is an absurd allegation, but they must respond to it.

C.J. can't deny anyone in the White House uses drugs; there are too many employees. Leo suggests they "look into it," which implies drug testing the staff.[143] Josh opposes drug testing and investigating the issue. Toby and Mandy support requiring the drug testing.

Sam gets an anonymous call and heads out.

Leo and the President are excited about meeting with Harrison. They want an easy confirmation, which will help their approval. The President asks, briefly, if they looked at Mendoza. Leo says they did but picked Harrison instead. The President asks Toby for information about Mendoza; "I don't want it to be like 'we had a Hispanic on the short list.'"[144]

Sam's phone call concerns an unsigned note, allegedly written by Harrison; unsigned notes are written by law students and published anonymously (hence "unsigned").[145] The views in the note indicate Harrison doesn't believe in the right to abortion or other unenumerated rights. Sam is certain the unsigned note was written by Harrison.

We learn Sam is the superstar lawyer on the staff. (Josh is also a lawyer, but did not practice law.)

Josh and Donna talk about Lillienfield and the hearings. Lillienfield is on House Government Oversight.[146] Josh isn't worried about Donna; she knows people use drugs but won't rat them out. Josh is the reluctant witch hunter.

Josh knows Lillienfield has a specific goal. Lillienfield is targeting someone.

The press directly asks if C.J. uses drugs. She uses the word "subpoena." Danny flirts with C.J. but tells her now everyone is going to ask about subpoenas. Josh asks whether Danny has any information about Lillienfield. Danny also thinks Lillienfield has a specific target.

"C.J. likes goldfish," Josh tells Danny. Danny thinks he means the pet (when he means the crackers) and buys C.J. a pet fish. This introduces the fishbowl for Gail (the fish), which is decorated thematically in different episodes.[147] The President reads the unsigned note, which argues there is no right to privacy.

Harrison confirms he wrote the note. Sam grills Harrison about the note. It is also clear Harrison believes he is entitled to the seat on the Supreme Court and is offended by the aggressive inquiry. Harrison would be confirmed easily, but the staff does worries about how he would rule on the Court.

Josh meets with Leo. Leo is a recovering alcoholic. Josh asks Leo if there was something else. Leo confirms there were pills. Lillienfield is targeting Leo.

Harrison argues there are no unenumerated rights.

Note on Constitutional Law

The 9th Amendment to the Constitution states there are unenumerated rights: "The enumeration in the Constitution, of certain rights, shall not be construed to deny or disparage others retained by the people." Harrison's argument takes us to Sam's monologue about the importance of privacy, but unenumerated rights are part of constitutional jurisprudence and disagreement.

Taken in tandem, the 9th Amendment entails there are some unenumerated rights and the 14th Amendment entails that neither states nor the federal government can circumvent such rights. In the majority opinion in Dobbs v. Jackson Women's Health Organization (the decision which overturned Roe and Casey), Justice Alito refuses to apply the 14th Amendment to a right to abortion because unenumerated rights must be "deeply rooted in this Nation's history and tradition" and "implicit in the concept of ordered liberty."

Rights of equal access to spaces, for example, were not "deeply rooted in this Nation's history and tradition" as civil rights law developed. This would exclude the right to equal access in education (Brown v. Board of Education) or non-discrimination in places of public accommodation. In advancing this argument, Justice Alito ignores the historical interpretation of the 14th Amendment in civil rights law, but even Alito doesn't deny unenumerated rights.

Synopsis, cont'd

After Harrison leaves the room, Sam addresses the President:

SAM: It's not just about abortion. It's about the next 20 years. '20s and '30s it was the role of government. '50s and '60s it was civil rights. The next two decades are going to be privacy.[148] I'm talking about the internet. I'm talking about cell phones. I'm talking about health records and who's gay and who's not.[149] Moreover, in a country built on the will to be free what could be more fundamental than this?

Fact checking Harrison's basic constitutional arguments

During the examination, Harrison refers to "freedom of expression" in defense of an obnoxious tie, in the 1st Amendment. There is no such enumeration. The relevant portion of the 1st Amendment enumerates "freedom of speech, or of the press; or the right of the people peaceably to assemble, and to petition the Government for a redress of grievances." It doesn't say anything about clothing. On the view Harrison endorses, there is no right to wear an ugly tie.

Sam's prediction that the next two decades (1999 to 2020) would be about privacy and extended into government surveillance, health information privacy, and other areas is totally right. Hrishi Hirway notes this episode is pre-Patriot Act. The discussion of surveillance and privacy in this episode can't foresee the changes after 9/11.[150] Hirway was commenting before the ruling in Dobbs overturned Roe and Casey; that also marks significant change, as abortion remains a major issue.

Synopsis cont'd

The staff plans to meet Mendoza. Mandy thinks Mendoza is a difficult nominee. Harrison was decidedly upper-class and privileged; Mendoza is working-class, a former cop who was shot in the line of duty and became a lawyer going to night school.[151]

Mendoza (Edward James Olmos)[152] is introduced to President Bartlet. He is a commanding presence, even opposite President Bartlet.

Harrison knows Charlie, who caddied at a country club where Harrison golfed.[153] This emphasizes Harrison's privilege in contrast Charlie and Mendoza. Leo tells the President about Lillienfield targeting Leo's pill addiction.

Toby asks Mendoza how Mendoza would rule about a White House staffer being forced to take a drug test. Mendoza says he would insist the employee be reinstated, as it violates the employee's rights against search and seizure. The President decides to appoint Mendoza to the Supreme Court.

In Excelsis Deo (1.10)

Aired on: December 15, 1999
Directed by: Alex Graves[154]
Written by: Rick Cleveland and Aaron Sorkin
Teleplay by: Aaron Sorkin
Plotlines:
  a) Toby gets a call from the police following the death of Korea veteran Walter Hoffnagle.[155]
  b) The staff prepares for the public release of Leo's drug abuse history.
  c) C.J. sends up a test balloon about possible hate crimes legislation.

It is December 23rd; this is a Christmas episode. The communications portion of the staff (Toby, C.J., Sam, and Mandy) are talking about Christmas, featuring Al Roker (he does not appear in the episode) as Santa.[156] They argue about whether it is "the new millennium," since it is going to be 2000, not 2001.

Toby gets a call from the D.C. police. C.J. discovers her Secret Service codename is "flamingo."[157]

Toby goes to the Vietnam War Memorial in D.C.[158] A man died. Toby was called because his card was in the man's pocket. Toby donated his jacket to Goodwill and the card was in the jacket. Toby notices a military tattoo. The man was a veteran of the Korean War. Toby is distressed that the body has not been taken to the coroner.

Josh and Donna banter about Christmas gifts. Leo is signing a stack of Christmas cards. Josh suggests fighting Lillienfield's release of Leo's drug abuse by approaching "Sam's friend" Laurie about her clients. Leo rejects this. Leo talks about a gay kid in Minnesota who was beaten, stripped naked, and pelted with rocks. [159]

C.J. "sends up a test balloon" at the press briefing, talking about a hate crimes bills. Toby learns about Walter Hoffnagle, the veteran who died. He tries to contact the Department of Veterans Affairs.

Donna knows about Leo's drug abuse. Leo's assistant Margaret told her. Donna wants Josh to act; Josh wants to act.

The President meets with children visiting the White House for Christmas. He is jovial and good with children. This is our first time seeing President Bartlet as a grandpa, though we heard about his grandchildren in the pilot. C.J. tells the President that Lowell Lydell has died. The President returns to his interactions with the kids; the President has to play different roles.

Sam is hesitant about hate crimes legislation; C.J. is not. Sam's Secret Service codename is "Princeton," and C.J. is irritated that she is "flamingo." Sam is going to Bermuda, though our heroes cannot have personal lives. Josh and Sam talk about approaching Laurie for Republican clients. Sam is against it.

Charlie and Mrs. Landingham talk. We learn her twin sons died in Vietnam on Christmas Eve. The holidays are difficult for her

Toby returns to the Vietnam memorial. He asks one of the volunteers if he knew Hoffnagle. The volunteer tells him where many of homeless people live.

Mandy wants to turn the President's Christmas shopping into a photo-op. They go to a rare books store. The President invites Leo over for Christmas, because Leo is divorced. Leo is concerned about Lillienfield's story. The President is not.

C.J. asks Sam what he and Josh are doing. Sam is evasive. They're going to meet Laurie.

Toby visits with the homeless, standing in line for soup. One homeless man (Raynor Scheine) knew Walter and introduce Toby to Walter's brother George (Paul Austin). Toby says they're going to have a funeral for Walter, with an honor guard. George Hoffnagle has mental health issues or disability, but another man promises to bring George to Walter's funeral. The scene ends with Toby giving the two men all the money out of his wallet.

TOBY: I'm sorry. This is absolutely none of my business, but your brother is entitled to a proper funeral with mourners, and I think he deserves an honor guard and you don't know me... but I'm... I'm an influential person. I'm a very powerful person... If I come and pick you up in the morning and bring you back after.
MAN: I'll make sure he's here.
TOBY: Thank you.

This is all Toby can do.

C.J. and Danny banter and flirt. Leo tells C.J. that he's not sure about hate crimes legislation. C.J. supports the hate crimes law.

Josh and Sam meet with Laurie. She is furious that they are asking her for information.

Leo and C.J. argue about hate crimes laws. Leo argues the punishment for the predicate crime is enough, that enhancing punishments based on hate crimes is not appropriate. C.J. points out that enhancements protect civil rights and it's good politics.

Leo yells at Sam and Josh for meeting with Laurie. Josh and Sam want to protect Leo. Leo is a father figure to them.

C.J. asks Danny what he thinks about hate crimes. Danny takes the position Leo endorsed on hate crimes. "One murder isn't any better or worse than another." C.J. suggests she and Danny go out and argue about it.

Josh bought Donna a book on skiing (because she wanted skiing equipment) for Christmas. Mrs. Landingham confronts Toby about using the Office of the President to secure an honor guard for Walter Hoffnagle.

Toby knows it was wrong but did it anyway. The President makes the same confrontation to Toby.

Mrs. Landingham goes with Toby to the funeral.

BARTLET: Apparently, I've arranged for an honor guard for somebody.
TOBY: Yes, sir. I'm sorry.
BARTLET: No, no. Just tell me, is there anything else I've arranged for? We're still in NATO, right?
TOBY: Yes, sir.
BARTLET: What's going on?
TOBY: A homeless man died last night, a Korean War veteran who was wearing a coat I gave to the Goodwill. It had my card in it.
BARTLET: Toby, you're not responsible—
TOBY: It took an hour and 20 minutes for the ambulance to get there. A lance corporal, United States Marine Corps, second of the seventh. I got better treatment at Pon Mun Yong.
BARTLET: Toby, if we start pulling strings like this, you don't think every homeless veteran will come out of the woodwork.
TOBY: I can only hope, sir.

Sorkin's "Both Sides" on Hate Crimes

The line about "not legislating what's in people's head" is a political throughline in discussion of hate crimes, as Sorkin wrestles with the Matthew Shepherd and James Byrd Hate Crimes Prevention Act.[160] The bill was eventually passed in the Obama administration, a decade later.

Sorkin comes back to this line about "we don't punish people for what's in their heads." It's not true. The law differentiates between crimes based on mental state. Prosecution and sentencing are responsive to what's in a person's head. A premeditated murder is different than a murder of passion.

Not all crimes are evaluated based solely on external circumstances. The argument Leo and Danny make is just nonsense. The argument is repeated in "Take Out the Trash Day". The policy chops in the show are often soft. Crimes which include targeting victims based on membership in a protected class (e.g. women, LGBTQ+, racial or religious minority, etc.) are subject to enhanced sentencing and additional charges for civil rights violations.

Lord John Marbury (1.11)

Aired on: January 5, 2000
Directed by: Kevin Rodney Sullivan
Teleplay by: Aaron Sorkin and Patrick Caddell
Written by: Patrick Caddell and Lawrence O'Donnell
Plotline:
   a) India and Pakistan have a military conflict in Kashmir.[161]
   b) C.J. loses credibility with the press when she denies the conflict.[162]
   c) Josh is subpoenaed about Leo's drug history.
   d) Zoey asks out Charlie.
   e) Mandy wants to take on a Republican client.

Production Note

   This episode introduces Lord John Marbury (Roger Rees), a beloved and eccentric character. Marbury's character is frequently involved in international affairs plotlines. Rees's performance as Marbury gets the most attention, but the episode is packed with excellent performances. Chinese Ambassador David is played by James Hong (*Chinatown* and *Big Trouble in Little China*) and most recently in *Everything, Everywhere, All at Once.*) Pakistani Ambassador Habib is played by Erick Avari (*The Beast of War; Heroes*). The Indian Ambassador is played by Iqbal Theba (*Glee; The George Carlin Show*). All three give strong performances in the episode.

Synopsis

   In a Navy yard, two satellite surveillance officers see military action in Kashmir.
   Josh is served with a subpoena by "Claypool." He is hostile to the process server, but signs for it.[163] "This is what I do now. I'm a professional hostile witness."
   The President and Leo went to the Situation Room. Admiral Fitzwallace informs the President that the Indian army launched an incursion into Kashmir,[164] including parts controlled by Pakistan.

ADM. FITZWALLACE: Approximately 300,000 troops.

BARTLET: In the last 25 minutes.

FITZWALLACE: Yes, sir.

BARTLET: 300,000 is an awfully large piece of troop movement to have been on a whim.

FITZWALLACE: Yes, sir.

BARTLET: This was long planned.

FITZWALLACE: Yes, sir.

BARTLET: All I'm trying to do right now… I'm trying to avoid making eye contact with the CIA Director.

It is an intelligence failure. Bartlet orders a national security briefing.

The staff, except C.J., meet in the Oval Office and receives a briefing on the military incursion. C.J. enters and the staff tells her (lying) there is no more news for the day. The conversation pivots to nuclear weapons.

Zoey asks Charlie out on a date.

Josh and Sam talk about the subpoena. Josh was charged with investigating potential drug use by White House staffers. Sam points out Josh is not a "real lawyer." Josh should bring a lawyer to the deposition. Mandy asks Sam about taking on a new client, a Republican. Mandy points out Sam is interested in getting things done, while Josh and Toby are more interested in "beating the other guys."

During the press briefing, a reporter (Colin K. Gray) directly asks C.J. about the incursion into Kashmir. C.J. denies there is an incursion.

The President is briefed in the Situation Room. C.J. is furious that no one told her. No one apologizes to her. Sometimes they need to send her in without the appropriate information. She needs credibility with the press. This damages her credibility.

Josh is in a hostile deposition. Claypool asks about his "investigation" into recreational drug use by White House staffers; Josh denies there was an investigation, then claims it wasn't serious. Josh attacks the examining attorney. The situation escalates.

C.J. is briefed by Ed and Larry (Peter James Smith and William Duffy)[165] and their briefing is straight from the Encyclopedia Britannica. C.J. is angry the staff lied to her. Sam asks Toby about Mandy working for a Republican. Toby is upset.

Bartlet, Leo, and Toby get a military briefing on nuclear weapons in

India. The White House does not know who has command of those weapons. Bartlet wants to bring in Lord John Marbury; Leo doesn't.

C.J. gets into an argument with Toby. Toby is her boss. "There's a concern that you're [C.J.] too friendly with the press."

Josh must go back to the deposition tomorrow. Toby tells Josh to take Sam as his lawyer.

President Bartlet meets with the Chinese Ambassador (James Hong). Charlie asks Bartlet if he can go on a date with Zoey. The meeting with the Chinese Ambassador emphasizes geographical tension. China does not like India, so the Chinese Ambassador makes clear that China will side with the Pakistan and may intervene on Pakistan's behalf.

Sam and Mandy talk about her prospective Republican client. Sam acknowledges that he advocated for her; he then points out Republicans are currently attacking Leo over his history of substance abuse. Sam agrees with Toby.

Bartlet meets with Pakistani Ambassador Habib (Erick Avari), who informs the President that Pakistan plants to retaliate in response to the incursion. The President and the Ambassador argue about whether Pakistan provoked the attack. The President has publicly condemned India's aggression. Bartlet's goal is de-escalation, but this may not be possible.[166]

Leo and the President talk about Zoey asking Charlie out. Leo asks if the President's concern is that Charlie is Black; the President insists he just doesn't like the idea of his daughter dating anyone, especially someone older.

The Indian Ambassador (Iqbal Theba) greets the President.

Josh and Sam go to the deposition. Claypool has records of Leo's stint in rehab, despite those records being protected by laws governing health information.[167] Sam ends the deposition.

The Indian Ambassador defends India's possession of nuclear weapons and the dispute with Pakistan.

BARTLET: Every time he talks about colonial western imperialism, I always want to remind him that the United States is also a revolutionary country that threw off its colonial masters.[168]
LEO: Why don't you?
BARTLET: I keep forgetting.

Lord John Marbury (Roger Rees) enters the room; he introduces himself to Leo, despite their having met several times. Leo and Marbury argue about the situation.[169] Leo is a military officer and a former pilot during Vietnam, while the President is not comfortable with military issues.

C.J. gives a list of Marbury's credentials to someone over the phone.[170] Toby enters and apologizes for leaving her out of the loop.

Marbury points out constant conflict between India and Pakistan. He proposes a solution to deescalate.[171] Bartlet asks Marbury to stick around to help with the situation.

Fact Check:

Bartlet and others refer to "Revelations" as the book in the Bible. Bartlet should know the last book in the Christian Bible is called "Revelation," singular.

Synopsis, cont'd

Bartlet gives Charlie permission to date Zoey, but he tells Charlie some people are going to have issues with him being Black and dating the President's daughter, Charlie should screen the mail and be careful.[172]

Marbury comes back with a temporary ceasefire. "And I looked and I beheld a pale horse and he that sat on him was Death and hell followed after." (Revelation 6:8, NIV) The passage is often discussed in the context of the development of the bomb, though the line attributed to Oppenheimer is from the *Bhagavad Gita*, "Now I am become Death, the destroyer of worlds."[173]

Chapter Six
Episodes 1.12-1.15

He Shall, From Time to Time (1.12)

Aired on: January 12, 2000
Directed by: Arlene Sanford
Teleplay by: Aaron Sorkin
Written by: Aaron Sorkin
Plotlines:
   a) Toby writes the State of the Union.
   b) The President has the flu.
   c) Josh picks a designated survivor.

The staff prepares for the State of the Union. There are typos and debates about how the speech sets up their political priorities and messaging. The President is sick and the First Lady (a medical doctor) has given him pills. He hasn't taken them.

The President collapses in his office, sick with the flu.

The medical team recommends some tests for the President. The President and Leo are called to the situation room. There is movement on the border of India and Pakistan, despite the ceasefire established in 1.11.

Mandy knows the story about Leo and pills is going to break; "it's on the Internet right now."[174] The President must be invited to appear before Congress to deliver the State of the Union, as a matter of procedure. That creates some mild tension despite being ordinary.

Toby and the President argue about inclusion of the phrase "the era of big government is over." Toby hates it, despite knowing the phrase is popular.

The First Lady is a medical doctor and takes responsibility for the President's care, asking the physician Admiral Hackett (Madison Mason) to leave the room. She implies something more serious than the flu. The President flirts with the First Lady; she is concerned and upset.

Josh wants to verify they have received an invitation to address Congress. Josh explains to Donna (in a tell-a-Donna) that he must pick someone to be the designated survivor in case the Capitol explodes, and the cabinet is killed.[175] He picked the Secretary of Agriculture. Leo prepares to address the press about his substance abuse and Leo acknowledges to the staff he is still attending Alcoholics Anonymous meetings (the Vice President's meetings); Sam wrote a draft of a statement of support for Leo. Leo tells Sam there should be no statement.

The First Lady takes care of the President. They banter and flirt.[176] The President is too sick to leave bed.

Leo addresses the press about his substance abuse issues.

Donna asks why Josh picked the Secretary of Agriculture. Josh notes the political considerations, that other cabinet members need to be there as political props.

JOSH: I really don't expect the Capitol building exploding.
DONNA: What percent of things exploding have been anticipated?[177]

Josh and Sam talk about Leo's press conference. Sam gave the statement of support to the President. Sam and Josh don't care about getting in trouble with Leo.

Democrats in Congress want the President to de-emphasize the role of the federal government in the State of the Union. Toby hates these meetings. The Democratic congressmen want to deemphasize the National Endowment for the Arts.

Sorkinism:
The NEA
is a theme in Sorkin's work. It comes up several times in *The West Wing* and is part of the opening monologue in the pilot for Sorkin's drama *The Newsroom*.[178]

Synopsis, cont'd

Mallory visits Leo. She is sad that she couldn't be at the press conference. Mallory saw the statement of support from the President. Leo is furious to discover the statement has leaked and berates Sam and Josh. Sam defends it and says he is going to defend Leo out of loyalty.

The First Lady and Mallory talk about Mallory's crush on Sam.[179] Leo and the First Lady talk about postponing the State of the Union; the First Lady is worried about the President's health. The First Lady tells Leo the President has multiple sclerosis.[180]

The President recuperates in bed, watching soap operas.

Leo and the President talk about the President having multiple sclerosis and choosing not to tell anyone. They withheld this from the public when he was running for President; this is a potential scandal. The President says he's proud of Leo for press conference about past substance abuse. The White House is going to put out the statement of support.

LEO: When I was lying on my face in the hotel parking lot, you were the one I called.
BARTLET: And you stood up there today, I was so proud. I wanted to be with you.
LEO: No, no.
BARTLET: I tried to get up and I fell back down again.
LEO: I know the feeling.

Toby wants to keep funding for the National Endowment for the Arts in the State of the Union.[181] Toby decides they should pivot the speech and trumpet the role of government, instead of trying to run from it. He wants to pitch this to the President.

The President and Leo meet with Marbury. Marbury suggests the White House "buy them [India and Pakistan] off." Foreign aid and incentives for investment can provide strong disincentive for going to war. It's a way of providing a "carrot" (Sorkin's analogy in the scene).

Toby brings his proposal for the State of the Union to the President.

TOBY: I want to change the sentiment. We're running away from ourselves. I know we can score points that way. I was the principal architect of that campaign strategy right along with you, Josh. But we're here now. Tomorrow night we do an immense thing. We have to say what we feel: that government no matter what its failures in the past and in times to come for that matter, government can be a place where people come together and where no one gets left behind. No one gets left behind. An instrument of good. I've got no trouble understanding why the line tested well, Josh, but I don't think that means we should say it. I think that means we should change it.

Josh and the President agree to this shift in the State of the Union.[182]
The President prepares to give the State of the Union. Sam, C.J. and Josh talk. Mallory finds out that Sam wrote the President's statement defending Leo; she kisses Sam and then walks away in confusing disgust. C.J. meets with Danny in her office.

The First Lady and the President flirt as he gets dressed.

C.J. kisses Danny and then leaves. It's the second kiss-and-run in a few minutes.

Lord Marbury, Leo, and the President look at satellite photos of Indian forces withdrawing from Kashmir.

The President addresses the staff. He is proud of the speech and praises Toby and Sam for writing it. He then greets the Secretary of Agriculture, who gives him a copy of the Constitution translated into Latin. "He shall, from time to time, give to the Congress information of the state of the union and recommend to their consideration such measures as he judges necessary and expedient." Bartlet says kind words about Leo.

Take Out the Trash Day (1.13)

Aired on: January 26, 2000
Directed by: Ken Olin
Teleplay by: Aaron Sorkin
Written by: Aaron Sorkin
Plotlines:
   a) Leo's history of drug abuse is public and becomes a central issue.
   b) A sex education report suggests not teaching abstinence-only.
   c) Lowell Lydell's parents are critical of the President.
   d) An advance man for the Vice President was misusing government resources.

C.J. prepares the press for a bill signing outside. They introduce the ritual of signing the bill with multiple pens, which are given away as souvenirs. Josiah Bartlet will sign the bill with 15 pens, including one to dot the I and another to cross the Ts.

The parents of Lowell Lydell, the boy beaten to death for being gay (1.10), are going to visit the White House to attend the bill signing. The press asks about whether the Lydells are supporters of the President and if they will be available to the press. Mandy mentions this might be dangerous. It's possible the Lydells are ashamed of their son being gay. C.J. plans to meet with the parents before the bill signing.

Josh needs C.J. to read a report about sex education, that Republicans will only agree to increase funding to teachers if the law stipulates only teaching abstinence.[183]

After the opening credits, C.J. and Danny banter as C.J. reads the report. Danny has a story about an "advance man" for the Vice President who used a Navy helicopter to play golf.[184]

Another tell-a-Donna. Josh explains to Donna that they call Friday "take out the trash day." The White House releases stories all in a big lump and they want them in the paper on Saturday, when people don't read the paper.[185]

Sam and Toby discuss a story in the Georgetown Hoya; Zoey is a student at Georgetown and her sociology professor is teaching racist content.[186]

Leo is cranky about the sex education report. Josh and Sam meet with a Republican Congressman about the White House budget and Leo's substance abuse. Mrs. Landingham lectures the younger assistants that they shouldn't gossip.[187] Donna and the assistants think they know who leaked the story about the advanced man. Toby and C.J. talk about the advance man. Toby tells C.J. about the sociology professor and they're going to "take it out with the trash."

Josh, Sam, and Toby talk about the woman Donna believes leaked the story about the advance man. Josh and Sam know she leaked Leo's substance abuse. She had FBI clearance.

The staff sets up a short plotline about Toby meeting with members of Congress disrupting appointments to the Corporation for Public Broadcasting. The President is concerned that Lowell Lydell's father is ashamed his son was gay. C.J. is concerned about the sex education report. The President instructs Josh and Sam to preempt a hearing about Leo's substance abuse.

Leo is going to meet with Simon Blye. The President thinks Blye is a fair-weather friend and warns Leo not to trust him.

C.J. asks Danny about whether a father could be ashamed of his gay son even after the kid was killed; she's talking about the Lydells with Danny, even though she can't without violating her professional responsibilities. Danny knows about take out the trash day. C.J. is going to trash Danny's story about the advance man.

Josh and Sam meet with Representative Bruno (James Handy). Bruno chews out Josh and Sam for handling the situation poorly, though he is trying to help them prevent an investigation.

Leo meets with Simon Blye (Dakin Matthews).[188] Blye plans to publish an editorial suggesting Leo should resign. Bruno is trying to be helpful, even though he's a Republican. "I'd like to hold hearings into the two of you being stupid." He's right about Josh and Sam in handling the Claypool deposition.

Toby's defends PBS. PBS's audience is more representative of the public than the general TV audience. While PBS doesn't collect money from the Children's Television Workshop, the goal of a public service isn't to make a profit.

C.J. meets with the Lydells (Ray Baker; Lynda Gehringer). Mandy and the President discuss the sex education report. Mr. Lydell is quiet, but snaps under questioning. His issue isn't his son being gay, but with American politics being homophobic and the White House failing to speak out for gay rights.

MR. LYDELL: The hate crimes bill is fine. Who gives a damn? It's fine. I don't care. If you ask me, we shouldn't be making laws against what's in a person's head, but I don't give a damn. It's fine. I don't understand how this President who I voted for, I don't understand how he can take such a completely weak-assed position on gay rights, gays in the military, gay marriage, gay adoption, boards of education. Where the hell is he? I want to know what quality necessary to being a parent the President thinks my son lacked. I want to know from this President who has served not one day in uniform—I served two tours in Vietnam—I want to know what quality necessary to being a soldier this President feels my son lacked. Lady, I'm not embarrassed that my son was gay, my government is.

C.J. is jarred. C.J. and Mandy take focus off the Lydell family and steer the press away. C.J. agrees with Mr. Lydell and wants to direct a reporter to the story, she cannot do that. She takes out the trash.

The Politicization of LGBTQ+ rights during the Clinton years

The speech from Mr. Lydell is an indictment of the Clinton administration. Bill Clinton was considered a supporter of gay rights, relative to the standards, but Mr. Lydell cites policies of the Clinton administration. Clinton signed the "Defense of Marriage Act" (DOMA) in 1996, which defined marriage as between one man and one woman for all federal purposes. This was a broad Democratic policy until Obama's first term.[189]

Synopsis, cont'd

Josh and Sam cut a deal to avoid hearings in the House of Representatives. Sam fires Karen Larson (Liza Weil)[190] for leaking about Leo. Larson confirms she leaked Leo's treatment history.

The President says they're going to bury the sex education report. C.J. is angry; they're making decisions about the rights and health of people for political reasons. They are doing the wrong thing for political reasons.[191] C.J. is disturbed by the White House's position on gay rights in a closing exchange with the President. She considers leaking Mr. Lydell's views. Danny won't take the lead because he likes C.J.[192]

Leo meets with Karen Larson; they talk about having alcoholic and abusive parents. Leo forgives her for leaking about his substance abuse; he reinstates her as an employee.[193]

Take This Sabbath Day (1.14)

Aired on: February 9, 2000
Director: Thomas Schlamme
Story by: Lawrence O'Donnell & Paul Redford[194] and Aaron Sorkin
Teleplay by: Aaron Sorkin
Plotlines
  a) The President decides whether to commute the sentence of a death row inmate on the eve of his execution.
  b) Josh is berated by a campaign manager for cutting off funding to her campaign.
  c) Toby wrestles with Jewish attitudes towards the death penalty.

Note on Religion in *The West Wing*

This episode is a prelude to a major theme in the second season, the struggle between Bartlet's religious and professional obligations. The show wrestles with religion, especially Bartlet's Catholicism. (Leo and C.J. are also Catholic.) This episode also wrestles with Jewish religious identity and theology; while Sorkin has some Jewish roots, he is not practicing and his knowledge of Jewish religious practice is limited.[195] Josh and Toby are both Jewish. Bradley Whitford is not; Richard Schiff is the only Jewish actor in the main cast until Joshua Malina joined in Season 3.

Synopsis

A stay of execution is denied by the Supreme Court. Several attorneys leaving the Court, including Bobby Zane (Noah Emmerich);[196] Zane knows Sam Seaborn from high school.

Josh wants to go to a bachelor party but needs to see Sam. Sam and Josh talk about "Joey Lucas," a campaign manager for "O'Dwyer." This dialogue has minimal context. Josh will meet with Joey Lucas. Sam is planning to go sailing, but is interrupted by Bobby Zane.

Sam and Bobby Zane talk about the death penalty case. Zane tells Sam he needs to direct the President to stay the execution; Sam points out that no one directs the President to do anything. The President has the power to issue clemency, to stay the execution, but the President "believes in the separation of powers" (according to Sam) and does not want to get involved in a judicial matter. As we see through the episode, it is not as simple as mere separation of powers; that is expedient to sidestep the issue.

Sam says Toby will be at shul and gives Zane the address.

Sam and Leo discuss the execution, which was supposed to be stayed and remanded to a lower circuit. Sam and Leo don't want to deal with the death penalty. Sam mentions the execution is 12:01 a.m. Monday morning. Leo asks why he is not being executed immediately. "Because we don't execute people on the Sabbath."

Notes on Death Penalty Practices

It is still true that the United States does not execute people on the sabbath. 12:01 a.m. is standard time for issuance of an execution warrant because the warrant is valid for one full day,[197] and scheduling at 12:01 a.m. gives the maximum amount of time if circumstances delay the execution.

Synopsis, cont'd

Josh is passed out on the floor of his office. Donna wakes him up for his meeting with Joey Lucas. Donna gets him a change of clothes, leaving him in Sam's sailing gear. Josh looks ridiculous. He is interrupted by Joey Lucas.

C.J. and the President are fighting because the President lectured C.J. on the fjords. Leo meets them on the tarmac, telling the President about the execution.

Toby is in shul. Rabbi Glassman (David Proval)[198] gives a sermon on vengeance. Toby's pager goes off.

RABBI GLASSMAN: We will sing not only to entertain our children but to be reminded by the Haggadah[199] the simple truth that violence begets violence. Vengeance is not Jewish.

Sam asks if Toby's rabbi is giving a sermon on capital punishment. He is. Sam realizes Bobby Zane contacted Toby's rabbi.

A voice yells at Josh. We realize quickly the voice is a sign language interpreter (Bill O'Brien) for Joey Lucas (Marlee Matlin). The interpreter is yelling. Joey Lucas is furious. Josh is hungover and disoriented. It takes him a moment to realize Joey Lucas is the deaf woman. Josh excuses himself to change clothes. Donna tells Josh, "The appeal was denied."

Sam, Toby, Mandy, and Josh discuss the appeal and they are nervous about the President making a decision on the death penalty.

Fact Check:

The staff notes '63 was the last federal execution; this was true when the episode aired. Victor Feguer was executed was executed by hanging for kidnapping and murder under President Kennedy. This informs the relationship between the death penalty and Bartlet's Catholicism. Since this episode aired, the United States has executed 16 people (three under George W. Bush, starting with Tim McVeigh in '01; 13 under Trump, all at the end of his presidency). All 16 were executed by lethal injection at the US Prison in Terra Haute, Indiana. The episode notes Lincoln was the last President to use clemency powers in a death penalty case; this is still true.

Most executions today are handled by state governments. The President cannot extend clemency in state criminal matters; that power lies with the governor of the state.

Synopsis, cont'd

Sam notes there are pretexts for the President to commute, issues with the prosecution. Toby is angry Sam told Zane about his temple. Toby says the President will not commute the sentence.

Leo briefs the President on the procedural elements of the case. The case is a federal crime because some drug related homicides are prosecuted by the federal government. "I'm not going to be very good at this, Leo," the President admits. He asks Charlie to bring a priest from Hanover, New Hampshire down and to schedule a call with the Pope. This sets up the tension between the President's religious and civil obligations.

BARTLET: If they did [find the guy who shot your mother] would you
    want to see him executed? Killing a police officer is a capital crime,
    I figure you must have thought about it.
CHARLIE: Yes, sir.
BARTLET: And?
CHARLIE: I wouldn't want to see him executed, sir. I'd want to do it
    myself.

Joey Lucas lectures Josh on funding the candidate she is managing. Their opponent (in the California 46th)[200] is a far-right figure; they have a chance at beating him. Josh explains they want to keep the far-right congressman as a cartoonish foil. Joey Lucas wants to speak to the President. Josh laughs at her. The President appears behind Josh and introduces himself. He invites Joey Lucas to walk with him.

President Bartlet brings Joey Lucas into the Oval Office. He asks her if he should commute the sentence; she wants the President to commute the sentence because she opposes capital punishment as a Catholic. The President points out that great Catholic thinkers supported the death penalty; she thinks those views are arcane, though the death penalty enjoys wide public support. "That's a political problem," not a moral problem. She asks the President about cutting off funding to her campaign.

BARTLET: I don't like guys who run for congress because they think it's a good gig. Find yourself a live one and I'll get interested. In the meantime, the devil you know beats the devil you don't, and I like the devil I got.

The answer ends the conversation.

Toby meets with Rabbi Glassman. The cantor is practicing in the background. Toby points out that the Rabbi knew about the looming execution and the Rabbi acknowledges this.

TOBY: You want me to go into the Oval Office and say, "vengeance is not Jewish."
GLASSMAN: Why not?
TOBY: Well for one thing neither is the President.
[…]
GLASSMAN: You spent the day hoping the President wouldn't call the Pope.
TOBY: You're damn right I did.
GLASSMAN: If he had commuted the sentence after talking to the Pope, the worst fears of every non-Catholic who voted for him would be realized.
TOBY: Congratulations, Rabbi Glassman, you may now join the White House communications staff.

Historical Context on Catholicism in American Politics

The exchange between Toby and Rabbi Glassman on "calling the Pope" evokes concerns about Catholic politicians and the Church, going back to Al Smith (the first Catholic nominated for President by a major party) and John F. Kennedy (the first Catholic elected President). There was a concern that a Catholic President would obey the Pope, rather than his civil obligation to the American public. This was salient when JFK allowed the execution of Fegeur in '63.

Iowa Governor Harold Hughes and other opponents of the death penalty advocated for clemency for Fegeur, which could only be granted by President Kennedy. Some advocates explicitly invoked Catholicism. Fegeur was convicted of kidnapping and murdering a doctor. Fegeur was executed by hanging in Fort Madison on March 15, 1963.

Synopsis, cont'd

Toby wrestles with the implications of capital punishment in Jewish ethics.

TOBY: The Torah doesn't prohibit capital punishment.
GLASSMAN: No.
TOBY: It says, "an eye for an eye."
GLASSMAN: You know what it also says? It says a rebellious child can be brought to the city gates and stoned to death. It says homosexuality is an abomination and punishable by death. It says men can be polygamous and slavery is acceptable. For all I know, that thinking reflected the best wisdom of its time, but it is just plain wrong by any modern standard. Society has a right to protect itself, but it does not have a right to be vengeful. It has a right to punish, but it doesn't have a right to kill.[201]

C.J. wrestles with talking about the execution from the podium, reading about the family of the man who is going to be executed. She grapples with knowing about the man's mother.

Toby and the President talk about the death penalty. "Even 2000 years ago, the rabbis of the Talmud couldn't stomach it... they made it impossible for the state to punish people by killing them."[202]

The President and Leo talk; the President wants to commute the sentence but recognizes he must act in accordance with the law.[203]

Sam and Leo talk about the case. Leo confirms the President is not going to commute the sentence. Sam asks Leo if the solution would've been to keep the President out of the country, rather than address the issue substantively. Sam vents his frustration with the lack of moral direction.

SAM: Leo, there are times when we're absolutely nowhere.[204]

Josh meets with Joey Lucas. The President sends Josh to apologize and say they were impressed with her. He suggests Lucas consider running in the future.

The President meets with Fr. Cavanaugh (Karl Malden). The President explains he prefers to be addressed as "Mr. President" in the Oval Office, because it helps to think of himself as the Office, rather than a man. This is at the core of the moral dilemma, where he is charged with enforcing the law. Cavanaugh explains there was an opportunity to commute the sentence, the President had the authority, and he should have done it, but he didn't. Cavanaugh tells a parable about waiting for a sign when others are coming to help; Fr. Cavanaugh reminds the President many told him to commute the sentence.

The man is executed. Fr. Cavanaugh hears the President's confession.

Celestial Navigation (1.15)

Aired on: February 16, 2000
Directed by: Christopher Misiano
Story by: Dee Dee Myers and Lawrence O'Donnell
Teleplay by: Aaron Sorkin
Plotlines:
a)   Sam and Toby get Judge Mendoza out of jail in Connecticut.
b)   The HUD Secretary accuses a member of congress of racism.
c)   Josh mishandles a press briefing.[205]
d)   C.J. has emergency root canal surgery.

Josh gives a lecture at Georgetown. Before Josh goes onstage, he talks to Sam because Judge Mendoza (their nominee for the Supreme Court) has been arrested for drunk driving; Mendoza doesn't drink.

Josh talks to the students about his day.

The staff talk about Mendoza being arrested. Sam suspects it is racial profiling. Toby and Sam go to Connecticut to get Mendoza out of jail.

Josh tells a story about the last few days and how the news cycle has been difficult. The day was supposed to be about education reform and recruiting teachers. C.J. has a dentist appointment for pain. The Secretary for Housing and Urban Development Deborah O'Leary (CCH Pounder)[206] called a congressman racist.

The President gives remarks after signing a bill on education.

Danny asks the President if he agrees with Secretary O'Leary that the congressman is racist. The President avoids it; Danny pushes and the President says he will ask the Secretary to apologize.

Josh takes a call in the middle of his story. It is Sam and Toby, lost in Connecticut.

The HUD Secretary yells at Leo. She was right to call the congressman racist; the President shouldn't have suggested she apologize. She is humiliated by the prospect of apologizing. Leo acknowledges the President isn't angry about the comments.

C.J. had emergency root canal surgery at the dentist's office. She cannot speak. Josh decides he will handle the press briefing. Josh gets combative with the press. The briefing is a disaster. He implies there is an unpublished plan to fight inflation.[207]

Sam and Toby are still lost in Connecticut. Toby mocks Josh's "secret plan to fight inflation."

Sam and Toby go into the police station. Sam asks to see the watch commander. Sam explains to that he needs to release Mendoza; the junior officer sees a picture of Toby in the newspaper next to the President.

Toby and C.J. both yell at Josh for screwing up the briefing. Sam tells the staff that Mendoza commented on Secretary O'Leary's remarks; Mendoza said the President was wrong to make the Secretary apologize. This creates another scandal.

Josh explains the second-hardest job in the White House is Charlie's job, the personal aide to the President. He wakes the President up in the morning. They try to get the President out of bed. Bartlet chews out the staff, especially Josh.

The police officer defends the decision to pull Mendoza over. Sam points out Mendoza could not have been drinking. Mendoza has a liver disease that makes alcohol fatal.

Toby talks to Mendoza, sitting in a cell. Mendoza refused the breathalyzer test because it was an illegal search. He was racially profiled.[208] Mendoza plans to fight the case.

MENDOZA: My kid was in the car, Toby. They patted me down and they handcuffed me in front of my nine-year-old boy. Then he and his mother got to see them put me in the squad car and drive away.

TOBY: He's also seen you wearing a robe with a gavel in your hand.

MENDOZA: He doesn't understand that. He doesn't know what that is. He understands what the police are because he watches television. That's what he is going to remember. His father being handcuffed. So, America just got another pissed off guy with dark skin.

Toby talks Mendoza out of the cell. The officers will apologize to Mendoza, his wife and son.

Sorkinism:

This is one of two times the framing device through an interview is used in this season. President Bartlet is giving a talk in What Kind of Day Has It Been (1.22).

Chapter Seven
Episodes 1.16-1.18

20 Hours in L.A. (1.16)

Aired on: February 23, 2000
Directed by: Alan Taylor
Teleplay by: Aaron Sorkin
Written by: Aaron Sorkin
Plotlines
  a) The President attends a fundraiser in Los Angeles and has an issue with the organizer.
  b) The Vice President must break a tie in the Senate, but has misgivings about the legislation.
  c) The White House staff argues about whether to oppose a constitutional amendment banning flag burning.

The President prepares for a fundraising trip in Los Angeles; the whole of the trip will take one day. The Vice President is expected to break a tie in the Senate on the ethanol tax credit. Zoey has a new Secret Service agent on her detail, Gina Toscano (Jorja Fox).[209]

Note on the ethanol tax credit

The ethanol tax credit is a tax break to corn farmers in the Midwest, especially Iowa. *The West Wing* criticizes it regularly, arguing it was done for political reasons and was bad policy.[210] Ethanol is a corn-based fuel alternative, often criticized for being inefficient. *The West Wing* criticizes the ethanol tax credits because they received widespread support in Iowa, the first Presidential primary states. The show argues that the ethanol tax credit is an attempt to buy presidential primary votes in Iowa.

Synopsis, cont'd

A Representative is going to introduce a bill on gays in the military. Ted Marcus is holding the President's fundraiser; Marcus is upset about the proposed bill. Zoey and Charlie are dating.

Agent Toscano is young; the President quizzes her. She is prepared to address white supremacist hate mail and threats against Zoey and Charlie. To keep Zoey's trust, Agent Toscano may need to keep secrets, even from the President. Protection requires trust.

Ethanol creates jobs in Iowa and people in Iowa support it; the rest of the country views it as a buyoff.

C.J. walks the press through the schedule for the trip. The President is going to hear proposals to amend the Constitution to prohibit flag burning. Supreme Court jurisprudence (Texas v Johnson, 1989) is clear that flag burning is protected by the First Amendment. The only recourse is amending the Constitution. The major event is a fundraiser with Ted Marcus and celebrities.

Joey Lucas is staying in the same hotel. Josh has a crush on Joey Lucas. Donna says this explicitly. Donna tells Josh to "Gather ye rosebuds while ye may."[211]

Ted Marcus (Bob Balaban)[212] calls Josh. Marcus has a problem with a proposed bill banning gays in the military.[213] Marcus threatens to shut down the fundraiser unless the President comes out against the bill. Josh explains the President cannot come out against it; it would give the bill attention.

Leo and Hoynes discuss the ethanol tax credit. Hoynes opposes the ethanol tax credit, partly on principle and partly because he is a Texas oil guy. Voting for the tax credit would betray his history and look weak. Leo points out the ethanol tax credit creates jobs. Hoynes is concerned voting for the credit will have a political cost for him, flipping his established position.

The President hears speeches on flag burning. The President is bored.

Toby and Sam advise Josh to give Marcus time with the President.

They prepare to meet with Al Kiefer (John de Lancie).[214] President clears out a Mexican restaurant to have lunch with guacamole made next to the table. The President eats with his daughter. Toby and Sam meet with Kiefer.

Kiefer suggests the President should support the ban on flag burner, to score an easy political victory. Toby and Sam point out prohibiting protest is not consistent with democratic values. They don't support the ban. Kiefer suggests the amendment is going to happen either way. Kiefer comes across as a snake-oil salesman and is loathed by the staff.

The fundraiser is going on, several people approach the White House staff about jobs in Hollywood.

Fact Check: We find out in staff backstories (in 2.01 and 2.02) that C.J. used to work in public relations in Hollywood. In this episode, she doesn't know what a development deal is. In the backstories, she's not good at her job as a Hollywood publicist, so perhaps there's no inconsistency.

Synopsis, cont'd

Jay Leno and David Hasselhoff appear as themselves. Josh and Joey Lucas flirt. Josh is awkward; Joey Lucas is working through an interpreter.

Leo and Hoynes talk about breaking the tie in the Senate. Leo does not want Hoynes to vote against the tax credit; it would be devastating for the Vice President break with the President. The White House staff and the President don't trust the Vice President; Leo does. Hoynes thinks the White House arranged for the tie to humiliate him because of his past disagreements; Leo assures him that's not true.

Leo talks to the President. The President wants to fire Hoynes. Leo points out the President cannot fire the Vice President. Hoynes is right about the ethanol tax credit. Sam suggests that they let some other Democrats vote against the tax credit to let Hoynes off the hook. The President agrees.

Government nuts and bolts

The President cannot fire the Vice President because the Vice President is an elected officer. The Vice President can only be removed through resignation or impeachment, as specified in Article II, Section 4. No Vice President has ever been impeached. John C. Calhoun and Spiro Agnew both resigned.

Synopsis, cont'd

Josh and Joey Lucas talk about the flag burning amendment. "I heard. I hear everything," Joey Lucas jokes about her own deafness. Joey explains very few people care enough to swing their vote and Kiefer was overselling his data. Joey Lucas came to the fundraiser with a date.

Bartlet and Marcus talk about the bill banning gays in the military.

MARCUS: Why won't you say that [you'll veto the bill] publicly?
BARTLET: Because I know what I'm doing, Ted. Because I live in the world of professional politics, and you live in the world of adolescent tantrum. Don't you ever slap Josh Lyman around again. That guy is the White House Deputy Chief of Staff. He's not one of your associate producers… Right now, the worst thing that could happen to gay rights in this country is for me to put that thing on the debating table, which is what happens the minute I open my mouth. Do you get that? I'm a human starting gun.

Bartlet and Marcus commiserate over their shared dislike of fundraisers.

Josh goes to wish Joey Lucas goodbye. Her date is Al Kiefer, in her room in a bathrobe. Bartlet calls Hoynes. He admired Hoynes' honesty about the ethanol tax credit.

Note on Democrats and LGBTQ+ Rights in the '90s

Many Democrats say they were quiet in the '90s on LGBTQ+ rights out of political expedience and tactical awareness. Some attribute Bush's victory in his '04 reelection campaign to focus to so-called "culture war" issues (including gay rights) popular with his white evangelical base.[215] There is a substantive historical question as to whether the relative silence of Democrats during the period was a matter of tactics or moral failure.

The White House Pro-Am (1.17)

Aired on: March 22, 2000
Directed by: Ken Olin
Written by: Lawrence O'Donnell & Paul Redford[216] and Aaron Sorkin

Plotlines:
a) The chairman of the board of the Federal Reserve dies and the President must name a replacement.
b) The First Lady campaigns against child labor.
c) Charlie and Zoey fight about not being able to attend a club opening.

The First Lady does a television appearance with a boy campaigning against child labor. Sam disapproves of the appearance and the First Lady's press strategy.

Bernie Dahl, the Chairman of the Federal Reserve, died. The President must appoint a replacement.

Government Nuts and Bolts

The Federal Reserve is the central bank of the United States. It is independent of the executive branch from the White House, but the President appoints the Board of Governors, who are approved by the Senate. Governors of the Federal Reserve serve staggered 14-year terms.

The Federal Reserve has several functions. They set some banking resolutions, and provide financial services to depository institutions (including banks which handle public savings). The Federal Open Market Committee sets monetary policy for the country, including determining how much currency should be in circulation; the FOMC is constituted by the Board of Governors and the heads of the 12 regional Federal Reserve Banks. The Federal Reserve lends money to banks as a financial service. This lending and setting of interest rates on those loans is economic guidance to the financial sector.

Synopsis, cont'd

President Bartlet is an economist. Selecting a new Chairman of the Federal Reserve is important to him. The stock market crashes following Dahl's death; Leo suggests Bartlet name his replacement immediately.[217]

Leo is under the impression that Ron Ehrlich will be the nominee; Bartlet doesn't want to announce it.

The staff suggests saying they are waiting a day to announce a new Chair out of respect for Dahl. Toby notes Dahl's death was not surprising, as he was old and not in good health. Toby goes to a meeting about a bill they already have a clear majority to pass, but they want support from several liberal Democrats (Richard Fancy; Kathleen Garrett).

C.J. briefs the press. Danny asks about the First Lady's preference for Ron Ehrlich, which catches C.J. off-guard. We learn the First Lady dated Ehrlich before she dated the President.

Sam is furious with the First Lady's Chief of Staff Lilli (Nadia Dajani),[218] assuming she leaked Ehrlich's. She denies it. Sam reminds her the First Lady was not elected.

Bartlet lectures on abstract ideas in economics. He discourages C.J. from "handling my wife." C.J. wonders if this is the President telling her to "handle" the First Lady while maintaining personal deniability.

The President explains to Zoey the Secret Service is concerned about threats made against her by white supremacists.

Josh defends the free trade policies in the bill to Democrats. Toby gets frustrated and browbeats them, criticizing them for not buying American cars.

Context on Free Trade

Free trade was prescient in the late-'90s when the Democratic Party had a free trade wing (led by President Clinton) and a protectionist wing that thought free trade would harm union labor (led by, among others, Senator Bernie Sanders).[219] That fight is basically over now. There was some revival of these issues under the Trump administration. Trump opposes free trade policies, but there is a broad bipartisan consensus in favor of free trade.[220]

Synopsis, cont'd

C.J. also thinks the First Lady's Chief of Staff is the leak. She wonders out loud to Toby and Josh whether she should handle the First Lady, "but not because [the President] told you to." C.J. sends Sam back to talk to Lilli.

Congresswoman Reeseman (Amy Aquino) tells Sam that she is going to add a child labor amendment to the trade bill. This means the vote must be reevaluated.

Leo arranges a meeting between Danny and the President off the record.

Josh and Toby argue the merits of free trade with lefty Democrats. Has the ability to import cars hurt Ford? Toby argues it pushed Ford to make better cars.[221]

Sam tells Josh and Toby about the child labor amendment. Sam says he'll ask Lilli if the First Lady can convince Congresswoman Reeseman to withdraw the amendment.

Zoey tells Charlie about the threats. Charlie is furious about not going to a club opening. Agent Toscano calms Charlie down, reminding him Zoey doesn't like it either.

Sam goes to Lilli's office, but the First Lady is waiting for him instead. Sam gets blunt with the First Lady.

SAM: Mrs. Bartlet, you can't go on national television and have a kid sit next to you on a whim. You have got to vet this stuff through my office.

ABBEY: What was the problem with the interview?

SAM: There was no problem with the interview, except it looked like you discovered there was a child labor problem because a 14-year-old boy named Jeffrey just told you about it this morning.

ABBEY: I do not believe that is true.

SAM: And I do not believe exercise is going to make me any healthier. But I didn't go medical school. You did. You say so and I go to the gym.

The First Lady agrees to talk to Congresswoman Reeseman about the amendment. Sam decides not to ask about the statement of support for Ron Ehrlich.

Mrs. Landingham banters with Danny. Danny suggests to Charlie that he be nice to Zoey, since the security issues are worse for her.

DANNY: … I don't think the problem is that you're Black. I think the problem is you're stupid.

CHARLIE: Well thanks, Danny, you pick me right up.

DANNY: You bet. The Hardy Boys in these letters they're talking about, they may be heavily armed, but I wouldn't put a lot of money on their marksmanship. One of these days they're going to miss her and hit me.[222] 2,000 marriage proposals, 2,000 death threats, a dozen bodyguards, everyone wants to get close. Everyone wants a thing.

Plus, and I say this standing 15 feet away from the Oval Office, life with father couldn't have been a real company picnic, you know? If it was me, just for now, I'd make sure I was the one guy in her life who was totally hassle free.

The President tries to get Danny to say who leaked the First Lady's preference for Ron Ehrlich. Danny won't give up a source; Bartlet wants to know before talking to his wife.

The First Lady checks in with Congresswoman Reeseman about the child labor amendment. Reeseman agrees to withdraw the amendment. Reeseman wants to run for the Senate. The First Lady promises support.

The First Lady and the President argue about leaking Ehrlich to the press. The President did want C.J. to talk to the First Lady. The First Lady does not like the staff handling their personal issues; the President knows the First Lady was the one who leaked Ehrlich, not someone on the First Lady's staff. The President was going to name Ron Ehrlich anyway, but he doesn't like that Ehrlich had once dated the First Lady.

BARTLET: No "however." Just be wrong. Just stand there in your wrong-
ness and be wrong and get used to it.

They talk about child labor and the importance of defending kids. The First Lady cares about the issue and wants to make it a major focus, the way Betty Ford did with mental health or Michelle Obama later did with childhood nutrition and obesity.

Charlie apologizes to Zoey. They settle into her dorm for the night.

Six Meetings Before Lunch (1.18)

Aired on: April 5, 2000
Directed by: Clark Joseph
Written by: Aaron Sorkin
Plotlines:
  a) Mendoza is confirmed to the Supreme Court.
  b) Josh meets with a civil rights lawyer about confirming that lawyer at the Department of Justice.
  c) Zoey is confronted by a reporter on campus.
  d) Sam and Mallory argue about public education.
  e) Mandy tries to get a panda for the National Zoo.

The episode opens with the confirmation of Mendoza; Toby refuses to let anyone celebrate until they have 51 votes in the Senate. Toby is concerned about tempting fate, which is understandable for someone who lives in a universe written by Aaron Sorkin.

Josh needs to talk to Mandy about getting two new pandas for the National Zoo. Mallory is angry at Sam because Sam wrote a position paper on school vouchers. Leo has an issue with a Justice Department appointee who appears to support reparations for slavery.[223]

Jeff Breckenridge (Carl Lumbly)[224] wrote a positive comment about a book in favor of reparations for slavery. Leo instructs Josh meet with him because Toby is exhausted. C.J. is going to lip synch "The Jackal."[225]

Leo gave Mallory a position paper on school vouchers that Sam wrote.

Danny finds out the son of a Democratic donor was arrested for dealing drugs at a Georgetown frat party and Zoey was at the party. He warns C.J.

Mandy wants China to give the United States panda bears for the National Zoo. Josh redirects her to Toby as a practical joke since Josh is meeting with Breckenridge.

A reporter (Christopher Wynne) harasses Zoey about the arrest of the donor's kid.

Sam meets with Mallory. Mandy made an appointment to discuss his position paper in favor of school vouchers.

Josh meets with Breckenridge. Josh's father, who passed away,[226] was a partner at a law firm when Breckenridge was an intern. Breckenridge wrote a blurb for a book about reparations for slavery. Breckenridge walks through how his family was enslaved; he puts the estimated value of reparations at $1.7 trillion.[227]

Charlie tells C.J. that Zoey was harassed by a journalist on campus.

Toby is in an unusually good mood because of Mendoza's confirmation. Mandy is going to annoy him about a panda bear.

Sam and Mallory argue about school vouchers; she wants to massively expand public education. Sam criticizes public education for failing to provide adequate services to many at risk students. Cathy (Suzy Nakamura) cancelled Sam's later meetings, so he has more time for his awkward argument with Mallory.

C.J. asks Danny about Zoey getting harassed. C.J. realized Zoey lied to the reporter.

Breckenridge points out there were supposed to be reparations for slaves, most notably Special Field Order 15,[228] and those reparations were overturned during reconstruction. President Andrew Johnson returned land to former Confederates and granted those confederates amnesty.

Zoey kisses Charlie intensely as she comes into the White House. C.J. asks why Zoey lied to the reporter. C.J. meets with Agent Toscano to talk about Zoey's security. Agent Toscano points out the situation happened fast, and Zoey was trying to protect her dad. Agent Toscano also refuses to give C.J. any information about the night of the party, because of her commitment to confidentiality.[229]

Note on White Supremacists

The Secret Service uses the "14 words" in white supremacist threats to Zoey. The 14 words are a slogan popularized by American white supremacist David Lane, a leader in the Colorado chapters of the Klu Klux Klan and Aryan Nation; Lane was a founding member of The Order, a white supremacist terrorist group active in the '80s. Lane was convicted for his activities in The Order, including the murder of Jewish radio host Alan Berg. Lane also wrote the 88 Precepts. The number 88 is a numerical representation of "Heil Hitler" (H is the 8th letter of the alphabet). Fourteen and 88 are common in American neo-Nazi and white supremacist symbolism.

Agent Butterfield refers to the World Church of the Creator (also called the Creativity Movement), a white supremacist group. The Creativity Movement underwent significant fragmentation in 2003. The Creativity Movement lost its rights to use the name "World Church of the Creator" in 2002 (after this episode aired), in a lawsuit brought by an Oregon based group who had filed a copyright in the early '80s. The Creativity Movement believes in a coming "racial holy war" (RaHoWa) between white people and non-white people.

Synopsis, cont'd

Sam and Mallory argue. Sam points out that Mallory had a private education. Sam points out that public education and school vouchers are a class issue. Public education is for poor kids; no one is concerned about private education for rich kids.

C.J. asks Sam what to do about the reporter who confronted Zoey. Sam says she may have to "get in the President's face," which C.J. finds unhelpful.

Toby realizes Josh is pranking Mandy; the panda bear request shouldn't go to Toby. Toby suggests Mandy get revenge.

Mallory talks to her dad about having lunch with Sam. Leo clarifies Sam wrote the position paper on school vouchers as opposition preparation, taking the opposing side. Sam is a vocal supporter of public schools. Sam and Mallory go out for lunch.[230] C.J. gets in the President's face to stop him from attacking the press. He must deny he heard about it.

Breckenridge points out the United States paid reparations to the Japanese who were interned during World War II. Josh points out that his family are Holocaust survivors.[231] Breckenridge acknowledges this is a complicated conversation. The issue must be addressed through open and honest debate; that's why he wrote a blurb for the book.

BRECKENRIDGE: We have laws in this country. You break 'em, you
    pay your fine. You break God's laws, that's a different story. You
    can't kidnap a civilization and sell them into slavery. No amount of
    money will make up for it and all you have to do is look 200 years
    later at race relations in this country.

Chapter Eight
Let Bartlet Be Bartlet to the End of Season One

Let Bartlet Be Bartlet (1.19)

Aired on: April 26, 2000
Director: Laura Innes
Story by: Peter Parnell and Patrick Caddell
Teleplay by: Aaron Sorkin
Plotlines
  a) The White House staff explores putting two members on the Federal Election Commission to address campaign finance reform.
  b) Sam meets with military and congressional figures about gays in the military.
  c) Congressional staffer Steve Onorato threatens Josh with a legislative agenda designed to hurt the President's approval.

Toby and Sam discuss whether it will rain. The President has a speech about being outside; if they move the speech inside, they have to change the reference. Sam is confident it won't rain, and he is immediately wrong. The press asks about a "piece of paper," but the staff doesn't know about it. Mrs. Landingham tells the President to eat more vegetables. The President doesn't change the opening line in the speech, referring to a "magnificent vista" after the speech has been moved inside.[232]

Note:

The comments about diet are partly influenced by George H.W. Bush publicly saying that he wouldn't eat broccoli. Sorkin brings this back as a minor plot-point in Galileo (2.09).[233]

Synopsis, cont'd

The Congressional Budget Office revised their projection on the budget; two seats opened on the Federal Election Commission. The FEC oversees elections, including campaign finance law.[234] The CBO is responsible for investigating and projecting whether the budget will produce a deficit or surplus.[235] Bartlet is excited about putting new commissioners on the FEC, against Leo and Josh's objection; the commissioners on the FEC are technically appointed by the President, but the Senate leadership from each party usually make the decision because they lead the congressional delegations. Congress is impacted by the FEC, because congress regularly runs for reelection (with the whole House running every two years).

Josh explains to Donna: there are six commissioners on the FEC; they're required to be equally representative of each party, three Democrats and three Republicans. The President has an opportunity to make changes on campaign finance reform. Senate leadership makes the decision; the President asked Josh to look at some candidates, though Josh is confident the President won't appointing FEC commissioners who upset the status quo.

C.J. talks about the Easter Egg Hunt and Easter Egg Roll.[236] C.J. doesn't know anything about the piece of paper going around. We find out Mandy wrote the paper as an opposition memo on beating the President while working for Senator Russell (in 1.01).

Margaret has a "reply all" issue, no doubt familiar to all of us on big listservs.[237]

Josh finds two people in favor of campaign finance reform. Leo instructs him to meet outside of the building. Josh and Leo don't expect to push for campaign finance reform.

Toby and Sam meet with military brass regarding gays in the military. The military brass and members of Congress strongly oppose it; one argues it takes an act of Congress to change the Uniformed Code of Military Justice.

Fact Check

While it is true that UCMJ is only changed by Congress, the President (as Commander-in-Chief) determines enforcement. Bill

Clinton signed "Don't Ask, Don't Tell" (DADT) in 1993, which this episode addresses; in 2010 (10 years after this episode) Barack Obama signed the "Don't Ask, Don't Tell Repeal Act." Both went through the normal legislative process.

Synopsis, cont'd

Mandy gives C.J. a copy of the memo. Some reporter has it, but they don't know who.

Josh talks to members of the Senate leadership, including Steve Onorato (Paul Provenza),[238] about the FEC appointment and "soft money." Soft money is not subject to campaign finance regulations; there is no limit to the amount given and no transparency in who gives it. The Senate leadership likes soft money because they take soft money contributions. "Money isn't speech," Josh says. The President is considering candidates to fill seats on the FEC. He is rebuffed by Senate staffers. Josh is motivated by spite; he wants campaign finance reform.

Note on Changes in Campaign Finance Law post-Citizens United

Campaign finance law was rewritten by the '09-'10 Supreme Court case Citizens United v. The Federal Election Commission. Citizens United was a political organization that produced a political film critical of Hillary Clinton during the 2008 Democratic primaries. The 2002 Bipartisan Campaign Reform Act prohibited certain kinds of non-profits from making "electioneering communication" within 30 days of a primary; the FEC would not allow Citizens United to advertise the film. Citizens United sued the FEC for violating their First Amendment rights and won.

Many people claim the Citizens United decision is holds "corporations are people" and "money is speech." This is based in part on Justice Kennedy's majority opinion: corporations have a free speech right under the First Amendment, including political statements, just like individuals.[239] The result has been a proliferation of independent expenditure committees which can produce ads independently of campaigns, Super PACs.

Synopsis, cont'd

Sam and Toby continue to meet on the gays in the military issue;[240] Don't Ask, Don't Tell resulted in many more soldiers being harassed and discharged.

C.J. tells Sam and Toby about Mandy's opposition research memo. The memo is devastating to the White House.

Josh doesn't want to talk about the FEC with Donna. He asks Donna to research "English as the national language," because Onorato threated to make it an issue.

Note:

The United States does not have a national language. Legislation is introduced to make English the national language regularly; it has never been successful.[241]

Synopsis, cont'd

Toby, Josh, and C.J. read Mandy's memo. It is critical of the administration and the senior staff especially. It criticizes as incoherent in messaging and weak on follow-through.

Leo and Admiral Fitzwallace meet. Toby waits to tell Leo about Mandy's opposition memo. Toby tells Fitzwallace about the meeting on gays in the military.

Toby tells Leo about the opposition research memo. Leo acknowledges Mandy was playing for an opposing team, Senator Russell. Toby tells Leo the assessment in the memo is that Leo pushes the President "to the middle," away from controversial positions.

Josh snaps at Donna; the whole staff is in a bad mood. "Why is everyone acting like they've already lost?" This is the crux of the episode: combatting fatalism. Mandy tells Josh "English as the national language" is going to look bad; Josh chews out Mandy for letting the memo leak.

MANDY: You shouldn't let the President get into a debate on English as the national language.

JOSH: Mandy, it's not going to happen. Don't worry about it. The President's not going to nominate who he wants to the FEC.

MANDY: Why not?
JOSH: Because that's not what we do.

Sam continues to argue about gays in the military, that many of the statements made by members of the military admitting to being gay were coerced or are otherwise involuntary. Admiral Fitzwallace enters the meeting; the military representatives stand at attention. Fitzwallace is commanding and universally respected.[242] Fitzwallace checks the officers on gays in the military.

FITZWALLACE: We're discussing gays in the military, huh? What do you think? [...] You just don't want to see them serving in the armed forces, because they pose a threat to unit discipline and cohesion. That's what I think too. I also think the military wasn't designed to be an instrument of social change. The problem with that is that's what they were saying about me 50 years ago. Blacks shouldn't serve with whites. It'll disrupt the unit. You know what? It did disrupt the unit. The unit got over it. The unit changed. I'm an Admiral in the US Navy and Chairman of the Joint Chiefs of Staff. Beat that with a stick.

Sam thanks Fitzwallace. Fitzwallace tells him that the meetings aren't going to change anything. Fitzwallace was right; it was a decade before Don't Ask, Don't Tell was repealed.[243]

C.J. asks Danny who has Mandy's memo. Danny has it. He defends writing about it and points out the staff is upset because the memo is right.

Sam concludes the meeting on gays in the military. One Congressman points out they wouldn't be meeting if the President was serious about changing the law; if he wanted to change the law, this would involve more prominent people.

Toby and Leo talk about the President's low approval rating; they haven't felt empowered to do anything. We learn the President got less than 50% of the popular vote.

Note on political context before the 2000 Presidential election

When talking about candidates elected with less than 50% of the popular vote, it is most common to talk about George W. Bush in 2000 and Donald Trump in 2016, both cases where candidates won the electoral college but lost the popular vote. However, this episode precedes those elections. What Sorkin has in mind are the '92 and '96 Clinton campaigns; Clinton was elected with a plurality of 43% in '92 and 49% in '96, as the third-party campaign from Ross Perot drew 18.9% of the popular vote in '92; 8.4% in '96. Clinton won the popular vote, with a plurality and not a majority.

The show considers a candidate losing the popular vote and winning the electoral college in season seven, after the 2000 Presidential election, when it happened to George W. Bush.

Synopsis, cont'd

TOBY: One victory in the life of an administration stinks. But it's not the ones we lose that bother me, Leo. It's the ones we don't suit up for.

Leo and the President talk about Mandy's claim in the memo that Leo pushes the President to the middle. Leo points out the President is the one who moves to the safe ground. Leo convinced Bartlet to run for President. The President and Leo decide they need to start being more politically aggressive and meet with the staff to decide on appointments to FEC. They are going to push their agenda, not play it safe. Bartlet says, "This is more important than reelection. I want to speak now."[244]

The rest of the staff enthusiastically agrees.

Mandatory Minimums (1.20)

Aired on: May 3, 2000
Directed by: Aaron Berlinger
Written by: Aaron Sorkin
Plotlines:
   a) The President announces his nominees for the FEC.
   b) The staff considers reforms on drug enforcement, treatment, and sentencing.
   c) Joey Lucas explains why Republicans won't pursue English as the national language.

The President criticizes mandatory sentencing and term limits. The President announces his nominees for the FEC, creating immediate backlash. Steve Onorato and his boss (Bruce Weitz) are shocked by the President's nominees. The boss calls Josh; Josh hangs up on him.

After credits, C.J. says the President nominated one Democrat and one Republican, "which he was certainly under no legal obligation to do." He is under a legal obligation; the FEC must be a balanced bipartisan body. Josh and Toby talk about bringing in pollsters, including Al Kiefer and Joey Lucas. The whole staff knows Josh has a crush on Joey Lucas.

Danny is in the doghouse with C.J. because he reported on about Mandy's memo.

The next morning, Sam and Toby talk about mandatory minimums in drug sentencing and expanding treatment for drug abuse.[245] The staff goes to breakfast. Leo asks Margaret to write down a list of names. The staff is nervous about polling. If their approval numbers don't improve then they will drop their plans to reform the FEC.

Al Kiefer yells about drug policy; sentencing reform looks like legalization. Mandy is not invited to the meeting about drug policy, the staff still furious over her memo. Sam argues focusing on treatment is good policy, supported by doctors who view addiction as a disease.[246] Joey Lucas sets up in the White House; Josh tries to flirt with her.

The White House Counsel informs C.J. the President is under a legal obligation to nominate a Democrat and a Republican; she needs to issue a correction.

Kiefer talks about bad polling around drug reform, despite the American Medical Association recommendations that addiction be treated as a disease, not a criminal issue.[247] The rest of the staff leaves the room. Leo asks Toby to speak to a member of Congress, Toby's ex-wife Andrea Wyatt.[248] Leo asks for representatives from the list of names to meet with him later in the day.

Josh talks to Joey Lucas about "English as the national language."

Sam argues incarcerating drug offenders is bad policy; it's more expensive than treatment and produces worse outcomes and long-term costs. Again, Kiefer responds with public perception, not substance.

Steve Onorato meets with Sam to talk about the FEC. Sam suggests Steve should meet with Josh.

Toby and Congresswoman Wyatt (Kathleen York)[249] banter over a picnic. Toby doesn't like being outside. Wyatt does not foresee issues with the FEC, she wants to address mandatory minimums, which sentence heavier for crack cocaine than powdered cocaine, resulting in longer sentences for Black defendants than white ones. This is a part of the Reagan, H.W. Bush, and Clinton era policies on drug enforcement.[250] Wyatt wants attend Leo's meeting. Toby is severe; Congresswoman Wyatt pokes fun at him.

Leo talks to C.J. about the mistake over "under no legal obligation." Danny is upset that C.J. has him in the doghouse. C.J. yells at Danny.

Leo meets with representatives of members of Congress on his list in the press briefing room. Each member of Congress has family who got lenient sentencing in drug cases. Leo makes clear the White House won't tolerate hypocrisy if their bosses oppose drug reform legislation. Leo ends the meeting by letting the press back into the briefing room.

Leo wakes the President up in the night. Josh and Toby realize Onorato was trying to bait Sam out so they could hit him with the scandal around Laurie. Sam is angry;[251] Toby and Josh laugh it off.

Josh flirts with Joey Lucas.

Leo admits he's uncomfortable talking about drugs after coming out as a recovering addict. Bartlet wants to talk about drug treatment because of Leo, because everyone should get the help he did. C.J. apologizes for her mistake. The rest of the staff comes into the bedroom and the President wants them all to leave so he can sleep.

Lies, Damn Lies, and Statistics (1.21)

Aired on: May 10, 2000
Directed by: Don Scardino[252]
Written by: Aaron Sorkin
Plotlines:
   a) The staff prepares for polling on the President's approval.
   b) The President prepares to appoint his picks to the FEC and change campaign finance.
   c) An ambassador is tangled in a scandal; the President fires him.

The staff prepares for a poll. Toby and C.J. argue about "question six," because it contrasts "right direction" and "wrong track." C.J. points out the question is a reliable predictor of voting behavior.[253] The staff wants to see if the public is responding to their aggressive policy strategy. If their polling has improved, they can push their agenda. Public support is power. C.J. is the expert in polling models.[254] She predicts they have improved significantly; everyone else hopes they hold steady.

Only about 1-in-4 people respond to calls from pollsters, which is why it takes 48 hours to gather responses.[255] Sam can't go to Laurie's law school graduation.

Leo meets with FEC member Barry Haskell (Austin Pendelton).[256] Haskell is intimidated; Leo is friendly, which intimidates Haskell more. Leo knows Haskell supports campaign finance reform, that he's "one of us." Leo identified Haskell in anonymous; "I went to drug rehab on the condition of anonymity. Maybe you read about it in the papers." Leo takes Haskell into the Oval Office where the President is meeting with the Treasury Secretary (Conrad Bachmann), Attorney General (Sherry Houston),[257] and CIA Director (M.G. Mills); Haskell is overwhelmed. The President privately mentions to Leo campaign finance reform only matters if the polling is good.

Laurie is studying for the bar, even though she is graduating tomorrow. Sam calls Laurie; he can't attend her graduation. He warns her about Onorato.

The President is angry his views on drug treatment are being taken as favoring legalization. He asks for the staff's predictions on polling; C.J. is the lone optimist. The President will promote the current Ambassador to the Federated States of Micronesia. They can shift people up because they need to fire the Ambassador to Bulgaria, Ken Cochrane; Cochrane is having an affair with the Prime Minister of Bulgaria's daughter.[258] The President orders Cochrane back to the United States; Charlie knows who Cochrane is, drawing suspicion from the President.

C.J. is furious at Danny. The White House staff is angry about Danny covering Mandy's memo, and C.J. believes some of the staff blame her because of her relationship with Danny.

C.J. meets with Leo and asks why Leo had not told the President about her optimistic prediction. Leo suggests it's not an issue.

Josh and Joey Lucas argue about English as the national language; Joey insists the Republicans won't bring it up, despite the threat from Onorato. The Republican party needs Latino support to be competitive in the electorate.[259]

Sam visits Laurie and gives her a good pen and briefcase. Laurie is drunk from celebrating her graduation. Sam was tailed by a photographer. Toby and Leo are furious with Sam.

C.J. confirmed there was a picture; a British tabloid paid a waitress "friend" (Reiko Aylesworth) to set Sam and Laurie up. They tell the

President about Sam and Laurie; Toby insists they not fire Sam, despite his prior anger. The President asks Sam to make sure he didn't break the law; the White House will help Laurie get admitted to the bar if she passes the exam.

The President suspects that Charlie knows Ken Cochrane. The President meets with Ted Mitchell (Thom Gossom Jr.) to ask him to hire Cochrane as soon as the President fires Cochrane or Cochrane resigns. The President goes asks Ken Cochrane (Lawrence Pressman) to resign. Charlie and Ken Cochrane have met when Charlie was a waiter at the Gramercy Club. The Gramercy Club is "exclusive," code for racist; Cochrane clarifies he resigned his membership. Charlie points out that Cochrane was a member of the club initially and Cochrane asks to speak to Charlie's "supervisor."

CHARLIE: Well, I'm personal aid to the President. So, my supervisor is a little busy right now looking for a back door to this place to shove you out of. But I'll let him know you'd like to lodge a complaint.

The President reenters the room and Cochrane insists Charlie must have poisoned the President's view of Cochrane. This tells the President Cochrane and Charlie knew each other, which Charlie initially denied.

The President meets with Senator Max Lobell (David Huddleston)[260] to talk about soft money.

BARTLET: We agree on nothing, Max.
LOBELL: Yes sir.
BARTLET: Education, guns, drugs, school prayer, gays, defense spending, taxes. You name it, we disagree.
LOBELL: You know why?
BARTLET: 'cuz I'm a lily-livered, bleeding-heart liberal egg-head communist.
LOBELL: Yes sir. And I'm a gun-toting, redneck son of a bitch.
BARTLET: Yes, you are.
LOBELL: We agree on that.
BARTLET: We also agree on campaign finance.

Lobell will support the President's FEC nominees, which will mean four votes for soft-money reform on the FEC. Because the rules governing soft money were created by the FEC, they can be changed by the FEC without Congress.

Lobell agrees.

Note:

The West Wing is optimistic about bipartisanship. The idea that a hardline Republican would break with his party to work with a Democrat on a single issue is hard to imagine today, when partisanship in congressional behavior is especially severe. The President appeals to Lobell's sincerely held views on the issue of campaign finance reform, not on quid pro quo or strong-arm tactics.

Synopsis, cont'd

Toby offers one of the FEC members the Ambassadorship to the Federated States of Micronesia.

Josh and C.J. are nervous about the polling. C.J. is concerned about her position in the White House, after Mandy's memo and her various missteps in front of the press. C.J. expects the polling bump. Josh points out the President likes her and listens to her.

The staff waits nervously until C.J. comes in with the polling. She is vindicated; it is better than she expected.

What Kind of Day Has It Been (1.22)

Aired on: May 17, 2000
Directed by: Thomas Schlamme
Written by: Aaron Sorkin
Plotlines:
  a) A pilot is shot down over Iraq; the military mounts a rescue mission.
  b) There are issues with a space shuttle returning to earth.
  c) Josh tries to get Hoynes on board with campaign finance reform.

Note:

The title of this episode is a Sorkinism. It's the title of episodes in *The Newsroom* (3.6), *Studio 60 on the Sunset Strip* (1.22), and *Sports Night* (1.23). It is the season finale each time it appears and the series finale for both *The Newsroom* and *Studio 60.* Josh Malina notes the line comes from Broadway producer Robert Whitehead, who produced *A Few Good Men*; it was how Whitehead began meetings with production staff.[261]

Synopsis

The President speaks at the Newseum in Rosslyn, Virginia.[262] The President responds to a question (which we don't hear) that the 18-to-25-year-olds are "the most politically apathetic generation in American history.[263] President Bartlet is candid and engaging in the interview; Toby gets a call, but Sam answers. He gives Toby some sort of signal, but we don't know what it is. There's confusion about which "thing" the signal is for.[264]

C.J. gives Danny a tip about the space shuttle Columbia.[265] The President leaves the talk but is not planning to "work the rope line," engaging with people outside. He does anyway. Charlie tells Josh the President used some information Charlie found in the talk and Charlie is pleased. "You were right. It doesn't go away."[266]

Agent Toscano sees something; there is ominous music before credits.

Title card reads "12 Hours Earlier." Leo and Fitzwallace are talking in the situation room. There is a missing American pilot in Iraq; Leo must inform the President.[267] The President prepares for the talk at the Newseum; the President asks Sam why the space shuttle Columbia didn't land last night. Toby's brother is on the shuttle.

Toby rehearses a question about the positive disposition of the Bartlet administration towards China while being hostile to Cuba, since both are communist, authoritarian countries. Sam asks Toby about the space shuttle and his brother; Toby forgot his brother was supposed to return from space.

Josh is going jogging with Vice President Hoynes.

The President gets a blunt question from Mandy during his preparation regarding the lack of health care proposal to provide insurance to Americans, especially children, in need.[268] Leo interrupts to bring the President to the Situation Room. They need to find the pilot before the Iraqi Republican Guard does. If the pilot is killed, the President will take military action against Iraq.[269] There is a rescue mission, but C.J.

must cover it up and lie to the press. They refer to the previous refusal to brief C.J. on India and Pakistan; they are telling her, they need her to lie.

Sam explains the reason the space shuttle didn't land is because of a technical issue and they are trying to fix it. Toby asks Sam to tell him if it lands.

Josh talks to Hoynes, while jogging, about the collapse of the banking industry because of the savings and loan crisis (S&L) and subsequent bailout, as well as the corruption around politicians who deregulated the S&L industry.

Note on the S&L Bailout Scandal

While the show doesn't refer to contemporary political figures often, the exchange between Josh and Vice President Hoynes refers to the S&L crisis from the mid-80s until 1996.[270] The S&L bailout corruption scandal in '89 involved the Keating Five, four of whom were Democrats (Alan Cranston, Dennis DeConcini, John Glenn, and Donald Riegle); the fifth was John McCain (R-AZ). Following ethics investigations, Cranston, Riegle, and DeConcini were all found responsible to some degree in the scandal; Glenn and McCain were cleared.

Synopsis, cont'd

Josh wants Hoynes to get on board with campaign finance reform; the rise in the President's popularity will result in Hoynes losing the fight. We learn Josh used to work for Hoynes; Hoynes didn't listen to Josh during the Presidential campaign that Bartlet (who hired Josh) eventually won.[271]

JOSH: You've had some experience battling Jed Bartlet when he's right and you've had some experience battling him when he's popular. Why on earth would you want to try it when he's both at the same time?

HOYNES: You know something, Josh, sometimes I wonder if I'd listened to you two years ago, would I be President right now? You ever wonder that?

JOSH: No sir. I know it for sure.

C.J. briefs the press and says there have been no military actions taken, which we know is a lie.

Mandy prepares the President for the town hall; the staff argues about the President taking his jacket off. The President laughs at the absurdity of discussing his jacket. The President invites Zoey to the talk. She doesn't want to attend because it'll be embarrassing for her. Zoey says Charlie wanted to help prepare the President prepare.

Sam and the President discuss a signal in the event the pilot is rescued during the President's talk at the Newseum.

Leo is furious that Josh mentioned the political implications of rescuing the pilot downed in Iraq. Leo flew in Vietnam; he takes this personally.

Charlie is upset Zoey went to the President. Josh falls down because Donna removed his chair to have it repaired. The issues with the space shuttle continue and are worse than anticipated; Toby is nervous about his brother, though he admits he had forgotten his brother was on the mission.

Charlie gives the President information about a report on the perceptions of younger and older people. The President asks to see the study.

Fitzwallace comes into the Oval Office as they wait for news about the pilot. Fitzwallace provides the urban legend about how the eagle in the seal in the oval office carpet changes which direction he is facing in peacetime and wartime.[272] The rescue of the pilot was successful; the pilot is safe. The President thanks Fitzwallace. Danny is angry that C.J. called on him when she had to lie.

The President suggests Toby go to see his brother when the Columbia lands. Toby is worried. We get the same clip from the beginning of the episode during the talk at the Newseum. We find the signal originally created for the pilot's rescue now means the Columbia shuttle has landed safely.

Bartlet ends his remarks at the Newseum by noting that his family has deep roots going back to the founding of the country.[273] The staff celebrate as ominous music plays; there is a gunshot. Agent Toscano yells "gun" and gets everyone down. "Who's been hit?"

Introduction to Season Two, Plotlines, and New Characters

The second season of *The West Wing* continues themes developed in the first season; it also focuses on civic and moral responsibility.

The beginning of season two introduces Ainsley Hayes (Emily Procter), a Republican who disagrees with the staff on issues[274] but shares their civic and moral responsibility. Hayes emphasizes reasonable disagreement. Hayes disagrees on policy and she is a member of the team the staff often wants to "beat." Today, Ainsley Hayes is a case-in-point that Sorkin is too optimistic about politics. The idea of someone from across the partisan crevasse working in a Democratic doesn't seem plausible.

By contrast, the brief appearance of Ann Stark (Felicity Huffman) is cynical about political cooperation. Toby hopes he can have a serious and candid conversation about the issues with a Republican friend, only to be (metaphorically) stabbed in the back.

Ainsley and Ann Stark are sides of a coin. Sometimes we find people we can work with, despite serious disagreements. Sometimes we get played for suckers. Cynicism is the safer gambling strategy; never trusting anyone reduces the likelihood of harm, but it cuts us off from good people, like Ainsley.[275]

Sorkin argues that solving moral problems, making progress, and carrying out good government requires some optimism about the capacities of other people. Lame-duck Senator Pat Marino says, "More and more, we've come to expect less and less of each other."[276] Some political actors are cynical and manipulative, others are ideologues entrenched in their own worlds, and others still are trying to do what they think is right. No attitude is going to work across the board.

The West Wing is optimistic about working together across parties, but it isn't optimistic about the good intentions of others. There are more people like Ann Stark and fewer like Ainsley Hayes. Where *The West*

Wing is too optimistic is on the role of argument and whether the "other side" of an issue is reasonable; sometimes, Sorkin has to completely change arguments to make the character likeable. When Ainsley Hayes argues the ERA is redundant because of the 14th Amendment's equal protection clause, she's likeable. She agrees in equal rights; she disagrees about how to achieve them. But Hayes' argument isn't the one ERA opponents made; it doesn't square with the arguments made by Phyllis Schlafly and other opponents of the ERA. The argument advanced by Schlafly, that the absence of women's equal rights is necessary for privileges women enjoy, and gender roles are good and proper for government to reinforce.

The show delves into our staff's personal lives and how their experiences influence political positions; we saw this in "Take This Sabbath Day" and "In Excelsis Deo." The season illustrates the personal moral cores of many of our staff members. Some of those are religious, including President Bartlet; some are humanistic, with Sam's faith in the goodness of people and Toby's sense of care and responsibility. In those episodes, we get some glimpse into how their personal beliefs and private lives play and how they drive characters to duty and service.

President Bartlet's moral center and personal history is developed throughout the season, culminating in Sheen's performance in the season finale "Two Cathedrals" (for which he won a Golden Globe). Bartlet's Catholicism comes up throughout the season, as does his relationship with his abusive father (played by *West Wing* writer Lawrence O'Donnell in flashbacks). The President wrestles with the suffering around him, people he cares about, people who haven't done wrong. He sets out to reconcile that with his religious commitments to a loving God and his best efforts to do what is morally right.

He wrestles with an old philosophical problem, that others suffer because of his moral failures.[277] Bartlet feels the suffering around him is the result of his moral failures. In "Two Cathedrals" Bartlet wrestles with his own understanding of Catholicism and God's intercession.[278] In "Someone's Going to Emergency, Someone's Going to Jail," Sam Seaborn wrestles with discovering his father had a mistress for decades, with betrayal. The first season and the two-part opener of the second season establish Sam as an optimistic character who joined the Bartlet campaign out of his belief that he could do good, leaving behind a corporate legal job.

In "Noel", Josh wrestles with post-traumatic stress from the shooting and residual guilt about the death of his sister in a fire when he was a child. Like Toby's arc in "In Excelsis Deo," Josh's struggle with post-traumatic stress occurs over a Christmas episode, which heightens the sense of joy and celebration around him for contrast.

The show also discusses family and religion outside of central cast, in "The Stackhouse Filibuster" and "Shibboleth."

The United States has a non-sectarian government with people from different religious backgrounds. While the Constitution forbids establishment of religion, people in government are sometimes often by religious views about their moral or civic obligations. This includes President Bartlet.

The opening three episodes of the first season and the final five episodes of the second create thematic bookends. While the show often focuses only on the professional lives of our heroes, those episodes address the personal life of the President. In the pilot and proportional response arc (1.01-1.03), the President is denied privileges of private life. His grandchildren insulated from harassment by religious zealots; his friend's death influences his military decision making and makes him irresponsible.

New Main and Recurring Characters

Nancy McNally (Anna Deavere Smith) is the National Security Advisor to President Bartlet. She is commanding and funny, often using humor to defuse the misogyny that accompanies being a woman in a male-dominated and jocular field. She also plays the comedic role to Admiral Fitzwallace's or Leo's straight-man.

Ainsley Hayes (Emily Procter) is a Republican lawyer from South Carolina who joins the White House Counsel's office (2.04). She is brilliant and comfortable challenging Sam and other members of the White House staff, often providing an instructive point of reasonable disagreement. She was an undergraduate at Smith College and completed her JD at Harvard Law School.

Mark Gottfried (Ted McGinley) is the host of *Capitol Beat*, a regular political panel show which features members of the White House staff.

Henry Shallick (Corbin Bernsen) is a Republican Congressman from Mississippi and Deputy Majority Whip.

Mickey Troop (Tony Plana) is an Assistant Secretary of State for Latin America. Troop is a critical advisor to the President during the abduction of FDA agents in Columbia.

Howard Stackhouse (George Coe) is a Senator from Minnesota. Stackhouse is not a friend to the President, apparently an antagonist from the left. His personal hero is Vice President Hubert Humphrey, also a Minnesota Senator.

Oliver Babish (Oliver Platt) is the White House Counsel, succeeding Lionel Tribbey. He is the President's fifth White House Counsel in two years and a native of Chicago.

Notable Single Episode Characters:

Lionel Tribbey (John Larroquette) is the fourth White House Counsel under the Bartlet administration. Ainsley Hayes indicates Tribbey is much more liberal than the President. He also has a serious temper.

Ann Stark (Felicity Huffman) is the Chief of Staff to the Majority Leader (a Republican). She is a friend of Toby Ziegler and leverages that friendship to score political points against the White House.

Recurring Plotlines

The Hiring of Ainsley Hayes (2.04-2.05)
FDA Agents are abducted by a drug cartel in Columbia
The President's Multiple Sclerosis (2.18-2.22)
The President prepares for reelection
Mrs. Landingham dies (2.21-2.22)

Chapter Nine
Episodes 2.01-2.02

In the Shadow of Two Gunman, Part I (2.01)

Aired on October 4, 2000
Directed by: Thomas Schlamme
Written by: Aaron Sorkin
Plotlines:
   a) The President and Josh Lyman are shot.
   b) As Lyman goes into surgery, he remembers the early days of the Bartlet campaign.

Production Note

According to interviews on *The West Wing Weekly*, the cliffhanger at the end of season one was partly the work of Tommy Schlamme and partly the studio. Sorkin hadn't decided who had been shot when the first season was completed. The secret was closely guarded until the two-part season opener aired. Schlamme was concerned with the flashback structure of the opener, so Schlamme was intent on directing these flashback episodes.

Synopsis

Agent Butterfield and President Bartlet rush into the car; Zoey is in a trailing car. She is vomiting, but she wasn't shot. Bartlet is panicked. Butterfield was shot in the hand, and his hand is quickly bandaged. The President was shot in the chest; the car takes them to the hospital.

Production Note

Michael O'Neill (who plays Agent Ron Butterfield) interviewed Secret Service agents in researching the role. Butterfield's behavior, including checking the body and clarifying if the blood includes bubbles (indicating damage to the lungs) is something he learned discussing the assassination attempt against President Reagan with former members of the Secret Service.[279]

Synopsis, cont'd

Toby and C.J. are still at the Newseum; C.J. hit her head. Sam isn't injured. Toby and Charlie are looking for Josh. Toby finds Josh clutching his abdomen, bleeding heavily.

The nurse asks if this is a drill; Butterfield says it's not. The emergency room calls a trauma code. The Secret Service clears the hospital ahead of the President's arrival. Hoynes is pulled out of a meeting with a USC women's sports team (probably basketball);[280] the First Lady rushes to the hospital.

The President is wheeled into the operating room on a gurney. He wants to talk to his daughter and Leo before going under anesthesia. Mrs. Landingham and Margaret see the news he has been shot on a television in the office. The President jokes to Zoey as he is prepared for surgery; he tells Leo to get the cabinet and security counsel together and take emergency measures. He is going under anesthesia and tells Leo to talk to Abby. Leo and President Bartlet don't know Josh has been shot.

Doctor Abigail Bartlet tells the anesthesiologist the President has multiple sclerosis.[281]

Leo talks to Agent Toscano about the shooter; she is still frazzled. Josh is brought into the hospital, crashing through the door. Josh is incoherent and in a neck brace.

Production Note

John Wells, producer of *E.R.*, was one of the producers of *The West Wing*. The shot of the door crashing open behind Leo is a *E.R.* move. Schlamme notes changes in pacing is a major difference between *E.R.* and *The West Wing*.[282]

Synopsis, cont'd

Sam is standing over Josh as Josh talks incoherently about New Hampshire. Fade to white.[283] Josh and Hoynes are talking around a table. Josh says Hoynes should support social security reform and be open about it, but Hoynes believes proposing social security reform is political suicide.[284] Josh is combative with the rest of Hoynes' staff.

JOSH: Senator, you're the prohibitive favorite to be the Democratic Party's nominee for President. You have $58 million in a war chest with no end in sight[285] and I don't know what we're for. I don't know what we're for; I don't know what we're against. Except we seem to be for winning and against somebody else winning.

HOYNES: Josh, we're going to run a good campaign. You're going to be very proud of it. And when we get to the White House, you're going to play a big role. In the meantime, cheer up and get off my ass about social security.

Leo meets with the Josh. He didn't come to see Hoynes; he came to see Josh. Josh's dad has cancer and is in the hospital but won't stop working.[286] Leo tells Josh to come to Nashua, New Hampshire, to hear Jed Bartlet. Josh thinks Hoynes is going to win; Bartlet running for President is bad politics, suggesting Bartlet (then Governor of New Hampshire) wants a cabinet post.

Sam is in a meeting. He's explaining to clients how he is limiting their liability on oil tankers they are buying.[287] Josh is in Sam's office. Sam is at a prestigious New York law firm. Josh is frazzled. Josh wants Sam to come work for Hoynes, to leave the firm. Sam is getting married and isn't going to leave the firm.

SAM: Josh. Hoynes, he's not the real thing, is he?
JOSH: The thing you got to know about Hoynes is—
SAM: O.K.
JOSH: No, I'm saying, the thing you gotta know about Hoynes—
Sam: Josh, what are you doing?
JOSH: I don't know. What are you doing?
SAM: Protecting oil companies from litigation. They're a client. They don't lose legal protection because they make a lot of money.

JOSH: Can't believe no one ever wrote a folk song about that. If I see the real thing in Nashua, you want me to tell you about that?

SAM: You won't have to. You've got a pretty bad poker face.

In the present, President is going to be fine. His injuries from the gunshot are relatively minor (despite being hit in the lung).[288] Josh is in bad shape and will stay in surgery. Dr. Abigail Bartlet explains the medical situation to the staff in the hospital.[289]

Leo and Fitzwallace enter the Situation Room, followed by National Security Adviser Nancy McNally (Anna Deavere Smith)[290] and then Vice President Hoynes. The Joint Chiefs brief the Vice President on the shooting; the shooters expected to be killed and were not carrying their wallets or identification. There is some military movement in Iraq; McNally refers to the downing of the plane and the successful recovery mission in the previous episode. Hoynes suggests the military stay restrained and sends a message to Iraq that they shouldn't try anything given the unstable situation in the United States.

Donna arrives in the emergency room; she doesn't know Josh has been shot. Toby tells her Josh was shot and is in surgery.

C.J. briefs the press. Danny asks whether there has been discussion of the 25th Amendment; C.J. responds that the President is not going to die.[291] Another reporter (Jane Lynch)[292] asks about the identity of the shooters and follows up about possible accomplices. Another reporter asks why there was no canopy; C.J. won't comment on secret service procedure. The press is frustrated; C.J. is frazzled.

Danny tries to follow-up with C.J. as she leaves the briefing room.

Leo and Nancy argue about whether the United States should change DEFCON posture. There's a question whether the Vice President can order military actions; Nancy clarifies the Secretary of Defense might have those powers instead, because there is vagueness in the law regarding who can make national security decisions in the President's absence.[293]

C.J. is scratching at her neck. She asks Toby about the canopy. Toby and Ginger hug; she is distressed, but happy to see Toby.

We flash back to Toby in a bar, talking with a woman who didn't know Bartlet was running for President. Bartlet is Governor of New Hampshire. The title card tells us we are in Nashua. Toby admits he's never won a political campaign. He's about to be fired, which is why he's drinking.

Bartlet is speaking at a Veterans of Foreign Wars center. He is giving a complex answer on economics. One of the advisors asks Toby what Bartlet is going to say on the "New England DFC."[294] Apparently, Toby told the President to tell the truth about his vote, which was viewed as bad politics.

DAIRY FARMER: Governor Bartlet, when you were a member of Congress, you voted against the New England Dairy Farming Compact. That vote hurt me, sir. I'm a businessman and that vote hurt me to the tune of maybe ten cents a gallon. And I voted for you three times for Congressman. I voted for you twice for Governor. And I'm here, sir, and I'd like to ask you for an explanation.

BARTLET: Yeah. I screwed you on that one. I screwed you. You got hosed. And not just you. A lot of my constituents. I put the hammer to farms in Concord, Salem, Laconia, Pelham, Hampton, Hudson. You guys got rogered but good. Today for the first time in history, the largest group of Americans living in poverty are children. One-in-five children live in the most abject, dangerous, hopeless, back-breaking, gut-wrenching poverty any of us could imagine. One-in-five, and they're children. If fidelity to freedom and democracy is the code of our civic religion then surely the code of our humanity is faithful service to that unwritten commandment that says we shall give our children better than we ourselves received. Let me put it this way: I voted against the bill because I didn't want to make it harder for people to buy milk. I stopped some money from flowing into your pocket.[295] If that angers you, if you resent me, I completely respect that. But if you expect anything different from the President of the United States, then you should vote for somebody else.

Josh looks on as the President gives this answer.

We cut back to a meeting with Bartlet campaign staff in New Hampshire. Several of the staffers argue Bartlet shouldn't say "his opponent's" name. The President responds that referring to the frontrunner, John Hoynes, as "my opponent" is going to make him look old and addled.[296]

Leo fires the campaign staff, except Toby. Toby is perplexed.

Bartlet is upset Leo fired the staff and kept Toby. He doesn't know Toby. Leo doesn't care. Bartlet's family founded the state of New Hampshire and Leo makes fun of Bartlet winning offices there.[297]

BARTLET: Why are you doing this Leo? You're bigger in the party than I am. Hoynes would make you party chairman. Tell me this isn't one of the 12 Steps.

[...]

LEO: Because I'm tired of it. Year after year after year after year, having to choose between the lesser of "who cares?" Of trying to get myself excited about a candidate who can speak in complete sentences. Of setting the bar so low I can hardly look at it. They a good man can get elected President. I don't believe that. Do you?

Leo has more confidence in Bartlet than Bartlet does. The press clips cover the shooting.

In the Shadow of Two Gunman: Part II (2.02)

Aired on October 4, 2000
Directed by: Thomas Schlamme
Written by: Aaron Sorkin
Plotlines:

a) Josh is still in surgery. Bartlet has a successful surgery and is in recovery.

b) We continue to get flashbacks of the White House staff joining the Bartlet campaign.

The signaler from the shooting is captured by the FBI in a diner.

C.J. briefs the press. She can confirm they have taken a suspect into custody but cannot say more. Another woman in the crowd was shot; the President is recovering; Josh is still in surgery. Abby, Sam, Toby, and Donna are all in the hospital waiting room. Abby comforts Donna.

C.J. is in the office; she asks Sam to talk to Nancy McNally about the letter transferring power and Toby offers to follow-up with the Secret Service about the tent.

Sam is in the law firm. He suggests the company he is representing not buy the oil tankers,[298] as they're in poor condition. The liability protection means the company will not take financial damage, but there is still moral responsibility. Sam is laughed out of the meeting. He sees Josh, who was blown away by Bartlet; Sam decides to join the Bartlet campaign.

Back in the present, C.J. is still disoriented about being pushed down when the shooting started. Sam talked to Nancy about the letter; they still do not have an answer. C.J. doesn't want to do morning talk shows. Danny asks again about the letter.

We flash back again. A phone call startles C.J. awake. She is called into an office and yelled at by a Hollywood producer the public relations firm represents.[299] She is fired.

C.J. gets home and Toby is waiting for her. C.J. falls into the pool. Toby asks her to join the Bartlet campaign as Press Secretary; it is not much money, but she was just fired. C.J. and Toby have a friendly relationship that predates the campaign. C.J. worked for Emily's List.[300] Toby still thinks Bartlet is a jerk but wants Bartlet to win.

Abby and Butterfield explain the shooters used handguns, which were less effective at that range. Charlie enters; the President, Abby, and Butterfield explain Charlie was the target. Zoey comforts Charlie.

Margaret mentions she can forge the President's signature if they need the President's signature for a letter. Leo points out forging the President's name on a document removing him from power would be a coup.[301] Leo suggests someone do the morning shows; C.J. isn't ready, so they agree to send Sam. Leo says he'll see Danny to discuss letter; Toby wants to talk about the canopy; the Secret Service doesn't comment on procedure.

We flashback to Manchester, New Hampshire. Bartlet did well in Iowa; the staff watches a botched interview where Bartlet did not show up. Bartlet still doesn't know the staff. Bartlet is combative, even as they discuss strategy for the rest of the primary. They're going to win in New Hampshire, because Bartlet is a popular former Governor, so they are trying to him up for the nomination. Bartlet is a jerk to the staff.

Donna is in Josh's office in New Hampshire. Josh doesn't know her; she is answering calls on his behalf. Donna lies about a range of things and quickly gets caught. He ends up taking her on as an assistant anyway.

Sam and C.J. take a walk; C.J. has been disoriented and checking her neck, still dealing with the trauma and missing her necklace. Sam knocked her down during the shooting to keep her out of the way. He has her necklace.

Toby talks to Butterfield about the tent; Toby asked to have the tent removed. Butterfield explains the Secret Service doesn't comment on procedure.

BUTTERFIELD: It wasn't your fault. It wasn't Gina's [Toscano] fault. It wasn't Charlie's fault. It wasn't anybody's fault, Toby. It was an act of madmen. You think a tent was going to stop them? We got the President in the car. We got Zoey in the car. And at 150 yards and five stories up, the shooters were down 9.2 seconds after the first shot was fired. I would never let you not let me protect the President. You tell us you don't like something, we figure out something else. It was an act of madmen. Anyway, the Secret Service doesn't comment on procedure.

C.J. briefs the press and notes there is a serious gun violence problem in America.

We flashback to the Illinois primary; Bartlet is going to win. Bartlet is combative; Josh and the staff are frustrated. Josh celebrates the win until he finds out his father died.

Josh goes to O'Hare to fly back home.[302] Bartlet meets him at the airport, says he's sorry Josh's father died. Bartlet is finally friendly, talking to Josh about his dad. Bartlet tells Josh he is sure Josh's father was proud of him. Josh tells Bartlet to go back to the hotel. Bartlet apologizes for being a jerk to the campaign staff.

Josh wakes up after surgery. Bartlet and Leo are with Josh as he wakes up.

The Midterms (2.03)

Aired on: October 18, 2000
Directed by: Alex Graves
Written by: Aaron Sorkin
Plotlines:
  a) The staff prepares for the midterms.
  b) Toby wants to persecute white supremacist groups.
  c) Sam convinces a friend to run for Congress.
  d) Bartlet obsesses about a school board race in New Hampshire.

Production Note

The episode airs on the eve of a real-world general election, not a midterm election. While the world of *The West Wing* is largely analogous to our own, one of the features is the election schedule is different. Bartlet was elected in '98, runs for reelection in '01-'02, while the midterms occur in '00. The election schedule is still even years, but the West Wing Presidential elections fall on our midterm years and vice versa.

Synopsis

Josh talks to C.J. Cregg about the "theory of everything" over the phone, as C.J. prepares for her briefing. She says "psychics at Cal Tech" are writing on the theory of everything.[303] Toby explains the consumer price index increases; the consumer price index is outdated[304] because it was developed prior to the advent of computers and shifts in cost. Leo asks C.J. to include technical material on Housing and Urban Development; Sam informs C.J. that Congressman Grant Samuels died.

C.J. gives a briefing but slips on "psychics at Cal Tech" again. Josh is still recovering from his gunshot wound but is watching the briefing while in recovery.

The group talks about the job approval numbers being "soft" because they reflect public sympathy following the shooting. The group discussed the midterm strategy and is enthusiastic about the prospect of winning back the House of Representatives and picking up some seats in the Senate. They talk about strategy and how to allocate campaign funds.

Zoey visits Charlie at work. Zoey is frustrated Charlie didn't return her calls.

C.J. doesn't want it to look like the President is taking advantage of the popularity from the shooting. Toby wants to use their public support to pass gun control legislation and target hate groups through the FBI. Toby is brushed off.

Bartlet is bothered by a former political opponent running for school board in New Hampshire. Leo discourages the President from asking for polling data on that race; the President does it anyway.

Sam meets with an old friend Tom (James Denton) and Tom's wife Sarah (Rebecca Creskoff).[305] Sam wants to convince his friend to run for Congress in a competitive district. Sam shows again that he doesn't know the history of the White House building. Tom should run for Grant Samuel's seat in Congress; he's a prosecutor with a good record that will poll well in the district. Sam knows everything, despite initially giving the impression that he didn't.

C.J. and Toby argue about whether to target hate groups. Toby wants to get aggressive; C.J. doesn't. Toby says they should investigate and prosecute West Virginia White Pride through the FBI. Sam points out targeting organizations is a common way to get around the Bill of Rights, especially free association.[306] Donna takes Josh his lunch; Toby cannot come with her.

Zoey is looking for her father; President Bartlet makes campaign calls from the residential wing of the White House.[307] C.J. and the President argue that Bartlet's old opponent is polling well for school board.

BARTLET: All they have to do is get themselves on boards of education and city councils, because that's where all the governing that really matters to anybody really happens.
C.J.: We do a little governing here, Mr. President.

Sorkinism:

"He has grown back, not by the root, but by the other thing." "The other thing" is a Sorkinism. One of the most common Sorkinisms is his use of "thing" or "other thing" in contrast with aggressive, detailed dialogue. This includes "Tempting the wrath of the whatever from high atop the thing."[308] The term "Sorkinism" sometimes refers to idiosyncratic ticks; I use the term broadly to include Sorkin's literary style and choices as well. This phraseology and the use of "thing" illustrates both. Sorkin's writing is often specific; his metaphors are direct and careful. The contrast to the throwaway of "the thing" or "whatever" highlight this by contrast.[309]

Synopsis, cont'd

Zoey and Bartlet talk about Charlie. C.J. is avoiding doing aftermath stories.

Toby still wants to go after white supremacist groups. Sam points out a potential constitutional issue, violating free association, and such tactics were pioneered partly to attack the civil rights movement.[310]

C.J. tells Sam his friend Tom "likes white juries for his Black defendants."

Bartlet explains to Charlie that he doesn't want to look like he's using the White House to raise money, even if it is an empty gesture. Charlie mentions a reception for talk radio.

Charlie meets Andrew MacIntosh (Alfonso Freeman) and his son Jeffree (Myles Kilpatrick).

Leo tells Sam his friend's campaign is over following allegations Tom was in an all-white fraternity. Sam advocates for his friend, but Josh and Leo are clear they need to cut bait on his campaign.

Josh still wants to talk about physics, now superstring theory.

C.J. and Toby talk about the President's remarks. Toby is still agitated and C.J. is worried there is post-traumatic stress among the staff, especially Toby.

C.J. meets with the President. C.J. tells the President he cannot get involved in the school board race in New Hampshire; it would inappropriate. The President says he doesn't care about winning back the House; he is fixated on this school board race. He loathes his former opponent.

On election day, the White House is buzzing. Sam meets with Tom and Sarah who are furious the White House threw Tom under the bus when he was labeled a racist.

C.J. attends the reception for talk radio. She slips out of small talk with talk show hosts to check the exit polling of the midterms.

The President talks about discovering the eggcream; Toby is from Brooklyn, where the eggcream originated. Toby wants to leave the White House for a while, recognizing the post-traumatic stress, and the President suggests he instead get back to work. The President shoots down the Attorney General prosecuting hate groups.

TOBY: Why does it feel like this? I've seen shootings like this before.
BARTLET: It wasn't a shooting. It was a lynching. They tried to lynch Charlie right in front of our eyes. Can you believe that?

Bartlet thought about ordering the FBI to arrest the organizations. The two are struggling with anger. Bartlet is wrestling with the school board race, which his old opponent is going to win. Bartlet is going to stop by the talk radio reception.

The President starts to give remarks, before turning on a Christian theocratic talk radio host with a frustrated, angry rant after the host stays seated.[311]

BARTLET: Good. I like your show. I like how you call homosexuality an abomination.

DR. JENNA JACOBS:[312] I don't say homosexuality is an abomination, Mr. President. The Bible does.

BARTLET: Yes, it does. Leviticus.

JACOBS: 18-22.

BARTLET: Chapter and verse. I wanted to ask you a couple of questions while I had you here. I'm interested in selling my youngest daughter into slavery as sanctioned in Exodus 21:7. She's a Georgetown sophomore, speaks fluent Italian, always cleared the table when it was her turn. What would a good price for her be? While thinking about that, can I ask another? My Chief of Staff Leo McGarry insists on working on the Sabbath. Exodus 35:2 clearly states he should be put to death. Am I morally obligated to kill himself or is it okay to call the police? Here's one that's really important, 'cause we've got a lot of sports fans in this town: Touching the skin of a dead pig makes one unclean. Leviticus 11:7. If they promise to wear gloves, can the Washington Redskins still play football? Can Notre Dame? Can West Point? Does the whole town really have to be together to stone my brother John for planting different crops side by side? Can I burn my mother in a small family gathering for wearing garments made from two different threads? Think about those questions, would you? One last thing: While you may be mistaking this for your monthly meeting of the Ignorant Tight-Ass Club, in this building, when the President stands, nobody sits.

Sorkinism:

Sam says "I'm just gonna take my crab puff." This food exchange is normal after a big speech. Ainsley Hayes does it a lot.

Synopsis, cont'd

Charlie meets with Mr. MacIntosh, who tells him that he [Charlie] almost got the President killed. Mr. MacIntosh acknowledges he is proud of Charlie. "If they're shooting at you, you know you're doing something right."

Charlie apologizes to Zoey for being absent; Zoey acknowledges his life (including the job as the President's bodyman, the shooting, the death of his mother, and so on) are overwhelming for someone Charlie's age.

Josh is in pajamas. The rest of the staff sits with him on his stoop. The balance in the House has stayed the same, despite the midterm campaign. "After four months and $400 million, everything stayed the same."[313]

Chapter Ten
Episodes 2.04-2.05

In This White House (2.04)

Aired on: October 25, 2000
Directed by: Ken Olin
Story by: Peter Parnell and Allison Abner
Teleplay by: Aaron Sorkin
Plotlines
  a) Sam gets beaten in a televised debate; the President hires the woman who beat him.
  b) Josh and Toby mediate between an African President and pharmaceutical companies.
  c) C.J. accidentally leaks a story and panics about potential legal consequences.

Sam goes on a television program. He is introduced to his opponent on the debate program, who is a "young, blonde, leggy, Republican" named Ainsley Hayes (Emily Procter).[314] They debate federal education spending. Ainsley kicks Sam's ass in the debate. The staff watches, amused.

C.J. briefs the press on the summit between President Nimbala (Zakes Mokae)[315] and the heads of pharmaceutical companies[316] on drug costs in Africa. Nimbala is President of the "Republic of Equatorial Kundu," a fictional country.[317] The focus is on HIV/AIDS cases and deaths in Africa. Toby argues about the pharmaceutical industry and drug pricing; drug companies are gouging in Africa.

C.J. makes fun of Sam for losing the debate with Hayes. The entire staff is making fun of him over the incident. A reporter privately asks C.J. about whether an energy company is violating sanctions by selling drilling equipment to Iraq;[318] C.J. accidentally confirms a grand jury investigation into the matter, but the reporter does not realize this confirmation. C.J. panics, worried she has broken the law.

The President and Leo talk about the pharmaceutical summit and concerns about misinformation regarding HIV/AIDS.

Historical Context on HIV/AIDS and African Politics

The President mentions "You have people like Mbeki saying that AIDS isn't linked to HIV, it's linked to poverty." This is a reference to statements made by then-South African President Thabo Mbeki. Leo defends Mbeki, saying people are more likely to progress from HIV to AIDS without the financial resources to treat HIV. AIDS is diagnosed when the patient's CD4 T-cell count drops below 2,000 or the patient has certain complications. Leo is right; progression from HIV to AIDS is linked to poverty, both in the US and internationally. However, he is wrong to attribute such a sophisticated view to Mbeki. Mbeki is an HIV/AIDS denialist;[319] as President of South Africa, Mbeki failed to distribute and antiretroviral drugs and delayed mother-to-child transmission programs. A seminal study by epidemiologist Pride Chigwedere concluded that Mbeke's administration contributed 330,000 excess HIV/AIDS deaths from 2000 to 2005 from governmental failures.[320] Leo has a reasonable point here; Mbeki did not.

Synopsis, cont'd

The President and Leo talk about Sam losing the debate with Hayes; Bartlet wants to hire Hayes. Leo objects, because Hayes is a Republican.

The President meets with President Nimbala for a photo-op. They take questions.

REPORTER: President Nimbala, what's the best you could hope to come away with from this summit?

NIMBALA'S TRANSLATOR:[321] There are people who make miracles in the world. One of them lives right here in the US. He realized that vital elements could be harvested from the stalk of the wheat and in his hands India, which at the time had been ravaged by drought and overpopulation, in his hands their wheat crop increased from 11,000,000 tons to 60,000,000 tons annually.

BARTLET: That's right. His name is Norman Borlaug, and he won the Nobel Prize in 1970.[322]

[...]

BARTLET: I think you're absolutely right about the kind of miracle we need. I think we're going to make a lot of progress in the next couple of days.

NIMBALA: I hope so, Mr. President. My country is dying.

The President insists Leo hire Ainsley Hayes in the White House Counsel's office. Charlie makes fun of the President.[323]

Ainsley and her friends rewatch the debate between her and Sam. Ainsley gets a call from the White House. Her friends think she's going to be a star for attacking Democrats.[324]

C.J. got lost on her way to work, because she is anxious about accidentally leaking the existence of the grand jury to a reporter. She almost asks Sam about her legal exposure on the issue but stops herself. Leo tells Sam and C.J. about hiring Ainsley Hayes; they yell in protest.

Josh explains to Donna: African countries have high rates of HIV/AIDS; antiretroviral drugs are too expensive. African people in need of drugs turn to the black market. Black market drugs circumvent patents held by American drug companies, which companies don't like. There is conflict over the need to lower prices and black market antiretrovirals; pharmaceutical companies want to shut down the black market, which would prevent many people in Africa from being able to access antiretroviral medication at all.

Josh attends the meeting with the pharmaceutical industry executives. They fill the room; Nimbala is alone, aside from his translator. A pharmaceutical industry executive (Michael Cavanaugh) insists the price differences between African countries and European countries are the result of agreements with local pharmacies, not price gouging. Industry executives also note reports of corruption and incompetence in African countries that prevent drugs from getting to people who need them. The pharmaceutical company executives do not like being demonized and insist they are not doing anything unethical.[325]

Leo meets with Ainsley Hayes. Ainsley expects Leo to yell at her for beating Sam. She is shocked when he offers her a job in the White House Counsel's office.

C.J. is still stressed and cannot sleep. Sam asks what C.J. is stressed about.

Ainsley is a lifelong Republican; she is uncomfortable working for a Democratic President. "The President likes smart people who disagree with him."

Josh points out patent treaties will be enforced, because pharmaceutical companies donate enormous amounts of money to Congress and the White House doesn't have any leverage. Toby points out pharmaceutical companies take federal money in tax breaks and grants. Nimbala is "cursed by geography." He's a good leader who cannot get ahead.

Ainsley attends the press briefing where a reporter asks Ainsley about the grand jury investigation, the investigation C.J. accidentally confirmed to the reporter. He also mentions C.J. isn't sleeping, an odd thing for a reporter to know.

The pharmaceutical company executives bring up Mbeki's comments on the relationship between HIV and AIDS. Nimbala points out that he is not Mbeki.

EXECUTIVE: If tomorrow we made AIDS medication free to every patient in your country, as much as they needed for as long as they needed it, it would likely make very little difference in the spread of the epidemic.

JOSH: Why?

EXECUTIVE 2: Anti-HIV drugs are a triple cocktail. It's a complicated regimen that requires 10 pills to be taken every day at precise times. Two protease inhibitors every eight hours; two combination RTI pills every 12 hours.

JOSH: What's the problem?

TOBY: They don't own wristwatches. They can't tell time.

Ainsley tells C.J. there are no legal consequences for confirming the existence of a grand jury and C.J. should not be worried. Ainsley also says she is not taking the job in the White House Counsel's office.

Toby and Josh meet privately with Nimbala and offer executive action.

NIMBALA: It's a terrible thing, to beg for your life. Terrible. My father was a proud man. He built homes. He wouldn't like what I came here to do.

TOBY: Yes, he would, Mr. President. I swear to God he would.

Sam and Ainsley meet in the hallway; Sam is angry about losing the debate. Josh and Sam mock her for not taking the job. She has issues with the White House including the position on guns. She says this in front of Josh, who was recently shot.

The staff gets a memo and interrupts their conversation with Ainsley. There is a national security issue; Leo informs the staff and Nimbala that there was a coup in his country. Bartlet offers Nimbala asylum. If Nimbala returns home, he will be executed. He is going home anyway. Ainsley sees part of this exchange.

Ainsley meets with her friends, who denigrate the White House. Ainsley chews out her friends and tells them she took the job in the White House.

The President talks with Toby about Norman Borlaug and the Green Revolution. Nimbala was killed in the airport parking lot upon arriving back in Kundu.

On Public Health Infrastructure

Problems in public health look easy if you reduce them down to the point of delivering treatment; "get people antiretrovirals" is a simple solution to addressing the HIV/AIDS crisis, but it ignores medical and public health infrastructure, the major block for many people accessing care. Providing a complicated drug cocktail like the antiretrovirals of the early 2000s requires medical distribution centers capable of receiving and storing medications, clear communication with patients about the protocol, and the resources to follow-up and track progress. When Toby says, "they don't have wrist watches," he's missing the point. It's not about wristwatches; it was about roads and medical centers and nursing, pharmaceutical, and administrative staff.

In Africa, infrastructure development has been an ongoing, massive intergovernmental effort through the African union.[326] The United States' PEPFAR program helps fund HIV/AIDS services in Africa; PEPFAR was created by President George W Bush in 2003, a few years after this episode. PEPFAR was a major vehicle for funding and distributing antiretrovirals in Africa. It has controversies, including its abstinence-first ABC model and its failure to fund needle-exchange programs, but (on balance) PEPFAR is widely recognized as helping to substantially reduce the number of HIV/AIDS cases and deaths.

One of the reasons that PEPFAR works is its inclusion of a range of United States government groups, including the logistical support of the Peace Corps and the Department of Defense. Most importantly, though, the African Union's development of roads, water distribution, computer systems, has helped urban areas develop the medical infrastructure necessary to treat HIV/AIDS cases and reduce transmission.[327]

The HIV/AIDS epidemic is ongoing, but the number of new cases is decreasing and people who contract HIV are living longer. WHO data shows that HIV/AIDS related deaths in South Africa have decreased from 250,000 per year (in the early 2000s) to 45,000.[328] These projects make a difference, but they often require literally laying foundation.

And It's Surely to Their Credit (2.05)

Aired on: November 1, 2000
Directed by: Christopher Misiano
Story by: Kevin Falls & Laura Glasser
Teleplay by: Aaron Sorkin
Plotlines:
  a) Ainsley Hayes meets hostile colleagues in the White House Counsel's office.
  b) Josh and Sam consider suing the Klu Klux Klan.
  c) The President and First Lady discuss the President's multiple sclerosis.
  d) A retiring general prepares to criticize the President.

Josh gets a bill for $50,000 from his health insurance company. Sam and Donna talk about the President's radio address. Donna takes guests in to listen to the recording of the President's radio address. The President repeatedly flubs, joking he's going to "do it in one."

Toby and C.J. discuss Ainsley Hayes. C.J. is supportive of Hayes and thinks the staff is sexist;[329] Toby informs C.J. that General Barrie is doing a range of shows as he prepares for retirement. He is going to attack the President.

Leo and Ainsley discuss her hiring. The White House Counsel Lionel Tribbey (John Larroquette)[330] storms into Leo's office; he is furious about a memo and thinks hiring Ainsley Hayes is terrible. Brookline and Joyce lied to Congress. Tribbey had to skip his vacation to fix their mistakes. Ainsley Hayes clerked for a Supreme Court Justice, who Tribbey thinks is an idiot. Tribbey takes the issue up with the President, interrupting the recording of the radio address in front of tourists visiting the White House.

Toby and Sam talk about Josh's insurance company. Josh can sue the insurance company but not the people who shot him. Sam thinks Josh could sue the white supremacist groups.

The President didn't complete the radio address. Sam and Josh discuss suing the white supremacist groups.[331]

The First Lady asks Charlie to tell the President: they [the President and First Lady] can have sex now that the President's laboratory values are stable. The President barges in, excited. The President and First Lady put off having sex for other things on their schedule.

General Barrie sent a staff aid (Daniel Roebuck) to meet with C.J.; she chews the staff aid out and demands the General come down.

Leo takes Ainsley to her office in the "steam pipe trunk distribution venue," a basement. Ainsley acknowledges she wrote an op-ed calling for Leo to resign because of his alcoholism. They have a good rapport; Leo assures her not to worry about anything except doing her job.

Tribbey and Ainsley fight. He doesn't trust her. She feels a sense of duty. Tribbey cites "For He's an English Man," wrongly attributing it to *Pirates of Penzance*. Ainsley corrects him; it's from *H.M.S. Pinafore*. Tribbey sends Ainsley to fix Brookline and Joyce lying to Congress. Tribbey left a lot of money to come to work for a President he disagrees with, and he understands duty.[332]

Sam and Josh discuss suing the Klan, because the shooters had an affiliation with West Virginia White Pride, an affiliate organization.[333] Sam is going to talk to Brookline and Joyce; Leo tells Sam that Ainsley Hayes will address the issue with Congress. Toby tells Sam to drop his issues with Hayes.

The President leaves the radio address to meet with the First Lady. The First Lady left for Pennsylvania early, so he goes back to the radio address.

General Barrie (Tom Bower) yells at C.J. and insists he can do what he likes as he retires. C.J. points out there are pictures of him wearing medals that he was not awarded.[334] C.J. implies she will leak this to the press if he goes on television and disparages the President. It will cause embarrassment and a potential investigation for stolen valor.

Ainsley Hayes meets with Brookline and Joyce (Steven Flynn and Paul Perri, respectively), to correct their lies to congress. They blow her off.

The President and First Lady get ready to have sex. The President says she didn't need to go to Pennsylvania, at which point the First Lady pivots to the importance of women in American history and why she went to a statue dedication for Nellie Bly.[335]

Sam walks Josh through suing the Klan and the Southern Poverty Law Center's record of suing white supremacist groups.[336] Sam and Ainsley have a disagreement, but Ainsley is upset about something, borderline crying. Ainsley got a package from Brookline and Joyce calling her a "bitch." Sam finds out about this package and goes to meet with Brookline and Joyce. He fires them while defending Ainsley. Tribbey affirms Brookline and Joyce are fired.

The President gives a different radio address, this time about women in history, and does it live. The President says General Barrie can criticize him on the morning shows (instructing C.J. not to retaliate by leaking the stolen valor story).

Josh doesn't want to sue the Klan. He wants to focus on his job. He will sue the insurance company, though. The staff sings to Ainsley Hayes, "For He is an English Man." They accept Ainsley Hayes as one of them.

Optimism, reasonable disagreement, and Ainsley Hayes

Ainsley Hayes represents optimism about reasonable disagreement. Ainsley has substantive, principled disagreements with the White House and whose positions viewers may think are wrong but can still be the subject of reasonable disagreement. Ainsley is often criticized as unrealistic; she is an imagination of a conservative political commentator by liberals who want to believe others are sincere and committed; in many cases in modern politics, there isn't sincere interest or engagement.

The real-life inspiration for Ainsley Hayes is often cited as Ann Coulter,[337] claiming Coulter was not as obviously racist, antisemitic, and homophobic during her early career.[338] Coulter's most famous bigoted remarks didn't happen until later, her claim women shouldn't have the right to vote or "gays value promiscuous sex over monogamy." The character Hayes fictionalized is (at this point in American political life) a powerful illustration of the conspiratorial transformation of American political discourse into reality television with no commitment to any recognizable principles or theory.

Some critics refer to Ainsley Hayes as a liberal fiction of a Republican, but I've met many Republicans who identify with Ainsley, just as I've met Democrats who identify with the West Wing's main cast. They think of themselves as reasonable person who are swayed by the open exchange of ideas. Even if we acknowledge some people are unreasonable, some people who disagree are reasonable.[339]

In the philosophical literature on disagreement, there's length discussion of what makes someone reasonable in a disagreement. Ainsley[340] Hayes usefully captures reasonable disagreement. She understands the facts; she agrees with the White House staff about core values. There are people like Ainsley Hayes; one problem in contemporary politics is that there aren't many, and there are bad faith actors who exploit the idea of reasonable disagreement for political gain. There's a problem when many people insist on being treated like Ainsley Haynes when they're not engaging in good faith.

Chapter Eleven
Episodes 2.06-2.07

The Lame Duck Congress (2.06)

Aired on: November 8, 2000
Directed by: Jeremy Kagan
Story by: Lawrence O'Donnell
Teleplay by: Aaron Sorkin
Plotlines:
  a) The President considers recalling Congress before the newly elected Congress is seated, to vote on a nuclear test ban treaty.
  b) Ainsley and Sam argue over the White House's position on small businesses and employee theft.
  c) A Ukrainian politician shows up to the White House unannounced and very drunk.
  d) Donna and Josh talk about OSHA rules and carpal tunnel.

C.J. briefs the press. Mr. Konanov is not meeting with any cabinet officials while he is in Washington. The press corps asks if the President is considering a lame duck session of Congress to pass a treaty banning nuclear tests, because an incoming Senator (elected during the midterms) will disrupt a treaty during the new Senate. C.J. cannot confirm or deny the President has considered the lame duck session; she will have to ask.

Donna badgers Josh about OSHA regulations and how many people get carpal tunnel every year. C.J. and Josh discuss the lame duck session; Sam says they should consider it, because the disruptive Senator-elect may get a seat on the Foreign Relations Committee. Toby and Sam say no one else in the Republican caucus wants the seat on Foreign Relations, because "there's no money in it."[341] They propose a lame duck session to the President.

The staff meets with the President in the Oval Office. The treaty will not pass in the new congress and so must be addressed immediately.[342] Toby suggests they can use the threat of nuclear proliferation to argue there is an imminent need for the treaty. Leo suggests they start meetings to prepare for a lame duck session. Sam mentions legislation on fraud awareness for small business owners.

The President is clear Konanov should have "no high-level meetings." Leo points out they cannot call the vote and lose, they must win if they call the lame duck session.

Leo and C.J. discuss a forthcoming op-ed that the President's time is not being used efficiently.[343] Leo points out the meeting about the lame duck session was a mess and took longer than it should. He requires the staff provide a summary and run that summary by him if they intend to brief the President, to ensure the President's time is being used efficiently.

Toby, Sam, and Josh are planning to meet with members of Congress. Sam must summarize a memo before briefing the President.

C.J. yells at Danny because his paper ran the op-ed on the President's time management. Danny points out news and editorial staff are separate.[344] C.J. leaks the possibility of the lame duck session to Danny.

Donna points out ergonomics shows poorly designed keyboards contribute to carpal tunnel. Donna wants the White House to implement new OSHA rules; Josh explains it would cost small businesses and the White House doesn't want to upset those businesses.

Charlie tells Josh that Vasily Konanov is at the White House. Josh cannot meet with Konanov because he is a senior official.

JOSH: I can't see him. Make sure he's not in the bullpen.
CHARLIE: He's not. He's in the driveway.
JOSH: What do you mean?
CHARLIE: He's sitting in the car in the driveway. He's refusing to get out unless he can speak to the President.
JOSH: This is a joke?
CHARLIE: No.
JOSH: He's sitting in the driveway?
CHARLIE: Josh, they're saying… you know…
JOSH: What?
CHARLIE: They're saying he's drunk.

Sam meets with Ainsley to ask her to summarize his memo on fraud detection. Sam is a bit misogynistic; Ainsley makes fun of him for asking for her help. Ainsley agrees if she can attend the meeting on the Hill. Sam agrees.

Josh tells Leo that Konanov is drunk in the driveway. They need to move Konanov into the building, but Josh cannot talk to him. Leo gives Josh permission to talk to Konanov but orders him to keep the situation quiet and contained.\Toby takes a lunch meeting with two congressional staffers. They are not going to vote to ratify on the nuclear test ban treaty. The treaty is overwhelmingly popular, but not in states these staffers represent. One of the staffers suggests the White House may have lost votes they thought were safe.

Donna asks Leo why they're not going to implement the OSHA rules. Leo tells her it costs too much, to "type slower." Leo suggests Danny should get access to the President for a feature story. C.J. objects to giving Danny access, because of his paper's editorial.

Toby is worried about the votes that they lost. Toby is going to meet with Senator Marino, who lost his seat in the midterms. Vasily Konanov (Evgeniy Lazarev)[345] is in Toby's office, blustering incoherently.

Josh explains to Konanov that the White House can only deal with the government of Ukraine.[346] They support Konanov becoming leader of Ukraine, but they cannot meet with him while he is outside of the government.

Sam and Ainsley meet with congressional staffers to encourage them to try to shift their boss's position. The staffers won't move. Ainsley suggests that the reason the congressmen won't move on the test ban treaty is because they cynically want to beat the White House. She knows the staffers well and the comment stings.

Margaret is typing slower in protest of Leo's remarks to Donna. Josh is panicking about the Ukrainian government's response to news that Konanov (an opposition leader) met with the White House. Leo suggests they can have the President bump into Konanov in the hallway and this will allow Konanov to say he met the President while allowing the White House to brush it off as a mistake.

LEO: Here's what we're going to do. All this guy wants is to be able to say he met the President while he was here.
JOSH: He can't meet the President.

LEO: He can meet the President accidentally.

JOSH: How do you meet the President accidentally?

LEO: When I was Labor Secretary, we did it with the Dalai Lama. Obviously, Beijing doesn't want the President to have any diplomatic contact. So, they arrange a low-level meeting. Keep the door open. The President wanders by. "Hey, how you doing, Dalai Lama?"

JOSH: That's the most crazy-ass thing I've ever heard.

LEO: It works.

JOSH: This is how the world is run?

LEO: Yeah.

Leo does not like calling the lame duck congress. It is cynical and manipulative to hold a vote after many of them have been removed.

Josh tells Donna to stop causing problems for Leo over the OSHA policies. Donna points out that the regulations would prevent more than 30,000 injuries a year. Leo responds the White House is exempt from all workplace regulations that it passes.[347] Josh sets up Donna as the meeting with Konanov, which the President will interrupt.[348]

Sam and Ainsley return from their meetings. Sam thinks they may be able to win with the help of Senator Marino. C.J. debates giving Danny access to the President; Ainsley suggests she should, because "he's cute."[349] Ainsley gives Sam the summary she wrote. The summary reverses Sam's position.

Toby meets with Senator Marino (Mike Starr).[350] Marino is the vote that jumped ship. He won't to override the will of the voters, who just voted him out of office.

MARINO: Toby, it seems that more and more we've come to expect less and less from each other, and I think that should change. I'm a Senator for another 10 weeks and I'm going to choose to respect these people and what they want.

Toby interrupts a White House tour and rants about the importance of the nuclear test ban treaty. "We're all gonna die."

Ainsley explains many small businesses fail because employees commit fraud or steal. Sam is upset she reversed his position. Ainsley makes a convincing case for expanding checks on employee fraud.

Danny and C.J. wait to meet with the President; Charlie ignores them as they argue. The President points out editorials in the Washington Post aren't Danny's fault. The editorial writers are jerks, but separate from the news side. The President tells Danny the columns were bad and cancels his personal subscription.\

Danny got an offer to be an editor. C.J. is upset he won't take the job, because she wants to date Danny and will not date him while he is a reporter in the White House.

Donna explains the OSHA regulations and the problems with the QWERTY keyboard ergonomics and carpal tunnel.[351] The President interrupts and asks everyone to leave the room except Konanov. The President chews out Konanov for coming to the White House when he knows the President cannot talk with him. Bartlet wants Konanov to be President of Ukraine and Konanov can say they met.

Sam and Ainsley meet with Leo. Sam recommends Ainsley's position on employee fraud prevention; they will make the recommendation to the President. Ainsley is shocked they are going to make the recommendation. Leo said yes and so now the recommendation goes to the President.

The President and Toby talk about Senator Marino. The President suggests public opinion about something as complicated as a nuclear test ban treaty isn't useful and people who don't have expertise are not adequately informed. They agree not to call the lame duck session of congress. The President points out it's a Republic, a representative democracy.[352] Leo and the President go to the residence to have a cigar and play some chess.

The Iran Nuclear Agreement
and Mainstream [Mis]-Understandings

Nuclear nonproliferation agreements have stalled over the last several decades; most nuclear powers either not threatening or not inclined to sign a deal. Several former Soviet states (including Ukraine) disarmed after the end of the cold war. Since then, nuclear powers haven't disarmed.

The exception is the "Iran Nuclear deal," the Joint Comprehensive Plan of Action, signed by seven countries and the European Union. The deal was signed by China, France, Germany, Iran, Russia, the United

Kingdom, and the United States and implemented in January of 2016. The JCPOA was controversial in American politics, as the political right made a range of claims (many false): it allowed the accumulation of nuclear materials by Iran (not true), didn't allow oversight (not true), and provided various incentives to Iran (true, but complicated).

The basic agreement is straightforward.[353] Iran agreed to restrictions on proliferation of nuclear weapons, including limiting the amount of uranium enriched and submitting facilities to inspections by independent inspectors on short notice, in exchange for lifting economic sanctions. Economic sanctions on Iran had been in place for years, damaging Iran's economy and infrastructure (including health care), and limiting private sector development.

Following the election of President Trump, the United States reimplemented sanctions on Iran, breaking the American side of the agreement. The agreement stayed intact because of other countries. The American right supported the withdrawal from the JCPOA despite the possibility that Iran might refuse to allow inspections, because the US had violated the agreement. Fortunately, that has not happened. Public opinion on nuclear agreements are often not grounded in how such agreements work; but track domestic political factors.

The Portland Trip (2.07)

Aired on: November 15, 2000
Directed by: Paris Barclay
Story by: Paul Redford
Teleplay by: Aaron Sorkin
Plotlines:
  a) The President travels to Portland, Oregon.
  b) Josh meets with Rep. Skinner to discuss a ban on gay marriage.
  c) An oil tanker carries oil that may have been purchased illegally.
  d) Sam wants to rewrite an upcoming speech on education.

The Presidential motorcade drives through. An Assistant Secretary of Energy is taking a trip with the President to meet with the President on the flight back from Portland. C.J. briefs the press on several people traveling on Air Force One. Sam Seaborn and C.J. are both on the trip as well; off-the-record, C.J. is on the trip because she made fun of Notre

Dame, the President's alma mater, before a Notre Dame football game against Michigan. Leo gives the President a hard time; Leo tells the President the United States is going to board an oil tanker in "the gulf."[354] C.J. is forced to wear a Notre Dame hat.

Leo and Josh stay behind in Washington. The President likes long flights at night. Josh meets with Representative Skinner. Donna is going on a date, but Josh stays behind. Josh needs Donna to come back after the date. None of our characters can have personal lives. Josh suggests Donna has bad taste in men and no sense for how romantic relationships work.[355]

Sam and Toby are on the flight. Sam is "not writing well" and doesn't want to distribute his draft to the press pool. C.J. has already distributed the draft. "It's very bad writing. It's got my fingerprints all over it." Sam wants her to get it back.

The President tells C.J. the United States has stopped an oil tanker from Cyprus which the U.S. believes is carrying Iraqi oil, which would violate United Nations sanctions on Iraq.[356] We get some exposition.

C.J.: What do we do when that happens?
BARTLET: We board the ship. We test the oil. We determine its point of origin and if it's black market, the oil company gets fined.
C.J.: Don't they also get to sell the oil?
BARTLET: Yes.
C.J.: Doesn't the profit from the sale exceed the fine?
BARTLET: It dramatically exceeds the fine.

They dislike the policy, but there is little they can do.[357] The President asks C.J. to lead the press in the Notre Dame fight song as they fly over South Bend.

Ainsley is working late; the White House doesn't have Fresca.[358] Ainsley tells Leo it is too hot in her office, which is where the heating equipment in the building is.

Josh meets with Skinner. They have a beer. Skinner and Josh held off the meeting. The two discuss a law providing a federal definition of marriage as between one man and one woman, meaning the federal government would not recognize gay marriage.[359] Skinner suggests this would allow marriage equality at the state level.[360]

Josh pivots the conversation to the homophobia surrounding this bill.

JOSH: Matt, when this bill was being discussed on the floor there were some very ugly things said about homosexuals.

SKINNER: Yes.

JOSH: They were said by members of your own party. In fact, they were said by one of the guys who escorted you here tonight, who is sitting out in the lobby.

SKINNER: Yes, they were.

JOSH: You support this bill.

SKINNER: Yes, I do.

JOSH: Congressman, you're gay.

SKINNER: Yes, I am.

Leo is in the Situation Room, where he is informed the crew of the oil tanker obstructed American attempts to board the tanker, including firing with AK-47s.

Margaret is concerned Leo may drink as he finalizes his divorce. Leo tells her not to worry. He takes a call from the President about the tanker. They agree to fire warning shots, but the President worries about shooting the tanker. Sam doesn't like the writing in the speech, his writing. Sam suggests they should be talking about a "permanent revolution." Toby suggests quoting Chairman Mao is not a great idea. Toby points out they cannot write a speech about a radical and visionary approach to education, because putting one together takes time.[361]

Leo tells Donna what to order on her date, but her date didn't happen because she needed to come back to the office.

Skinner points out the bill passed Congress with veto-proof majorities.[362] The President could veto the bill, but the veto would be overridden. The public supports the bill; the public often opposes civil rights, including interracial marriage and school integration. Skinner then suggests the gay marriage debate is not like interracial marriage, interracial marriage is "legislating values."[363] Skinner suggests the country "isn't ready for" gay marriage; the country was homophobic into the 21st century. Josh points out many states are already banning gay marriage[364] and the federal government getting involved is impinges states' rights.

A reporter asks why the flight took off late. C.J. points out the President had a budget meeting and there was a concern it might run long. C.J. tries to get the drafts of the speech back, assuring the press there will not be a policy shift.

The crew of the oil tanker threw the ship's manifest overboard when boarded. Leo is frustrated and brings together military leaders to discuss the next action.

The President takes a meeting about the lack of light-rail transit outside of the northeastern United States.

The President pokes C.J. for making fun of Notre Dame. The President likes late flights. The President gets romantic about Mao and the phrase "permanent revolution." The President clarifies they left late because of worries the budget meeting would run long.

BARTLET: You don't like permanent revolution?
TOBY: It's a nifty phrase. But I think if we call for a permanent revolution than people are—you know—going to expect one.

Donna visits Ainsley in Ainsley's sweltering office. Ainsley is working on the constitutionality of gay marriage bans. Donna asks if she and Ainsley look alike, because apparently someone got them confused; this was her date.

Skinner suggests "the founders based the country on a Judeo-Christian morality" and Josh responds that they did not want Judeo-Christian morality[365] in government, which is why the First Amendment prohibits establishment of religion and restrictions on free exercise. Religious values cannot be the basis for curtailing the rights of others. Josh points out the ban would make gay couples ineligible for marriage benefits, including social security benefits; Skinner and Josh accept the government cannot pay those benefits out.[366]

Danny doesn't want to give his draft copy of the speech back. C.J. promises no substantive changes, but he refuses.

Charlie suggests tuition incentives for people who become teachers. Toby points out they don't have a plan to pay for tuition incentives.

Josh and Skinner argue the merits and public opinion on gay marriage. Josh argues the federal government cannot pass a ban on gay marriage because it would violate the 14th amendment, which is the view developed by Justice Kennedy (in part) in Obergefell v. Hodges in 2015.[367]

Skinner says the bill is going to pass anyway, over a veto.

SKINNER: Ask me the question.
JOSH: He compared homosexuality to kleptomania and sex addiction, Matt.

SKINNER: Yes.

JOSH: The Majority Leader, the leader of your own party.

SKINNER: He was wrong, and I told him so.

JOSH: For crying out loud—

SKINNER: Ask me the question, Josh.

JOSH: How can you be a member of this party?

SKINNER: You've been holding that in for way too long, man.

JOSH: This party that says who you are is against the law.

[…]

SKINNER: I agree with 95% of the Republican platform. I believe in local government. I am in favor of individual rights rather than group rights. I believe free markets lead to free people and that the country needs a strong national defense. My life doesn't have to be about being a homosexual. It doesn't have to be entirely about that.

On Rep. Skinner's defense, and the Log Cabin Republican view

Some gay rights groups are politically aligned with the Republican party, including the Log Cabin Republicans (founded 1977).

During the '90s, the American LGBTQ+ community outed closeted politicians and public figures for pressing for policies that harmed the community.[368] It's not clear if Skinner is closeted, but he would be targeted for outing because of his support for marriage restrictions, which prevented gay couples from accessing public services available to heterosexual couples.

At the time, the rule regarding outing among many LGBTQ+ journalists and activists was to respect the privacy of the closeted person unless they were doing harm to the community. This was developed by Michaelangelo Signorile[369] and Michael Rogers. In some cases, politicians and activists were outed by their own acts, as with Senator Larry Craig's arrest at the Minneapolis-St. Paul Airport (2007) or Exodus International[370] President John Paulk going to a Washington D.C. gay bar (2000).

Synopsis, cont'd

Skinner leaves with the Majority Leader. The President will sign the bill; Skinner tells the Majority Leader not to touch him.

Sam suggests they might float a new education initiative. Toby says they won't. C.J. protests because they got the draft back from the reporters (except Danny) on the assumption there would be no new initiatives or substantive changes.

Toby says they're not going to float a new policy initiative, because they cannot propose whims. Sam admits one reason he wants the initiative is because he froze up on the speech.

Ainsley explains to Josh that full faith and credit requires states recognize documents (including marriage certificates) issued in other states, but how they recognize these can vary. States can choose what privileges are tied to a marriage certificate in their own state. Josh tells Toby to reign in the President; Toby is considering the tuition incentives for teachers but knows they cannot propose it without research to figure out (among other things) what it would cost.

Donna explains to Josh that her date was terrible. Josh is kind to her and tells her she should buy the dress. Donna was planning to wear the dress and then return it.

Leo and the President suggest they are going to hold the ship and test the point of origin. The President is angry they cannot fine the oil company. Toby asks Danny for the draft back and explains it is because Sam is unhappy with the writing, and Danny complies. Danny complying annoys C.J. Danny went to Notre Dame and was ribbing her for making fun of Notre Dame before a Michigan game.

The President doesn't want to sign the gay marriage definition law because it is gay bashing. Josh suggests they do the pocket veto as a gesture to the gay community, even though they'll eventually have to sign it. Josh, Leo, and Margaret go home.

Bartlet went to Notre Dame because he was thinking about becoming a priest. He decided not to become a priest when he met Abby.

Toby wants to consider tuition incentives, but not put it in the speech. As they land, their discussion becomes grounded.

Chapter Twelve
Episodes 2.08-2.10

Shibboleth (2.08)

Aired on: November 22, 2000
Directed by: Laura Innes
Story by: Patrick Caddell
Teleplay by: Aaron Sorkin
Plotlines:
  a) Chinese refugees seek asylum in the United States.
  b) Toby urges the President to appoint Leo's sister to a position in the Department of Education.
  c) Charlie helps the President find a new carving knife.
  d) C.J. decides which turkey the President will pardon on Thanksgiving.

In San Diego, the Coast Guard stopping a container ship from Fujian, China.[371] Sam pitches Toby a show about pilgrim detectives. C.J. was sick last year during Thanksgiving; the staff doesn't remember because they check out during the holidays. Josh is flipping a coin that keeps coming up tails.[372]

Turkeys are dropped off for the turkey pardoning.[373] Sam, Toby, and Josh decide to leave them in C.J.'s office as a prank.

Josh is brought in on a call about "a boat from China."[374] There were almost 100 Chinese refugees stuffed into a container on a ship; 13 died in transit. Josh tells Leo not to mention he, Sam, and Toby are available on Thanksgiving, because the President will insist they attend Thanksgiving with the President. Leo laughs the suggestion off and focuses on the Chinese refugees. Josh briefs C.J. about the Chinese and a recess appointment of Leo's sister.

The turkeys are in C.J.'s office. Carol warns her, but they are free and wandering around the office. The Press Secretary chooses which of the turkeys will be pardoned, based on which is "more photogenic."

Charlie tries to find the President a new carving knife. The President decides he wants to try a German knife, sending Charlie out again. Sam briefs the President on the Chinese immigrants in San Diego. Toby insists they should appoint Leo's sister during the congressional recess; the President suggests they shouldn't use recess appointments to appoint controversial people. Toby and the President want to have a conversation about school prayer. Leo's sister Josephine McGarry will start that conversation.[375] Toby tells Leo he wants to appoint Josephine list; Leo objects. She's qualified but has a controversial record. Toby must take meetings on her appointment.

Josh and Sam brief the President; the Chinese immigrants are Christian Evangelicals who claim they are fleeing religious persecution.[376] C.J. briefs the press on the "credible fear interview," where the INS establishes whether the people have a credible fear of persecution. The White House staff will meet with Reverend Al Caldwall,[377] as well as American and Chinese governmental officials. C.J. announces the turkey pardon and Thanksgiving proclamation. The Press Secretary leads the children in song, which C.J. isn't prepared to do.[378]

A Christian Evangelical in the United States threatened to blow up a theater because of a play in which Jesus Christ was portrayed as gay. Sam and Josh meet with Reverend Caldwell and Mary Marsh.[379] Marsh insists the President doesn't care about persecuted Christians around the world, including China. Marsh threatens the White House with political retribution if it does not support the asylum request. Caldwell rehashes the persecution of Christian Evangelicals in China, evidenced by various human rights reports.

CALDWELL: China harasses Christians, Josh. The State Department says so. Amnesty International says so. I say so. It is fact.[380]

Sam redirects the conversation to the instance of a Christian threatening to blow up a theater and the ambivalence of the Christian right to the free exercise of religion by non-Christians. These Christian leaders only care when ideologically aligned Christians are persecuted.

Caldwell acknowledges Sam's point, taking Josh aside. He says his church will sponsor the refugees and pay their bail if necessary. Josh points out this is a considerable amount of money. Caldwell will raise the money.

Religious Persecution and American Evangelicalism

In both the pilot and this episode, The West Wing is critical of some Evangelical Christian[381] leaders (through Mary Marsh) while crediting others as morally sincere (through Al Caldwell). In the present climate, a liberal-leaning show crediting the Evangelical movement as good faith seems odd, but it reflects an important political reality.

For decades, Evangelical groups in the United States supported immigration measures into the United States to prevent religious persecution. During the Bush administration, Evangelical groups sponsored Christian immigration from Muslim- and communist-controlled countries. This posture shifted as the Republican party became anti-immigration in the later part of the Bush administration and afterwards, culminating in the anti-immigrant posture of the Trump administration.[382]

Christian Evangelical groups often framed this in terms of "religious freedom." Sorkin notes the hypocrisy in this framing.

In many countries, religious minorities are persecuted. Christians face persecution in China, Pakistan, Malaysia, etc. So do other religious minorities. Zoroastrians face religious persecution in Muslim-majority countries; Muslims (Uyghurs in particular) face persecution in communist China; Jews face persecution in Christian-controlled eastern European countries. In these cases, some Christians who advocate for religious freedom are far less outspoken.[383] These religious organizations aren't concerned with religious freedom generally; they're concerned with the religious freedom of Christians (and usually only Christians who are politically aligned with them).

The free exercise of religion is sacrosanct in the United States; this should inform our immigration policy. The episode (through President Bartlet and Reverend Caldwell) argues those who seek the free exercise of religion should be allowed to immigrate to the United States when they have reasonable fear of persecution, which was the dominant American policy position at the time. It is not the position of the current Republican Party, which wants to put those seeking refuge in other "safe" countries.

While Sorkin criticizes Evangelical leaders for failing to protect free exercise for non-Christians, he acknowledges some (like Caldwell) are sincere and doing their best.

Synopsis, cont'd

Toby meets with congressional Republicans. They are furious Josephine McGarry is being appointed. They are upset about her attitudes towards school prayer; Toby points out Josephine is deeply religious but upheld the law against organized prayer in school. The Republicans suggest 70% of the public opposes the law prohibiting organized prayer in schools; Toby points out constitutional protections don't consider popular opinion. The Republicans raise the same objection President Bartlet had: recess appointments shouldn't be used to avoid the Senate's advice and consent.

The Senate Republican representatives have an article with a photograph of a kid being handcuffed as Josephine McGarry looks on.[384] Leo meets with Toby and Leo points out the picture is disqualifying. Leo points out that the appointment was about picking the fight.

C.J. must choose which turkey to pardon; she must learn the song. C.J. asks Donna to help her learn the song "We Gather Together."

Sam and Josh meet with the INS, the INS notes sometimes immigrants are coached, they will claim to be Christians because it makes them more sympathetic. Sam points out they lived in a container for months with dead bodies.

The President doesn't like the German knife. He pardons the turkey. China claims Christians aren't persecuted in China; Josh and Sam warn the President about coaching. The President explains the term "shibboleth;" a shibboleth is the way members of a group recognize one another. The President will meet with one of the Chinese refugees.

Leo meets with his sister (Deborah Hedwall).[385] Leo asks her to withdraw her name from consideration, because of the picture. Leo knows Josephine called the photographer, staged the photo; he recognized the photographer and the photographer mentioned his sister had called him for photos. She wanted the picture taken; Leo finds that repulsive. Toby comes into the room afterwards and explains why he want the fight on school prayer.

TOBY: I'll tell you why it should be front and center. It's not the First Amendment. It's not religious freedom. It's not church and state. It's not abstract.

LEO: What is it?

TOBY: It's the fourth grader who gets his ass kicked at recess 'cause he sat out the voluntary prayer in homeroom. It's another way of making kids different from other kids when they're required by law to be there.

Toby is speaking from experience.[386] Leo insists the President won't invite the staff to dinner.

The President meets with one of the Chinese refugees, Jhin Wei (Henry O),[387] a Chemistry professor. The refugee talks about his practice, that they give to charity and share bibles.

WEI: Mr. President, Christianity is not demonstrated through a recitation of facts. You're seeking evidence of faith, a whole-hearted acceptance of God's promise of a better world. "For we hold that man is justified by faith alone," is what Saint Paul said. Justified by faith alone. Faith is the true... I'm trying to... shibboleth. Faith is the true shibboleth.

BARTLET: Yes, it is.

Admitting the refugees would be a diplomatic disaster, but the Chinese refugees could "escape" from the INS detention facility and this would insulate the White House from accountability.[388] The President and Leo go along with the escape.

Toby invites C.J. to dinner with him, Sam, and Josh. A man comes to take one of the turkeys back to be killed. C.J. and Donna stage a presidential pardon to confuse the guy picking up the turkey. The President points out the President does not have any jurisdiction over turkeys. Mrs. Landingham gives the President a hard time because the President cannot use the intercom.

Charlie brings another knife, which the President doesn't like. The President reveals he is giving away the carving knife passed down through his family. He is giving it to Charlie. The knife was made for the Bartlet family by Paul Revere, hearkening back to Bartlet's old New England history; Charlie is a surrogate son to President Bartlet.

The President prepares to proclaim a day of thanksgivings; the refugees escaped in San Diego.

Galileo (2.09)

Aired on: November 29, 2000
Directed by: Alex Graves
Written by: Aaron Sorkin and Kevin Falls
Plotlines:
   a) The President prepares for an educational event for children with NASA about a probe landing on Mars.
   b) There is a fire at a Russian facility.
   c) The President doesn't like green beans.
   d) Josh and Toby decide who should be on a commemorative postage stamp.
   e) C.J. and Sam don't want to go to the symphony.

The President talks about how good NASA is at naming things, including the probe Galileo V,[389] which is going to land on Mars. C.J. takes the President to a rehearsal for a Presidential classroom event. Sam is cranky with draft remarks from NASA public affairs; the NASA public affairs staffer is defensive about it. The President is going to talk to school children with a panel of NASA experts. The President knows about Mars; C.J. suggests the President defer to experts. The President also decides the NASA remarks are inadequate; Sam does a rewrite on the fly.

Josh is eating lunch with Toby, who explains that a Martian day is 24 hours and 37 minutes. Toby is concerned about a report the President doesn't like green beans. Leo walks Josh and Toby out to talk about a stamp because Marcus Aquino[390] should be put on a stamp per the Citizen's Stamp Advisory Committee. Marcus Aquino favored statehood for Puerto Rico. Leo is concerned about political blowback.[391] Toby deputizes Josh to deal with the stamp. Toby tells C.J. to worry about the green bean story, but she blows him off.

Charlie briefs the President on his schedule. The President wants to read up on Mars and so will end his schedule at 6:30. Mrs. Landingham tells the President cannot spend the night reading. He is attending a concert by the Reykjavik Symphony Orchestra at the Kennedy Center. Leo explains attending the concert will placate the Icelandic Ambassador, and they want to convince Iceland to ban on whale hunting.[392]

The President gets a security briefing about an explosion at a Russian "oil refinery," but there is no oil refinery in that area. It's probably a missile silo. The President is concerned the missile may have been armed. The President suggests they would help with the silo fire, but the Russians will not ask for American support. The President waxes poetic about Galileo's discovery. The President wants a broader theme for the Presidential classroom; he suggests Sam and C.J. come to the symphony to discuss the broader theme.

Donna wants to put Marcus Aquino on a stamp.

C.J. admits she was wrong about the green bean story.[393] There are a lot of green bean farmers in Oregon; the President didn't win Oregon by a large enough margin, making it an electoral issue. Toby knows this already.

C.J. does not want to go to the symphony with the President, because she just rejected a bunch of people from the State Department. Sam doesn't want to go, because Mallory will be there. C.J. is pissed about people diminishing her intelligence.[394]

The President is briefed on the Russian missile silo. The Russian military is deteriorating after the collapse of the Soviet Union; the likely explanation is something went wrong due to incompetence. Leo meets with the Russian ambassador. The President finds out NASA lost the signal from Galileo V.

Josh and Donna argue about the stamp; the government must be officially neutral on Puerto Rico statehood.[395] Donna is strongly in favor of statehood for Puerto Rico.

Toby explains the spacecraft has gone into a non-transmitting mode.

C.J. and Sam go to the Kennedy Center.

Leo meets with the Russian Ambassador to the United States Nadia Kozlowski (Charlotte Cornwell),[396] who flirts with him. The Russian position is incoherent, both claiming the issue is merely an oil refinery and a matter of national security. Leo offers to help with the explosion.

Bartlet complains to Charlie about the "modern music," including a piece by a new Icelandic composer. The President likes "classical" music, but nothing modern.[397]

The President considers a broader theme for the classroom with C.J. and Sam. Mallory confronts Sam, and he babbles incoherently. Mallory is dating a hockey player.[398] Sam tells the President they have more information about the refinery fire, and they are still working on Galileo V.

Charlie mentioned the President doesn't like green beans to a reporter. He also points out it is silly to care about those things.[399]

CHARLIE: What the hell, C.J. He doesn't like green beans.

C.J.: We won Oregon by 10,000 votes. I don't know how many green bean farmers they have out there, but if there are 10,001 then we're screwed.

CHARLIE: C.J.—

C.J.: This is a serious thing now.

CHARLIE: Well, I'm sorry I mouthed off to a reporter, but you're out of your mind.

C.J.: No, I'm—

CHARLIE: Education is a serious thing. Crime, jobs, national security. In 18 months, I've been to Oregon four times and not a single person I've met there has been stupid.

C.J.: Everybody is stupid in an election year, Charlie.

CHARLIE: No, everybody gets treated stupid in an election year, C.J.

Toby acknowledges it may take a few days to deal with Galileo V. C.J. is approached by someone from the State Department she rejected for a job. He mentions they briefly dated and C.J. takes offense to the idea their dating may be relevant.

Sam and Josh talk about Mallory. Mallory suggests Sam is mad; she pretends to be ambivalent about the space probe to get Sam riled up.

Donna pushes for Aquino on the stamp. Leo and the Ambassador argue about the rescue mission. The President enters the room and points out the Russian missile system is falling into serious disrepair.[400] Soldiers were trying to steal the missile. The President is not going to accept conditions on United States inspectors, because the failure of Russian nuclear security endangers the entire world.

The staff decides, with C.J.'s leadership, to put Marcus Aquino on the stamp and let the green beans story fade.

The President enjoyed the concert and liked the new composition from the Icelandic composer. He wants to keep the classroom scheduled and talk about how sometimes even smart people fail. C.J. thinks it is important for children to hear smart people get things wrong, because it is an important life lesson.

Noël (2.10)

Aired on: December 20, 2000
Directed by: Thomas Schlamme

Story by: Peter Parnell
Teleplay by: Aaron Sorkin
Plotlines:
  a) Josh meets with a psychiatrist.
  b) An Air Force pilot disobeys orders and crashes.
  c) Toby hires musicians to play in the White House.
  d) A woman screams during a White House tour.
  e) The Energy Secretary mentions using the Strategic Petroleum Reserve instead of drilling in the artic.

On Christmas Eve, Josh meets with Dr. Stanley Keyworth (Adam Arkin)[401] and Kaytha Trask (Purva Bedi).[402] Josh has an injury on his hand; he says the injury is from a broken drinking glass. Keyworth and Trask are from ATVA, the American Trauma Victims Association.[403] Josh knows the organization. He is frustrated with Stanley playing dumb; Trask is here is because there are always two people, so one person can always keep watch on the patient.[404] Stanley knows Josh is lying about cutting his hand on a glass; he establishes himself as intelligent and capable.

Stanley and Josh talk about the shooting. Stanley tries to get Josh to tell him what happened, but Josh doesn't remember anything before waking up in the hospital. Three weeks ago, staffers worried about Josh's behavior. Josh mentions a pilot, Robert Cano.[405]

We flash back to a brass band in the White House lobby. Toby is trying to be more cheerful, though usually cranky. Josh mentions Energy Secretary Ben Zaharian[406] expressed potential use of the Strategic Petroleum Reserve.[407] A reporter asks about a woman screaming during a White House tour. C.J. points out using the SPR might be appropriate in the winter, when gas prices increase.

The President is in the Situation Room. An Air Force pilot left his group and is not responding. He has weapons and the plane has not crashed, as far as they can tell. They do not know what the goals or state of mind of the pilot are.

Josh tells Stanley he didn't hear about the pilot in the Situation Room. Josh knew about the pilot because he looked at the pilot's personnel file.

The pilot got through psychological screening. Donna continues to butter Josh up, because she wants to attend an event where YoYo Ma is playing. Josh and the pilot have the same birthday.

Sam spoke to someone from the Energy Department; Sam thinks the White House should change their position on the SPR.

Bernard Thatch (Paxton Whitehead)[408] meets with C.J. about the woman who screamed on the White House tour. The painting is by Gustave Cailloux.[409] Thatch says it is a minor work of. Thatch does not approve of the President's taste in art and is snobby about it.

The President worries about the missing plane. The President asks Charlie what they should do with the pilot once the pilot is on the ground. The President cannot sign all his Christmas cards, because he sends out 1.1 million Christmas cards, which includes everyone who writes a letter to the White House (except the death threats).

The pilot died. Josh was supposed to brief the President, but the pilot killed himself by crashing into a mountain before the President had time for the briefing. Stanley asks Josh what he learned about the pilot; the pilot had a purple heart for being shot at and ejecting over Bosnia.

Music in the White House lobby, this time bagpipes. Josh "can hear the damn sirens all over the buildings," a slip as he complains about the bagpipes. C.J. asks Carol to get her the report from the White House tour.

Stanley asks if Josh knew other White House staffers were concerned about him. Josh was agitated throughout the week and is agitated with Stanley through the questioning. There is no information about the pilot concerning a mental breakdown. C.J. shows Josh a picture and Josh recognizes the painting from the White House.

Donna is excited about seeing YoYo Ma play at the Christmas party.

Josh and Sam talk to the President about the SPR. Josh doesn't want the President to use the SPR; he yells at the President, crossing a line. Josh and Leo meet after Josh yells at the President. Leo suggests Josh meet with ATVA.

Stanley confronts Josh about how Josh injured his hand. Stanley knows about Josh's issues with trauma. Josh hurt his hand after coming home from the Congressional Christmas Party, where YoYo Ma was playing.

C.J. meets with the woman who yelled on the tour, Mrs. Housman (Etyl Leder).[410] Mrs. Housman is accompanied by her son (Michael Crider). C.J. explains the painting was owned by the woman's father and it was taken by the Vichy government when Jews were stripped of their property.[411] She offers the painting back to the women. They offer to display the painting in the White House, but the woman would like the painting back.

Stanley diagnosed Josh with post-traumatic stress disorder and Josh is concerned it will mean it can't work in the White House.[412]

YoYo Ma plays Bach's Cello Suite in G Major. "It's really quite something."[413] Josh is having an episode. Josh admits the injury wasn't caused by the drink. We see Josh smash the mirror in his apartment. Stanley assures Josh employment is not an issue; he should see a therapist but is otherwise fine. The music is the trigger for the episode.

Josh and Leo meet afterwards. Leo smiles.

LEO: This guy's walking down the street when he falls in a hole. The walls are so steep he can't get out. A doctor passes by, the guy shouts, "Hey, can you help me out?" The doctor writes a prescription and throws it down in the hole and moves on. Then a priest comes along and the man shouts, "Hey father, I'm down in this hole, can you help me out?" The priest writes out a prayer, throws it down in the hole and moves on. Then a friend walks by. "Hey Joe, it's me. Can you help me out?" and the friend jumps in the hole. Our guy says, "Are you stupid? Now we're both down here." The friend says, "Yeah, but I've been down here before and I know the way out."

Leo struggles with addiction, and he knows how to help Josh. Donna takes Josh to the doctor to have his hand examined as Carol of the Bells plays.

Chapter Thirteen
Episodes 2.11-2.14

The Leadership Breakfast (2.11)

Aired on: January 10, 2001
Directed by: Scott Winant[414]
Story by: Paul Redford
Teleplay by: Aaron Sorkin
Plotlines:
   a) Toby wants to use the Leadership Breakfast to talk about issues.
   b) C.J. has conflict with the new Chief of Staff to the Majority Leader.
   c) Sam suggests moving the White House Press Corps across the street.
   d) Leo has an issue with a reporter.

Josh and Sam build a fire in a fireplace as Donna objects. Sam talks about firewood. C.J. works on the seating chart for the Leadership Breakfast, which is an annual bipartisan event. Ginger smells smoke. The flue has been welded shut. The fire alarm goes off. Charlie wakes up the President; the President is cranky.

Leo and Toby talk about the Breakfast; they are not allowed to talk about policy at the breakfast. They can't talk about raising the minimum wage. They can't talk about the Patient's Bill of Rights.[415] They can't talk about a tax cut.

The President is about the fire alarm; the President had to evacuate to the balcony. Toby wants to change the Breakfast to allow substantive issues; these are rules and not (as Leo calls them) "guidelines." The President is annoyed they are serving Vermont maple syrup, since he's from New Hampshire.

Leo instructs Josh to go to a dinner at "Ben and Sally's" on Leo's behalf. Leo wants Josh to apologize to Karen Cahill[416] because Leo made a joke about her shoes. Josh delegates this apology to Sam.

C.J. and Carol meet with Republican staffers, including Ann Stark (Felicity Huffman).[417] They haggle over language. Stark insists the Majority Leader will brief the press in front of the Capitol, rather than the White House. C.J. fights over this and wins.

Toby takes Stark aside and complains about the rules for the Leadership Breakfast. He wants to junk the rules. They agree to meet for breakfast.

Sam and Donna talk about kicking the press corps out of the White House; Sam is apologizing to Karen Cahill on Leo's behalf; he is intimidated by Karen Cahill.

Toby and Leo talk about the rules; Toby wants them to talk about policy. He knows they will not come up with solutions, but they should try. Leo doesn't like negotiating with Ann Stark because she is new to her job. Toby vouches for her. Both Toby and Leo acknowledge that not talking about issues contributed to their failed marriages. This is a metaphor for the Leadership Breakfast rules.

Toby and Stark meet for breakfast; Stark brought him New Hampshire maple syrup, for the President. Toby and Stark banter; they are familiar and friendly.

C.J. tells Sam never to mention the prospect of moving the press. Sam wants space between the press and the President. C.J. points out neither the press nor the public want "space" between the press and the President; the public likes the press being as close to the President as possible. Sam goes behind C.J.'s back to add a question about moving the press to a poll they have commissioned.

Sam says his meeting with Karen Cahill went well. He talked about the nuclear weapons in Kyrgyzstan. Josh points out he meant Kazakhstan.[418] There are no nuclear weapons in Kyrgyzstan.[419]

Toby and Stark go back and forth on the minimum wage[420] to show the Leadership Breakfast should be able to dispute those issues. Toby and Stark agree to discuss the Patient's Bill of Rights, on the condition the Majority Leader can brief from the Capitol. Toby points out that he is C.J.'s boss.

Bartlet and Charlie talk about preparing remarks for the Breakfast. Bartlet reads the lines, "there is a lot more that unites Americans than divides them."

Sam and Donna talk about Sam's , worried that Karen Cahill will run a story about him being stupid. Sam is stressed. Sam suggests Donna meet with Karen Cahill to talk about how he obviously meant Kazakhstan.

Toby admits he let the Republican leader brief from the Capitol, over C.J.'s objections. C.J. is furious about the optics. Toby hates arguing about the seating arrangement all day and failing to talk about substantive issues. Toby orders C.J. to make the deal.

A pollster called a reporter to ask about moving the press briefing room. This is how C.J. finds out Sam and Josh polled on the issue.

C.J. watches the press conference. A reporter asks about a minimum wage increase and that the White House will attach the increase to "everything that moves." The quote is from Toby, to Ann Stark. C.J. is stunned by the comment and the Republicans use this to score political points.

Leo yells at Toby. C.J. prepares to brief the press on the statement. They strategize and agree to make a statement. Toby suggests they attack the Majority Leader by pointing out he used a sore throat as an excuse for not attending the press conference, while millions of Americans don't have health insurance. Josh gets a package and Donna is happy about her exchange with Karen Cahill. The package is from Karen Cahill and contains Donna's underwear, which slipped out of her pants in a row.[421]

C.J. chews out Sam and Josh for putting the question about moving the press out of the White House. C.J. is angry with Sam for not listening but proceeds to go the press briefing room and nail the response.

Toby meets with Ann Stark. "Shocked, shocked to discover there is gambling going on in this establishment," he quotes Casablanca. Toby is disappointed they cannot talk about issues in a substantive way. The Majority Leader is preparing to run for President.

Leo and Toby meet to talk about reelection, as Toby admits he made a serious mistake around the Leadership Breakfast.

The Drop-In (2.12)

Aired on: January 24, 2001
Directed by: Lou Antonio
Story by: Lawrence O'Donnell
Teleplay by: Aaron Sorkin
Plotlines:
  a) Leo advocates for a missile defense system.

b) Toby wants to include criticism of environmental terrorism in a speech, but doesn't want to argue about it with Sam.
c) The President welcomes new ambassadors to the United States.
d) Comedian Corey Sykes is invited to host the Will Rogers Dinner.[422]

Leo drags the President to the situation room to tests of a new missile defense system. The President is meeting with the new ambassador for Thailand to the United States (Alberto Isaac). Mrs. Landingham criticizes the missile defense system. The President thinks the Pentagon is jerking Leo around, comparing the relationship to Lucy and Charlie Brown.[423] The missile defense system doesn't work.

C.J. briefs the press on the ceremony welcoming ambassadors to the United States. The President accepts ambassadors in the order they arrive in Washington. The ambassador from the United Kingdom has not been named. C.J. studied up on the process; the press is not interested.

Sam tells C.J. the President is going to speak to the Global Defense Council, an environmentalist organization,[424] and announce a clean air program. Sam writes the speech; Sam is passionate about environmentalism, a tie-back to his departure from private practice protecting oil companies from liability (2.01 and 2.02). Toby is not happy about the speech; Toby and Leo were not told the President would be speaking to the GDC. Toby is upset, because they decided not to speak to the AFL-CIO. There is already tension between the labor movement and the environmental movement.

Donna tells Josh that Lord John Marbury is going to be the new ambassador for the United Kingdom to the United States. Josh is not excited about this, because Marbury is "eccentric."

Toby and Josh aren't excited about the Global Defense Council speech. Toby wants to criticize the GDC for not condemning environmental terrorism.[425]

Leo is briefed on the missile defense system test; the system missed by 137 miles. Toby wants a drop-in line on environmental terrorism. Toby and Leo are focused on reelection. Toby wants to go behind Sam's back with the drop-in. He doesn't want the line in the advanced text.

Sam walks through the speech, including cap-and-trade cash incentives for companies to lower greenhouse gas emissions.[426] Josh and C.J. talk about Lord John Marbury, who C.J. likes and Josh does not. Josh tells C.J. that Cornelius Sykes (a stand-up comedian) is going to host the Will Rogers dinner[427] and C.J. must ask him not to host.

The President greets the ambassador from Sweden (Peter Holland).

BARTLET: Sweden has a 100% literacy rate, Leo. 100%. How do they do that?
LEO: Well, maybe they don't, and they also can't count.

The President and Leo argue about the missile defense system. Leo pitches the drop-in line on environmental terrorism and points out the President criticized Reverend Caldwell for not admonishing anti-abortion terrorists (in 1.01).[428]

The President speaks to Toby about the drop-in line and acknowledges the environmental group is going to hate the line; he is going to be attacked afterwards for criticizing them. C.J. is going to New York to meet with Corey Sykes, under the pretext of accepting an award. Toby tells C.J. about the drop-in, "friends should be honest with each other." Ginger is cranky about how long Sam spent working on the speech.

Leo and Josh talk about the missile shield. Leo points out all failed tests are used as a reason to cut funding. Lord John Marbury barges into the room, greeting Leo as "Gerald." He compliments Margaret in his eccentric way[429] and says he's glad to see Josh after Josh was shot. Marbury derides the missile shield.

JOSH: Leo's trying to convince the President to give the NMD more time.
LEO: And you're an expert in the field. And I hope I can count on your support.
MARBURY: You may hope for it, but you'll not have it.
LEO: Why not?
MARBURY: Because the NMD is an absurdly wasteful military boondoggle that will never produce a working missile. It violates any number of elements of the ABM treaty[430] and any argument you make in its defense will surely be moronic.

C.J. meets with Corey Sykes (Rocky Carroll). Sykes is charming. C.J. asks Sykes to turn down hosting the Will Rogers Dinner.

Marbury points out the missile system doesn't work. The President leaves for the Global Defense Council. Donna babysits Marbury in the meantime.

Sykes made a joke about New York City police killing Black men at a fundraiser; the joke caused a scandal. C.J. insisted to reporters the President did not laugh at the joke. The President did laugh, and Corey killed that night.[431] He was offended by how the White House treated him. He is a supporter and raised money for the President. He agrees not to host the Will Rogers Dinner.

Sam is furious the President admonished the Global Defense Council; Toby gives Sam the "friends are honest with each other" line to spin. Sam is also upset about the lukewarm reaction to the speech.[432]

Donna and Marbury talk about his royal background and his relationship to the British kings. C.J. gives Sam the same "friends are honest with each other" line. Sam realizes that Toby added the drop-in line.[433]

Toby points out the missile shield takes money away from equipment in the Pentagon budget that works, like helicopters and tanks. Leo points out the missile defense shield serves a different function.

Sam is furious with Toby about the drop-in. He wants to speak to the President, but Charlie blocks the door.

Leo continues to argue about the missile shield with Marbury. Leo focuses on North Korea as a potential nuclear threat; Marbury points out the missile shield would only protect the United States, even if it eventually works.[434]

Toby sits down with Sam. Sam cannot go into the Oval Office angry.[435] The policy the White House proposed is going to be a law; the environmental groups are upset over the attack and ignoring public policy. Toby is trying to figure out how to deal with the public opinion. "We can't govern if we don't win."

The President wants to make sure Leo's support for the missile shield is not a political issue, not about looking "strong on defense," but a genuine policy commitment. The President meets Marbury to accept his credentials as ambassador. The President asks Marbury what Marbury thinks of the missile shield.

MARBURY: Well, I think it's dangerous, illegal, fiscally irresponsible, technologically unsound, and a threat to all people everywhere.

BARTLET: Leo?

LEO: I think the world invented a nuclear weapon. I think the world owes it to itself to see if it can invent something that would make it irrelevant.

MARBURY: That's the right sentiment, and certainly a credible one from a man who has fought in a war. You think you can make it stop? Well, you can't. We build a shield, and somebody will build a better missile.

BARTLET: Well, it's a discussion for serious men. They say a statesman is a politician who's been dead for 15 years.[436] I'd like us to be statemen while we're still alive.

Bartlet's Third State of the Union (2.13)

Aired on: February 7, 2001
Directed by: Christopher Misiano
Story by: Allison Abner and Dee Dee Myers
Teleplay by: Aaron Sorkin
Plotlines:

a) The President gives his third State of the Union address.
b) The White House prepares for a blue-ribbon commission on entitlements, including social security.
c) Capitol Beat is broadcasting from inside the White House.
d) Charlie tracks down an uncashed check written by the First Lady.
e) A police officer invited to the State of the Union has a reprimand for excessive force.
f) DEA agents are abducted in Columbia.

There is a television broadcast in the White House during the President's third State of the Union. Toby is editing the speech at the last minute. They have a "green light on the blue ribbon"[437] as they walk to the House. Josh and Donna are in the polling center; the poll is being run by Joey Lucas. The commentators claim the State of the Union is "the speech of the President's political life." C.J. tells the press the "blue ribbon" is a bipartisan commission to study the future of entitlement programs. Capitol Beat is broadcasting live from the White House immediately after the State of the Union.[438]

The staff waits as the State of the Union begins.

Josh and Donna watch the State of the Union from the polling center. The speech ends. Josh is wondering what he should tell the callers. Joey Lucas arrives and instructs the callers to start.

Mark Gottfried interviews C.J. and Minority Whip Henry Shallick (Corben Bernsen). Shallick suggests the President's skill as a public speaker is irrelevant; he is dismissive of the substance. After they go to commercial, we find C.J. is not wearing paints because she sat in wet paint. Sam tells C.J. that a police officer the White House invited to the State of the Union has a reprimand for excessive use of force,[439] and the White House didn't catch it ahead of time because the criminal and civil cases had been dismissed.

Charlie asks Mrs. Landingham about a note; the note refers to an outstanding check written by the First Lady. Charlie is sent to ask the First Lady, who will be angry about it. The check was written to a woman who left an abusive husband and couldn't afford Christmas presents for her children. Charlie agrees to track down the check to make sure the woman got it.

Sam and Leo talk about the police officer. Leo tells Sam to keep the police officer out of any photographs with the President.

Leo goes to the Situation Room and is informed several DEA agents have been abducted, likely by a drug cartel, in Columbia.

Josh explains the President invited Officer Jack Sloan at the last minute; Sloan was not vetted. He was invited because of an incident at an elementary school. Josh also badgers Joey Lucas about wanting to see numbers from the poll, and she tells him they have a good response rate and otherwise shuts him down.

Margaret informs a Cabinet Secretary (Tony Plana) that Leo wants the Secretary to speak to an "old friend." This is a code the White House uses in emergencies.[440]

Gottfried talks to Ainsley Hayes and an ACLU representative (Barbara Eve Harris) about the President proposing public schools adopt uniforms. Hayes defends the White House's position but concedes the ACLU may be right that requiring uniforms is unconstitutional. Ainsley acknowledges she hasn't met the President. Sam is surprised she hasn't met the President and wants to introduce her.

The First Lady addresses a party after the State of the Union, getting lots of laughs. She is uncomfortable, after her polished public remarks. She wants to see Toby.

Josh badgers Joey Lucas about the polling information because he wants it immediately. She blows him off. Donna wants to set Josh and Joey up on a date. The power goes out in the polling center.

Toby and Shallick argue about the White House's position on gun control and the Second Amendment. Toby sees the First Lady, who is furious they are appeasing a Republican with the commission, though the details are unclear.[441]

C.J. meets with Officer Jack Sloan (Richard Riehle) and asks about the alleged brutality incident. Sloan talks about pursuing the suspect and chasing him down, after which the suspect broke Sloan's hand and nose. Sloan points out the suspect was a former track and field athlete. The broken leg is the only way Sloan would have been able to catch the suspect, proving the broken leg could not have been the result of brutality.[442] Sloan didn't disclose it, because he assumed his success in protecting kids at the elementary school would make the previous incident irrelevant. C.J. needs to tell the press. Sloan objects.

Donna doesn't know when the power will be back on in the polling center. Joey continues to give Josh a hard time.

The President gets praise for his speech; Sam asks the President to introduce himself to Ainsley Hayes, because she is afraid of meeting the President. Leo pulls the President away to brief him about the kidnapped DEA agents. Leo thinks the cartel is just going to kill the DEA agents and there isn't anything they can do. The Joint Chiefs propose a rescue operation. Mickie warns the President that the drug cartel will strike back if they launch a military operation. Leo calls the staff back to the White House.

Ainsley Hayes also sat in paint and needs to meet Sam in her office. She is drinking and dancing in a bathrobe. The President introduces himself.

Gottlieb knows about the officer and C.J. says she is going to talk to him and give a statement. Toby uses the "old friend" code to pull C.J. away, as Gottlieb holds off reporting about Officer Sloan.

Abigail Bartlet is furious at her husband for cutting the Violence Against Women Act[443] from the State of the Union. She and the President agreed he would not run for a second term. He tells Abby about the DEA agents; she acknowledges the DEA agents and the military operation must be the priority. The episode fades to black.

The War at Home (2.14)

Aired on: February 14, 2001
Directed by: Christopher Misiano
Written by: Aaron Sorkin
Plotlines:
    a) The President launches a rescue mission to recover the kidnapped
        DEA agents.
    b) C.J. briefs the press about the Officer facing allegations of police
        brutality.

   The President smokes a cigarette on the balcony; Leo says he should
stop smoking. It sets a bad example.[444]
   The Joint Chiefs brief the President on the rescue mission. Mickey
suggests they continue negotiating with the cartel. The President gives
the order for the rescue mission.
   C.J. asks if Officer Sloan is willing to talk to the press. He is hesitant,
but the scandal is going to break anyway. C.J. briefs Officer Sloan on
how to conduct himself in the interview and he agrees.[445]
   The Capitol Beat broadcast ends. C.J. thanks Gottlieb for holding
off and gives him the interview with Sloan in the morning to thank him.
   Someone from Seth Gillette's office called to schedule a meeting
with Toby. Toby doesn't want to meet with Gillette, who is upset about
their blue-ribbon commission on social security. Toby thinks Gillette is a
lightweight. Gillette is popular with the left; Sam has already set up the
meeting. C.J. briefs Toby about Office Sloan; he lets her handle it.
   Josh and Donna wait for the power to come back on. Donna
encourages Josh to ask out Joey Lucas.
   The President sits on the balcony. He and Leo talk through a game
of chess. The President remembers caskets coming off the plane from
Vietnam,[446] worried about the DEA agents.
   Charlie explains the woman did not cash the check; she had it
framed.
   Sam also says Josh should ask Joey Lucas out. Josh is confused about
Donna being the one to encourage him. Sam and Josh eat breakfast with the
President. He cannot tell them about the possibility of the rescue mission.
Bartlet is concerned about the war on drugs and wants Sam and Josh to start
putting together a strategy for addressing excessive incarceration.[447]

Ainsley asks Sam to reintroduce her to the President, because she was embarrassed by the previous meeting. Sam set up the meeting that embarrassed her.

Toby meets with Seth Gillette (Ed Begley Jr.).[448] Gillette is angry about the blue-ribbon commission and the State of the Union. Gillette has proposed a reform bill for social security, but the proposal has only received support from far-left Senate Democrats and has no chance of passing. Gillette threatens to condemn the commission; Toby points out that the President is the leader of the party. Gillette points out the drop-in criticizing environmental terrorism (2.12) and the defense of the cop accused of brutality are both mistakes. Gillette then threatens to run as a third-party candidate.

TOBY: I was just thinking about this cartoon I once saw. A bunch of tiny fish are swimming through the leaves of the plant but then one of the fish realizes it's not the leaves of a plant. It's the tentacles of a predator and the fish says, "with friends like this, who needs anemones." Come at us from the left and I'm going to own your ass.[449]

The First Lady prepares for a trip. Charlie asks if he can draw cash and give it to the woman in the shelter who did not cash the check. The President and First Lady talk about reelection, but she does not want to distract him from the DEA agents in Columbia.

Josh is on hold. Donna asks why the polling the White House is doing is different than major news organizations. Josh is concerned with five congressional districts because the representatives from those districts are on the fence about gun control laws.

Sam brings Ainsley to meet the President. They meet in Leo's office and wait for the President. Ainsley asks to use the bathroom but steps into a closet as the President enters. The President waits. Ainsley is flustered. Bartlet settles her down and reassures her she is doing good work.

Mike Chrysler (Glenn Morshower) and Mickey inform the President the intelligence was wrong. Their special operations team was ambushed and shot down, leaving nine men dead. Bartlet is furious. Leo tries to calm him down, but it is unsuccessful. Bartlet speaks to the President of Columbia. The President of Columbia confirms the hostages are alive. The President of Columbia offers to release a cartel boss in exchange for the hostages. President Bartlet declines.

Sam and Toby argue about releasing the cartel boss in exchange for the hostages. They cannot negotiate with terrorists;[450] Sam holds there are lives at stake, though the policy is only ever relevant when there are lives at stake. It doesn't matter if the boss is in prison or not, because the boss continues to operate the cartel either way. Bartlet asks for military options.

A short tell-a-Donna explains the policy of not negotiating with terrorists.

Bartlet asks the Joint Chiefs what it would take to wipe out the cartel; Mickey estimates 200,000 soldiers. The mortality rate would be very high because they would invade and occupy the jungle and fight a guerilla war.

The President and First Lady talk. The President tells her about the dead commandos. The President hasn't made the decision to run again, though Leo and Toby have decided to get started on reelection. The First Lady insists he has made the decision; the President points out the default positioning of the White House and Congress is to campaign. The First Lady and the President agreed that he would only serve one term.[451] She is concerned about his multiple sclerosis. She walks through the symptoms of secondary progressive multiple sclerosis.[452]

Josh gets the early polling for the five districts. The support for the waiting period on gun purchasing is unpopular. Joey Lucas suggests the problem may be the public needs to hear more about the White House position on the issue. Joey Lucas points out polling requires interpretation; people will say they do not like sleazy coverage but buy newspapers featuring sex scandals. She uses it to talk about Donna. Joey thinks Donna wants to set Josh up because Donna has a crush on Josh and wants to distract by playing matchmaker.

Charlie is worried about the President.

Leo talks about fighting in Vietnam; a jungle war is terrible and unwinnable at a reasonable cost. Leo regrets the war in Vietnam and discourages the President from sending troops to Columbia. Instead, the United States should focus on drug treatment. The President can ask the President of Columbia to let the cartel boss out of prison. Bartlet argues going outside channels is difficult, that it inclines him to kill the cartel using the CIA.[453] The President agrees to make the exchange of the hostages for the cartel boss.

C.J. briefs the press on the abduction of the DEA agents and the deaths of the special operations team. The President salutes the caskets of those killed in the attempted rescue.

Chapter Fourteen
Episodes 2.15-2.17

In my view, these are three of the best nuclear episodes of *The West Wing*. They capture a core element of the show: the humanness of politics. Ellie (2.15) captures tension within Bartlet's family, with tension between being a father and being President. "Somebody's Going to Emergency; Somebody's Going to Jail" (2.16) focuses on Sam's wrestling with a betrayal by his father, against the backdrop of a "Big Block of Cheese Day"; we also learn about the personal lives of a Senator and the White House senior staff in "The Stackhouse Filibuster" (2.17).

Ellie (2.15)

Aired on: February 12, 2001
Directed by: Michael Engler
Story by: Kevin Falls & Laura Glasser
Teleplay by: Aaron Sorkin
Plotlines:
a) The Surgeon General comments on the health effect of marijuana.
b) Toby meets with the blue-ribbon commission on entitlement programs.
c) A right-wing group praises the President.
d) The President's middle daughter issues a statement to the press.

The Surgeon General (Mary Kay Place)[454] responds to questions about marijuana in an online chat. Donna sees the chat online in real time. The President is in Tokyo. The Surgeon General criticizes marijuana's classification as a Schedule I narcotic,[455] comparing it to tobacco and alcohol.

Josh meets with the White House communications staff. The staff needs to address the Surgeon General's statement immediately and tries

165

to figure out when the President will be back in Washington from Tokyo, wrestling with time zones. The Family Values Leadership Council praises the President for denouncing a movie; the staff does not know why this group is praising the President.[456]

Toby bounces a Spalding against the window to get Sam's attention.[457] Labor groups want to put Senator Seth Gillette on the blue-ribbon commission. Toby doesn't want to ask Gillette, because Gillette might say no; Toby has an adversarial relationship with Gillette. Sam points out they need Gillette on the commission because that would make it harder for Gillette to criticize the commission. They want him on the commission, but do not want to ask.

Sam and Charlie discuss the President "denouncing" a movie. Charlie says there was no denunciation; he decided not to screen the movie at the White House because the President wouldn't like it.

Josh and C.J. prepare for a press briefing that includes questions about the Surgeon General. C.J. needs to show public support for the Surgeon General without supporting her comments; Josh is considering pressing the Surgeon General to resign. The President is against legalization or decriminalization. Josh meets with the Surgeon General to ask for her resignation; the Surgeon General checks in about Josh's gunshot wound and health. The Surgeon General defends her remarks as accurate. Josh pushes on the politics of the issue; she was commenting on medicine. Josh points out that she did comment on the classification of marijuana, which is not a medical issue but a carceral one.[458] Josh asks for her resignation. She refuses.

A reporter asks about the Family Values Leadership Council praising the President. The President has not denounced the movie. The movie has religious imagery, sex, and violence. The movie producer "goes on Imus"[459] and takes a shot at the President, which spurred the Christian right organization to praise the President. The movie's producer Morgan Ross (Robert Knepper),[460] who C.J. knows,[461] criticized the President. Sam is bringing Ross out tomorrow for a meeting.

Danny asks for a comment about a statement in support of the Surgeon General by Eleanor Bartlet, the President's middle daughter.

Toby meets with labor groups, who press for Seth Gillette to be on the commission to study entitlements. Toby wants labor groups to support the commission regardless of whether Gillette is on the commission.

Josh tells C.J. that the Surgeon General declined to resign and C.J.

will have to walk back the support, because the President may have to fire the Surgeon General. C.J. says Eleanor is being quoted, "My father wouldn't fire the Surgeon General. He would never do that." Josh is shocked; Ellie does not speak to the press or have a public profile the way Zoey does.[462]

Bartlet talks about retaliatory steel tariffs in Japan.[463] Leo stops the President from talking to the press, because of Eleanor's comments. The President is protective of his children and does not want the press approaching them.[464]

Donna asks Josh why the White House doesn't support decriminalization of marijuana. Donna points out there is no strong reason to make marijuana illegal. Josh argues parents are trying to keep drugs away from their children.

The President yells at C.J. because Danny talked to Ellie. C.J. explains that Ellie called Danny. She actively sought him out. It was not Danny's fault.

Bartlet has the support of the religious right because of the movie and far-left stoners because of the Surgeon General. Ellie needs to come down to the White House immediately. Ellie is in medical school at Johns Hopkins, in Baltimore.

Sam wants to stand by the Surgeon General; so does Toby. Toby is meeting with his ex-wife, Congresswoman Andrea Wyatt of Maryland, to get support for the commission. Andrea points out announcing the commission made labor skeptical; this is why the labor movement is pushing for Seth Gillette.

Mrs. Landingham and Charlie talk about *Dial M For Murder*. Charlie explains the movie he declined is a retelling of Dostoyevsky's *The Idiot* with a scene where the main character has sex in a church. Ellie (Nina Siemaszko)[465] arrives to see her father.

Margaret asks the Surgeon General about cancer in white rats, and whether cancer rates are high in white rats.[466] Leo brings the Surgeon General into his office. Leo asks for her resignation, or the President will fire her.

Ellie is in medical school. Her mother is a doctor, and the Surgeon General is a family friend and Ellie's godmother. The President meets with Ellie. Ellie is studying at Johns Hopkins, which is nearby, but the President does not see her often. The President badgers her about talking to a reporter and how he has tried to insulate the children from the press.

ELLIE: She was doing exactly what she is supposed to do. She—I'm sorry. She was asked a question and she said what she knew to be true. And when you start firing doctors for that, you've crossed the line somewhere.[467]

JED: There is politics involved in this, Ellie. You knew it would make me unhappy and that's why you did it, and that's cheap.

ELLIE: I didn't do it to make you unhappy, Dad.

JED: Well, you sure didn't do it to make me happy.

ELLIE: I don't know how to make you happy, Dad. For that you have to talk to Zooey or Liz.

Danny points out that having Bartlet as a father is not easy; the man is a Nobel Laureate economist and career politician, not the most attentive father. Bartlet invites Ellie to stay over to watch a movie.

Toby and Congresswoman Wyatt argue. Wyatt points out the White House announcing the commission upset people on the left. Toby wants the commission to meet in secret to deliberate and make a recommendation without external political pressure. Andrea put Toby on a benefit for the child leukemia foundation without asking him; this gives Toby the idea to just announce Gillette joined commission.

The movie industry talks about parental content warnings; Sam pulls Morgan Ross out of the meeting to speak in private. Ross notes Hitchcock used sex and violence in his films; the White House chose not to screen Ross's movie because the President wouldn't like it. Sam threatens to publicly come after Ross if Ross criticizes the President.

The President and Ellie watch *Dial M For Murder*. Josh says the President usually talks during the movie but is quiet tonight.

The President steps out of the movie to meet with the Surgeon General, who has chosen to resign rather than be fired. Bartlet asks if the Surgeon General (who is Ellie's godmother) pressured Ellie to make a statement. She did not. Bartlet struggles with not being as close with Ellie as his other daughters. The Surgeon General points out Ellie did not like Bartlet's constant, imposing presence and Ellie had a different reaction to the public attention.

The Surgeon General says that Ellie knows she's not Bartlet's favorite.

BARTLET: No. No. No. I will bear with the nonsense of the Christian right and the Hollywood left and the AFLCIO and the AARP and the Cannabis Society and Japan. But I will not stand and allow someone to tell me that I love one of my children less than the others. She's frightened of me? [...] I wanted to be so mad at her. I heard the news and my first thought was—my God, *King Lear*'s a good play. "My father won't fire the Surgeon General. He would never do that." I wanted to be so mad at her. But the truth is it's the nicest thing she's ever said about me.

The President declines to accept the Surgeon General's resignation.

The President tells Josh they will support the Surgeon General. Josh points out it will seem like the President did it because his daughter asks. Bartlet is fine with that.

The President banters with Ellie about her medical specialty. He is happy when she visits, and he loves her. They jokingly argue about what endocrinology (Ellie's specialty) is.[468]

Somebody's Going to Emergency;
Somebody's Going to Jail (2.16)

Aired on: February 28, 2001
Directed by: Jessica Yu
Written by: Aaron Sorkin and Paul Redford
Plotlines:
  a) Sam's father has been having an affair for 28 years.[469]
  b) Toby attends a rally at the World Trade Organization.
  c) It's Big Block of Cheese Day.
  d) The President thinks about the Presidential Library.

Sam is sleeping in his office. The Eagles song "New York Minute" (from which the episode gets its name) plays in the background. Leo explains a lot of the city is shut down because of protests, including the National Geographic Society. Sam looks at pardon recommendations for the President. Leo suggests Sam should go home, but Sam refuses.

LEO: Josh told me what happened with your parents. Sam, my father had affairs.[470]
[...]
SAM: My father didn't pick up a cocktail waitress, Leo. He's had a woman in an apartment in Santa Monica for 28 years.

169

Sam found out on Tuesday; Sam has been sleeping in the office since Tuesday. Sam goes back to the pardon recommendations.[471] At 6:45 a.m., Ginger opens the communications office.

Josh and Leo talk about the Big Block of Cheese Day speech and Andrew Jackson. They talk about the protesters, include a protest at the World Trade Organization. Leo gives his speech; everyone groans.

C.J. meets with Cartographers for Social Equality. Several people suggest switching assignments, but Leo tells them not to switch. Toby vents about the protesters and is immediately told that he will meet with the protesters at the World Trade Organization.[472] C.J. got the protesters to agree not to let cameras into the WTO forum.

Donna meets with Stephanie Gault (Jolie Jenkins) who wants to meet with Sam Seaborn. Donna agrees to get her a meeting. Gault wants a pardon for her grandfather;[473] her father lobbied for a pardon for years; he is dying.

President Bartlet's brother is getting a site for the Bartlet Presidential Library. There is a historical preservation law preventing them from using the preferred site, a law Bartlet signed. Bartlet doesn't want to move on with the site.

Sam meets with Stephanie Gault; Gault is a professor of international relations at the Maxwell School[474] and advises the World Trade Organization. Her grandfather was Daniel Gault. Sam explains Gault was tried for perjury during the McCarthy-era red scare. Sam believes Gault was wrongly prosecuted. Gault was a foreign policy professional targeted because of his high-profile position in the State Department. Stephanie hopes Sam will add her grandfather's name to the pardon recommendations. Time is a factor because Stephanie's father is sick.

Toby goes to the WTO. A security officer (Roma Maffia)[475] is there to protect him. The two banter.

Sam explains the Office of the Pardon Attorney and the White House Counsel make pardon recommendations; he evaluates those recommendations. He is meeting with the FBI, who will oppose a Gault pardon. Stephanie wants to give her father some good news.

Josh knows Stephanie Gault. Josh mentions Lincoln's final pardon of Patrick Murphy, a union deserter. Sam is not laughing. Josh sets up a meeting with the FBI for Sam.

A raucous crowd yells at Toby. Toby doesn't care about the forum, because without cameras in the room it doesn't matter that the crowd is raucous. An organizer briefly organizes the crowd to ask a question, but they immediately break down again.

Sam meets with Agent Casper (Clark Gregg)[476] about the pardon. Casper is furious Sam is requesting the file on Daniel Gault. Casper is certain Gault is guilty and cites Joe McCarthy, who Sam points out also accused General Marshall and comedy writers. Many people were wrongly imprisoned. Agent Casper threatens Sam about leaking the absence of the canopy when the President was shot, a request Toby made. Sam is going ahead with Gault's pardon.

C.J. meets with the Organization of Cartographers for Social Equality (John Billingsley, Jordan Baker, Brent Hinkley), who explain putting the north on top of the map is entirely arbitrary. Some believe it marginalizes countries on the bottom of the map. They also explain that flat projections of the earth distort relative size[477] and location.[478] This has also resulted in bias against Africa and South America. They support public schools mandating the use of the Peters Projection over the Mercator Projection, because the Mercator Projection is worse on these biases.[479] Josh attended the meeting on a lark. Josh and C.J. are blown away.

The WTO protesters struggle to organize as Toby reads the newspaper. He explains why the White House supports the WTO and free trade policies to his security detail, when she asks. The protesters are overwhelming white, despite being a protest in favor of developing nations; she responds the White House isn't racially diverse either.

National Security Advisor McNally wants to see Sam. He meets her in the situation room, where she is alone on a conference call. She gives him a National Security Agency file, which shows Gault engaged in espionage.

MCNALLY: Sam, Daniel Gault was a spy.
SAM: Oh my God—
MCNALLY: He was a spy—
SAM: Based on what?
MCNALLY: Based on diplomatic cables intercepted by US Army signal intelligence in the 1940s.
SAM: If that was the case, why couldn't the US Attorney make espionage in the 1950s.
MCNALLY: Because the cables weren't decrypted until the 1970s.

SAM: You're telling me we cracked some obscure Russian code and suddenly we learned Gault was a spy?[480]

MCNALLY: Yes.

SAM: That's crap. If the FBI had proof on Gault, they would've told the world about it.

MCNALLY: No, they wouldn't have, Sam. No, they wouldn't have. Neither would the NSA. Neither would Central Intelligence. You don't show someone you've broken their ciphers unless you have to. Gault was long dead. But before he was, he was an agent called Blackwater, he was a delegate at Yalta, and he returned to the US by way of Rostov where he was awarded the Order of Lenin.

SAM: Yeah, well, I'll believe that when they show me the file.

The file is a highly classified NSA file and McNally lets Sam read through it, even though it is illegal; she has redacted the portions which would get them in trouble.

The Organization of Cartographers for Social Equality argues distorting size and position results in poor attitudes towards less advantaged countries.

Toby explains the White House supports the WTO because it keeps the cost of goods down and helps address conflict through economic means, rather than war.[481] Josh visits Toby. Toby satirically protests to Josh. Toby then decides to engage with them.

Leo and the President discuss the Presidential Library. The President is frustrated; he wants to do something important with his time in the White House, but is already being forced out of the door. Leo proposes thinking about reelection. Bartlet wants to put off that conversation.[482]

Sam sits in the White House commissary. Donna approaches him and he explodes, a combination of anger about discovering Gault was a spy and his father having an affair for 28 years. Daniel Gault was a spy and he killed a woman. Donna calms him down; he could not get Gault on the pardon list this year, but to reassure her dying father there has been progress.

Toby and Josh return from the WTO; Josh seems enthusiastic. Sam calls his dad.

The Stackhouse Filibuster (2.17)

Aired on: March 14, 2001
Directed by: Bryan Gordon

Story by: Peter McCabe
Teleplay by: Aaron Sorkin
Plotlines:
  a) An ornery Senator filibusters the White House's health care plan.
  b) Everyone wants to go home for the break.
  c) Toby wants the Vice President to stay silent on a dispute between the White House and oil companies.
  d) Sam wants to reduce the number of reports the government generates.

C.J. writes an email, explaining to her dad[483] that she is not with him because there is a filibuster in the Senate. We see Senator Stackhouse (George Coe)[484] reading from a recipe book as part of his speaking filibuster.[485] Sam wants to leave for a vacation, but can't because of the filibuster. C.J. needs Sam and Josh to stay for spin. Josh wants to see the Mets in spring training.[486] C.J. is keeping the press corps late. Toby is going to Telluride but can't leave until the Senate votes.

C.J. explains the talking filibuster applies so long as a Senator keeps the floor. Senate rules require a vote to end debate; while the filibustering Senator(s) refuse to yield the floor, they stave off a vote.[487]

We get a flashback to Josh discussing the health care bill. Josh has set up the votes to ensure the bill will pass. Leo is excited about the vote. A representative of the oil industry criticized the Bartlet administration for requiring additives and blamed them for an increase in gas prices; Toby says he will talk to Vice President Hoynes. The Vice President is a Texan and comfortable with the oil lobby.

C.J. has an Egyptian curse put on her. Hasan Ali is visiting; they want to display a statue given to the President. C.J. was given the statue by the gift officer. C.J. doesn't remember what happened to it.

Vice President Hoynes talks about flooding with women holding quilts. Toby meets with the Vice President and mentions the oil industry representative's comments about additives and emissions standards. The Vice President briefly defends the oil industry, then offers to criticize the oil industry representative. The Vice President says they should not send the Energy Secretary because the Energy Secretary criticizes the oil industry regularly; they should send Hoynes, because Hoynes is friendly with the industry.

Stackhouse continues to read from the recipe book. Stackhouse has been going for eight hours, speaking for hours at a time without leaning or stopping.[488] Sam listens to Stackhouse reading *David Copperfield*.[489] Sam's favorite writer is Toby; his favorite fiction writer is Dickens. C.J. and Sam talk about their emails to their respective fathers; Sam mentions his father's affair. C.J. mentions that Sam got beat up (metaphorically) by a 19-year-old intern at the Government Accountability Office.

Sam walks into a meeting with Josh about cutting government reports. Sam offers to take up the issue.

Toby tells Josh and Sam that Hoynes offered to criticize the oil industry. They are all surprised and Toby wonders what Hoynes is doing. Sam works through reports to cut. An intern (Cara DeLizia) groans.

HOOPER: You blow through these reports like they don't mean anything.
SAM: They don't mean anything.
HOOPER: You're an idiot!
SAM: Hey. Hey. You're talking to senior staff.
HOOPER: Gee. Genuflect when you say that, fella.
SAM: Report on the obstacles to state and local training needs in the solid
    and liquid waste management recovery—you know what this is?
HOOPER: Yes.
SAM: It's about career opportunities for garbage men.
HOOPER: And what's wrong with that?
SAM: I think it's a tough sell and I don't need a report to tell me that.

The intern shreds Sam's dismissiveness over the reports, pointing out areas like career opportunities for people in waste management require study to develop effective policy solutions. You can't address problems without understanding them. If we want policies that work, we need to invest work and money to study the issues and possible solutions, and that saves money over the long term.[490]

Hooper has read all the reports, because she is allowed to read them. They are in her office as an intern at the GAO.

C.J. broke the cat statue. Donna suggests gluing it back together.

Senator Stackhouse wants to add an amendment to the health care bill. Josh blows him off. Stackhouse leaves a message with Donna that "there's not going to be a vote while I'm alive."

Josh explains the filibuster to his mother. Josh meets with Senator Stackhouse, who wants $47 million for autism research.[491] Josh points out it is a multi-billion-dollar bill; Stackhouse points out in a bill primarily targeted at health care for children, there are appropriations for erectile dysfunction. Josh wants the bill to pass before people leave for the recess.

Donna notices the voiceover talking about Stackhouse mentions seven grandchildren. Donna gives Josh a hard time for his excitement about spring training.

Josh is confused about why Vice President Hoynes offered to take on the oil industry. Hoynes notes the environmental impacts of the White House position include improvements to air quality and lower asthma rates. The oil industry is gouging. Josh points out Hoynes almost became President; he is a savvy politician.

Leo and President Bartlet have dinner made by a famous French chef visiting the White House. The President vents about Stackhouse. Leo thinks Stackhouse is a good man. Stackhouse's wife died and Bartlet did not attend the funeral because he was running for President. The meal is romantically lit because they thought the President was going to be eating with the First Lady; they ignore that[492] as Stackhouse reads the rules of cards.

Donna notes Stackhouse has seven grandchildren, but the footage of campaign events only shows six. Donna thinks Stackhouse has an autistic grandson.

Bartlet and Abby agreed Bartlet would only serve one term, because of his multiple sclerosis. Bartlet also explains Hoynes knows about the deal; this explains why Hoynes agreed to criticize the oil industry, because Hoynes is preparing to run for President when Bartlet doesn't seek reelection. C.J. tells Leo and Bartlet that Stackhouse has an autistic grandson.

Bartlet would fight people over his grandchildren, hearkening back to the pilot. He suggests they help Stackhouse instead of letting him collapse on the Senate floor. Donna explains Senators can yield for a question.

Hoynes is going to leave. Toby asks why Hoynes agreed to take on the oil industry. Hoynes had polling which showed people were concerned about his ties to the industry.

TOBY: [...] why did you put the poll in the field at all? What do you know that I don't?

HOYNES: Toby, the total tonnage of what I know that you don't could stun a team of oxen in its tracks. Good night.

A Senator asks a question and Stackhouse yields. A group of Senators (all grandfathers) then open the debate back up and talk about autism. The White House reopens the bill and will presumably help Stackhouse with his amendment.

Chapter Fifteen
Episodes 2.18-2.20

17 People (2.18)

Aired on: April 4, 2001
Directed by: Alex Graves
Written by: Aaron Sorkin
Plotlines:
  a) Toby finds out about the President's multiple sclerosis.
  b) The staff prepares for the President to speak at the White House Correspondence Dinner.
  c) Ainsley Hayes attends a panel on the Equal Rights Amendment at Smith College.

Toby bounces a Spalding against a wall; a title card reads "Two Nights Later" and Toby throws away a paper at his desk; "Two Night After That" and Toby is typing at his computer before having a breakthrough, getting up, and going to meet with Leo.

Leo why Hoynes asked a polling question about his connections to oil; Leo suggests it is just a matter of Hoynes' ego. Toby asks if Leo and the President have considered dropping Hoynes from the ticket; Leo says they have not. "The Next Night," again bouncing the Spalding. Toby waits for Leo and then points out that, though Hoynes is going to eventually run for President, polling the question if he's going to run in six years would be silly. "That Night" Toby and Leo discuss the possibility of Hoynes challenging Bartlet. Hoynes is giving a speech in Nashua, New Hampshire, the site of the earliest primaries; Leo suggests he would mask the speech, which is exactly what he did.

TOBY: Why does Hoynes think the President isn't going to run again? What's going on, Leo?

Leo and the President need to tell Toby about the multiple sclerosis diagnosis. Bartlet is upset Hoynes scheduled the New Hampshire trip, because it provided the clues for Toby. Leo thinks he and Bartlet should consider the reactions of the staff.

Bartlet tells Leo to bring Toby into the Oval Office.

Josh and Sam read a speech that is supposed to be funny but isn't. Sam and Josh are going to work on jokes for the speech. Josh and Donna banter about whether it is her anniversary working for him. They argue about the anniversary because she left for a while. Ainsley is going to be on a panel at Smith College about the Equal Rights Amendment.[493] Ainsley opposes the Equal Rights Amendment. Ainsley's position shocks Sam.

Leo mentions the Correspondents Dinner speech is not funny. Toby cannot focus on it. Leo tells Toby to "take it easy in there." The President tells Toby the federal government stopped a terrorist. The President tells Toby that he has relapsing/remitting multiple sclerosis, recounting his symptoms and his diagnosis prior to the first campaign. Toby is concerned about cognitive function. Toby steps outside, clearly dumbfounded by the news.

The staff keeps working on the speech, though it is strange that they have not contracted any comedy writers.[494] Sam explains that Donna came to work for Josh and then left to get back together with her ex-boyfriend. We find out the host of the Correspondents Dinner is Bill Maher.[495]

Leo tells Toby that he found out before the State of the Union (2.13), when the President had the flu and passed out. Leo tells Toby 16 people know, but the doctors who give routine physicals do not know because multiple sclerosis does not appear on a routine physical.

LEO: It's in remission. Nobody lied.
TOBY: Nobody lied?
LEO: Nobody.
TOBY: Nobody lied? Is that what you've been saying to yourself over and over again for—Leo this is a deception of massive proportion— I can't even—he gets a physical twice a year at Bethesda. His doctors are Naval officers. Are you telling me that officers are involved in this?
LEO: Toby—
TOBY: These guys are going to be court martialed.
LEO: Nobody—listen to me, nobody lied. Nobody was asked to lie.

There's an ongoing hunt for other terrorists in New Jersey. Bartlet is trying to figure out if there is a credible threat. Toby is preoccupied with the multiple sclerosis.

Josh asks Charlie for feedback on a joke. Charlie shoots it down because the First Lady won't be at the dinner. Charlie doesn't discuss personal issues, to maintain confidentiality.[496]

Sam argues with Ainsley about the Equal Rights Amendment.[497] Ainsley suggests the 14th Amendment is sufficient. Josh says the President bombed at the Correspondents Dinner. Sam is confident Toby will help.

Toby asks the President about the attack prior to the State of the Union. The President was dealing with national security threats. Toby asks about medication; the President takes a medication to reduce the severity and frequency of attacks. Toby asks if the First Lady is medicating him. The tension between Bartlet and Toby escalates at the mention of the First Lady. Toby also raises concerns that there's no letter in the event of the President suffering a severe attack. The reason there is no letter is that it would draw press attention. Bartlet angrily blows this off.

Bartlet yells at Toby[498] and suggests Toby is angry because other people knew before him.

Sam, Josh, Donna, and Ainsley are uncomfortable with each other and their various disagreements. Sam and Ainsley go to the kitchen and argue about the Equal Rights Amendment. Ainsley argues the Pay Equity Act establishes equal pay for equal work, though women make $0.79 for every $1 men make.[499] She argues the federal government is not competent to address pay disparities. She also invokes choices women make about job flexibility, having children, and other personal considerations. Ainsley opposes the federal government passing redundant laws.

Toby knows the First Lady is angry because she believed the President wouldn't run. The State of the Union and other decisions by Toby and Leo have been oriented towards reelection. Toby and Leo agreed they were trying to get the President reelected. Leo still is.

Toby asks about the anesthesiologist at George Washington, worried the anesthesiologist may be under surveillance or leak information.[500] Toby points out Hoynes left enough of a trail for Toby to work out the problem. Hoynes has an obligation to the party and the country to prepare for a reelection bid, perhaps even to inform the public

Leo says they will break the story. Presidents have historically concealed health issues. Leo asks what Toby thinks will happen. He gives Leo a list of five things: not running; run and lose; run and win; he could resign; he could be impeached. Toby points out that one does not need to break the law to be impeached.

Ainsley argues the Equal Rights Amendment is "humiliating," because it implies women are not presently equal under the law.[501]

Fact Check:

Ainsley says she is protected by "Article 14." She means the 14th Amendment. As an attorney who works on the Constitution, that's a mistake.

Synopsis, cont'd

Josh and Donna settle their differences. Donna left her boyfriend because she was in a car accident and he stopped for a beer with friends, instead of coming to see her.

JOSH: If you were in an accident, I wouldn't stop for a beer.
DONNA: If you were in an accident, I wouldn't stop for red lights.[502]

Toby asks why they are not heightening security over the terrorism threat. It is a holiday weekend and there would be travel delays.

The President is not going to apologize to Toby, because the President has multiple sclerosis. It will appear as though they deceived and defrauded the public. Bartlet acknowledges this. Toby points out they will have to speak to lawyers about the scandal. Seventeen people knew; they hadn't been counting the President himself.

The President does apologize to Toby. Toby goes into the other room to help with the speech with the Correspondents Dinner.[503]

Bad Moon Rising (2.19)

Aired on: April 25, 2001
Directed by: Bill Johnson
Story by: Felicia Willson
Teleplay by: Aaron Sorkin

Plotlines:

    a) The President talks to the White House Counsel about disclosing his multiple sclerosis diagnosis.

    b) There is a leak in the White House.

    c) Josh negotiates a financial support package for Mexico.

    d) An oil tanker runs aground.

      White House Counsel Oliver Babish (Oliver Platt) is in his office reviewing a document before taking a trip to Borneo. He has a tape recorder stuck on record. The President and Leo come to meet with Babish; the White House has gone through five counsels in two years.[504] Leo is from Chicago; the President doesn't like lawyers. The President and Leo tell Babish about multiple sclerosis and Babish smashes his broken tape recorder with a gavel.[505]

      Josh is putting together a financial support package for Mexico after the country's economy collapsed.[506] There is a leaked quote about school vouchers; C.J. denies the President's position on school vouchers has changed. There has been an oil leak in Delaware. The ship is the Indio, one of the ships Sam helped the oil company acquire in 2.01. Toby is angry about the leak of the quote on school vouchers.

BABISH: Is it possible for someone with relapsing remitting MS to experience an attack that would include temporary loss of brain function but exclude any physical symptoms?[507] Let me put it a different way: Is it possible you could be sitting in this room, have an attack, and I don't know it?

BARTLET: I think what you're asking is, "Is it possible I could be sitting in the Situation Room, have an attack, and nobody knows it?"

BABISH: Yes.

BARTLET: Yes.

[…]

BABISH: Mr. President, before we go any further, there is something I want to make sure is absolutely clear.

BARTLET: What's that?

BABISH: You and I don't enjoy attorney-client privilege.[508]

      Babish is the attorney for the White House, not any person in the White House, including the President of the United States. The President is not his client and there is no privilege.[509] Babish then asks if the President may have been party to a lawsuit and required to give a deposition; if he did and lied about his health, then he committed perjury. He has not given such a deposition. Babish walks through the people who know about multiple sclerosis, concluding with Toby Ziegler.

Josh tries to fast track a relief package for the Mexican economy, because it will reduce international economic impacts. Representatives from Congress (Scott Lawrence; Michael Mantell) are unsure about the relief package.

C.J. tries to find the leak but can't. She is not going to find the leak, but Josh suggests she try anyway to placate Toby.

Donna doesn't want the White House to bail out for Mexico.[510] Josh blows her off.

Charlie is enrolling at Georgetown and is far along in college because of Advanced Placement credits. Sam meets with a member of the Navy (Jacqueline Kim) and asks about the Indio. There was a failure of the navigation and steering. The oil spill is bad, and Sam asks the Naval officer to inform him about any developments.

Bartlet acknowledges he does not have life insurance or health insurance, because he is independently wealthy, and the government covers his health care costs. He has never failed to disclose multiple sclerosis on a document for those purposes.

C.J. meets with a staffer (Robert Curtis Brown) who denies being the leak and says he would not tell C.J. even if he knew who it was. He is insulted and C.J. is embarrassed she is even asking.

Donna complains the bailout from Mexico is taking money from Americans in the manufacturing industry. Josh points out global economic crises are bad for American manufacturing because we export things like textiles to Mexico. He also points out this is a loan; we give the money in the short term and Mexico is obligated to pay it back, and these loans are always paid back.

DONNA: I'm not cheap, nor am I xenophobic. I just think it's time for some tough love.[511]

Sam visits Ainsley Hayes in her office. Sam has no exposure but feels guilty about the liability shield. Sam knows the state Attorneys General will sue Kensington Oil for damages; he also knows the liability shield will insulate Kensington. He considers allowing himself to be deposed and disclosing his attempts to discourage his former clients from buying the boat. Ainsley points out Sam is violating attorney client privilege.

Charlie plans his semester, just night classes. Margaret and Mrs. Landingham want him to consider a variety of classes. They seem to forget he is working in the White House full time. Charlie tells Margaret he needs to speak to Leo, using the "old friend from home" emergency code.

Leo and Babish talk about this case; Babish considers leaving.

LEO: In the two hours we've been sitting here, have you discovered one thing that he has done wrong?

BABISH: No.

LEO: Then what's your problem.

BABISH: That's my problem, Leo. Are you out of your mind? He did everything right. He did everything you do if your intent is to perpetrate a fraud.

Leo leaves the meeting with Babish after receiving the coded message. Charlie tells Leo the Bartlets would have to disclose the President's medical history on forms for college for Zoey. Charlie knew the President had health issues, because he was asked to look out for certain symptoms. Leo tells Margaret to get Zoey's the college paperwork.

C.J. interviews Donna about the leak. Donna makes fun of C.J. for being the interrogator.[512]

Josh explains the United States lent weapons and money to the allies during World War II, despite (prior to the bombing of Pearl Harbor) being isolationist. He talks about the Lend Lease Act. "If your neighbor's house is on fire, you don't haggle over the price of your garden hose."

Another person C.J. interviews (Shishir Kurup) suggests, "If you dunk the suspect in a deep well of water, it means they're not a witch."

Sam wrestles with his conscience over the oil spill.

Toby and C.J. talks about the leak; C the White House has leaks sometimes and that isn't a serious problem.[513] Toby understands, but he is nervous about much more serious leaks; he is worried about the multiple sclerosis, though C.J. doesn't know yet.

Charlie and Bartlet talk about the forms. Zoey told Charlie to look out for symptoms; Charlie figured it out from there. Bartlet is worried discussing the issue with Charlie will make Charlie legally vulnerable; he tells Charlie never to lie about it.

Bartlet tells Babish about the form that omitted multiple sclerosis from the medical history; the First Lady signed it. The President suggests Babish can resign if he wants to leave, but Babish agrees to stay if the President agrees to accept his advice. Babish insists the President will cooperate with investigations and appoint a special prosecutor to investigate the matter.[514]

The Fall's Gonna Kill You (2.20)

Aired on: May 2, 2001
Directed by: Christopher Misiano
Story by: Patrick Caddell
Teleplay by: Aaron Sorkin
Plotlines:
  a) The White House counsel interviews staffers about potential legal exposure from concealing the President's multiple sclerosis.
  b) Donna worries the sky is falling.
  c) The Department of Justice runs out of money for a lawsuit against the tobacco industry.

C.J. meets with Oliver Babish. C.J. was told about the multiple sclerosis the previous night and is still processing. Babish asks if C.J. has ever lied about the President's health. She does not trust Babish and the two fight. Babish points out there is potential criminal liability for the President and others on the staff. She has lied about the President's health many times.

Ed and Larry tell Donna that Ed just got a fax. A Chinese satellite is going to crash. The fax is for C.J., but she is meeting with Babish.

Toby, Josh, and Leo meet to discuss polling about the President's multiple sclerosis and the oncoming scandal. Josh trusts Joey Lucas and she is flying in to meet with him to talk about a poll, but she doesn't know anything. Toby does not want to tell Sam right away because Sam is writing another speech. Leo plans to tell him by the end of the day.

Donna is concerned about the satellite. Josh is not.

Josh meets with Martin Connelly (Lee Wilkoff), from Department of Justice. Connelly asks for money to fund the lawsuit charging the tobacco industry committed fraud. Connelly is concerned. "These people perpetrated a fraud against the public."

C.J. briefs the press on the President's health whenever the President is examined by doctors, including when he was shot and when he ran his bicycle into a tree (in the pilot). She asks the President for information because of doctor-patient confidentiality. Babish asks if C.J. uses the phrase "need to know" or "should know," as the former implies that there are things that she should know but the President shouldn't tell her. C.J. says she didn't consider the distinction. C.J. gets a note from Donna that "the sky is falling down," about the satellite.

Sam is writing a speech. The CBO projects a lower budget surplus, which means they will have an easier time fighting about who will receive tax cuts.

C.J. is aware the President had an attack before the State of the Union. She did not know the cause, because she is not a medical expert. She was told it was the flu.

BABISH: Do you know what time it is?
C.J.: It's five-past-noon.
BABISH: I'd like you to get out of the habit of doing that.
C.J.: Doing what?
BABISH: Answering more than was asked. Do you know what time it is?
C.J.: Yes.

Toby tries to encourage Sam on the speech writing. Sam tells Toby about the lower surplus projections. Sam doesn't want to include a change attacking the rich. Toby suggests Sam should talk to someone at ATJ (Americans for Tax Justice)[515] or the Progressive Caucus.[516]

Donna tells Charlie about the falling satellite. Charlie laughs it off.

The First Lady is back at the White House. The First Lady found out the staff was being informed about the President's multiple sclerosis. She and the President fight. The President tells her about the medical history form. The President didn't want to tell her over the phone, but took too long to tell her.

Josh and Leo discuss the President and First Lady fighting. Josh asks for more money for the lawsuit against tobacco. Leo points out the lawsuit is unwinnable, given the differences in resources.[517] Josh is meeting with Joey Lucas.

Sam meets with the Progressive Caucus about the speech. Sam points out the lines attacking the wealthy are a problem. The wealthy pay the most in taxes,[518] and it makes wealthy progressives (including Sam and members of the caucus) look silly and hypocritical.

Josh meets with Joey Lucas at the airport. She has a different interpreter (Jon Wolfe Nelson) than usual. Josh asks the interpreter to leave. Joey wants to know what's important.

The First Lady meets with Babish. He asks her about the health form. The First Lady explains they left the medical history blank. Babish points out the First Lady is an accomplished physician, but screwed up this basic medical history form. He questions her aggressively, and she argues the multiple sclerosis is not relevant because it is not hereditary. Babish points out that is different than leaving the form blank out of neglect. Babish points out the failure to disclose on the medical form is a big deal.[519]

Josh tells Joey Lucas they need a poll gauging public reaction; he tells Joey about the multiple sclerosis, and she agrees to put a poll in the field about opinions towards a "Governor of an industrial state" with a degenerative condition. She will be done in 96 hours.

Donna is worried about the satellite. Charlie jokes. The First Lady is stressed, walking through the West Wing. The First Lady meets with C.J. They commiserate about Babish being a pain in the ass. C.J. saw the First Lady give the President injections.[520] C.J. acknowledges she says "need to know" when asking about the President's health.

Leo asks Josh to report on the lawsuit against tobacco. Josh notes what Connelly said about perpetrating a fraud. Leo doesn't like the comparison to concealing Bartlet's multiple sclerosis.

Bartlet tells Leo about fighting with Abby; Leo tells Bartlet about the poll. Bartlet wants to make sure no one finds out. Bartlet is going to tell Sam about the multiple sclerosis. Toby tells Sam that he will be there to talk.

Josh talks to C.J. about the poll and worry it will look like the decision to disclose the multiple sclerosis was influenced by the poll. C.J. laughs. That is minor compared to the multiple sclerosis scandal itself. Josh tells C.J. that Donna was panicking about the fax on the falling satellite; C.J. says they get those faxes all the time and that nothing bad ever happens.[521] Josh knows but was enjoying the joke at Donna's expense.

Chapter Sixteen
Episodes 2.21-2.22

18th and Potomac[522] *(2.21)*

Aired on: May 9, 2001
Directed by: Robert Berlinger
Story by: Lawrence O'Donnell
Teleplay by: Aaron Sorkin
Plotlines:
   a) The staff sees polling numbers regarding the President' multiple sclerosis cover-up.
   b) There is a military coup Haiti.
   c) Josh tries to secure funding for the Justice Department's fight against big tobacco.
   d) Mrs. Landingham buys a new car.

   The President and Leo talk about polling. The President and Leo meet in the basement because Leo doesn't want them meeting in the Oval Office. Sam and Toby are skeptical the polling numbers mean anything. The numbers are bad. Most people think multiple sclerosis is fatal (it isn't)[523] and this influences their perception of the illness. Both the health condition and lying seem like unsalvageable political scandals.
   The President is briefed on a military standoff in Haiti; the military opposes newly elected President Dessalines[524] and shot two people while suppressing a rally. Dessalines cannot be located. President Bartlet orders the evacuation of non-essential personnel from the embassy.
   Sam and C.J. discuss how the President should announce the multiple sclerosis and whether he should do it through a speech (which Sam wants) or a softer interview format (which C.J. wants). C.J. points out they must get on the networks without telling the networks why. They

agree to a Wednesday, when the networks will not worry as much about lost advertising revenue. Sam points out the first question will be about reelection.[525]

Mrs. Landingham and Charlie talk about buying a new car.

Josh meets with Leo. The report on tobacco spending illustrates a wild disparity in funding between the tobacco companies and the government. They need a firm answer on whether the President will seek reelection, since that is the first question they expect at the press conference.

The Haitian military killed two of President Dessalines' body-guards. Dessalines is headed to the United States embassy to seek asylum.

One of the President's national security advisors Robbie Mosley (Gregory Alan Williams)[526] points out this is a domestic matter. International law and United States policies are against involvement in the internal affairs of other countries. The United States encouraged Dessalines to run for President and helped to secure a fair election.[527] Dessalines is at the gate of the embassy. President Bartlet orders the embassy to let him in.

Sam and C.J. continue the back and forth on the press conference, now arguing whether to have Vice President Hoynes there. Sam wants Hoynes to emphasize the President took these risks seriously; C.J. does not, because it emphasizes the health risks. C.J. has to brief the press about Haiti, leaving Toby (who has been silent) with Sam.

TOBY: Sam, can Josiah Bartlet function as President?

SAM: I'm not a medical expert.

[long pause]

SAM: Toby, there is a responsibility to the future and an obligation to the party and if he's not going to run, then he has to point to Hoynes and say, "this is our guy."

TOBY: What if they ask Hoynes, "in the meantime, can Bartlet function as President?"

SAM: He'll say, "yes."

TOBY: What if he says, "I'm not a medical expert."

Josh meets with a Senator Ritter (John Rubinstein) about funding the tobacco lawsuit. The Senator tells Josh the funding won't get a vote in committee, because the committee members take money from tobacco. There are two Democrats who oppose the lawsuit and Josh agrees to meet with them over their "ideological objections" to the lawsuit.

Toby meets with Donna and tells her about the President's multiple sclerosis. Donna goes back to work, flustered but functional.

Mrs. Landingham resists Charlie's advice about negotiating the price, which she believes is inappropriate for a White House employee.

Leo meets with the Joint Chiefs, including McNally. The Haitian army is taking the embassy[528] and the Pentagon prepares military action. C.J. will not acknowledge the military junta in Haiti from the podium.

C.J. meets with a network news executive Paul Hackett[529] (Peter Michael Goetz), brought in through the basement. She needs 30 minutes and cannot tell him why. Hackett agrees.

Josh meets with Senators Warren and Rossiter (Richard McGonagle; Robert Walden)[530] about the tobacco lawsuit. They do not take contributions from tobacco. Both are former United States Attorneys. Surgeons General have provided warnings on tobacco products for decades; tobacco companies withheld information about the dangerous nature of their products from the government and the public.[531] The Senators maintain the lawsuit is hopeless; the White House supports it for political reasons.

The First Lady joins the meeting in the basement. Sam explains questions about the medical history to prepare her for the interview. The First Lady walks through the symptoms in clear medical terminology; Sam tries to get her to speak in ordinary language. Sam acknowledges they are separating the President and First Lady to check their stories, both for the press and because the senior staff is concerned about deceit.

Charlie and Mrs. Landingham argue about taking a discount when purchasing a car.[532]

The President and Leo meet. United States marines shot three Haitian soldiers who boarded an Air Force plane. The President is upset, but Leo notes this was what the military was supposed to do.

The President points out to Mrs. Landingham that accepting discounts available to the public (like negotiating at a car dealership) is allowed. The President asks if Mrs. Landingham feels guilty or self-conscious about buying a new car. The President wants to talk to her after she picks up the car. She hasn't been told about the multiple sclerosis.

The First Lady continues to explain the basics of medical practice to Sam. Babish enters and asks Sam to leave. The First Lady insists she be referred to as "Dr." Bartlet. She loathes downplaying her medical background for political reasons. Babish suggests the First Lady needs to retain her own lawyer. She shouldn't take questions, because all medical questions are also legal questions; treating family members is a violation of the American Medical Association code of ethics and is illegal in several states, because she wrote the prescriptions to herself and had them shipped across state lines.[533] These are federal crimes involving medical fraud, and violate state board rules of New Hampshire, Arizona, and Missouri.[534]

Josh and Donna talk about tobacco; Donna knows about the multiple sclerosis and the meeting in the basement.

C.J. sends the press home. Toby meets with Leo; they discuss reelection. Josh is upset Toby told Donna, but Donna took the news well. Josh notes they're going to lose the vote on tobacco. Leo suggests Josh throw harder with Senators Warren and Rossiter; they are not going to tiptoe.

In the closing scene: Charlie tells Leo a drunk driver hit Mrs. Landingham as she was driving back to the White House. Mrs. Landingham is dead. Leo enters the Oval Office and tells the President that Mrs. Landingham has died. We see their exchange only through the distorted glass of the portico.[535]

Two Cathedrals (2.22)

Aired on: May 16, 2001
Directed by: Thomas Schlamme
Writer: Aaron Sorkin
Plotlines:
  a) The staff considers their options ahead of revealing the President's multiple sclerosis diagnosis. They don't know whether he will run for reelection.
  b) Bartlet reels from the death of Mrs. Landingham.
  c) The Haitian army continues to attack the United States Embassy in Haiti.

Leo meets with members of Congress (Harry Ornstein; John Bennett Perry)[536] about running for reelection. The congressmen are upset about the multiple sclerosis scandal. One of the Congressmen suggests the President should consider not running for reelection. Leo says this is being discussed.

Sam and Toby prepare for the interview, the same day as Mrs. Landingham's funeral. Toby has a meeting, despite wanting to focus on the funeral, interview, and press conference.

Josh tells C.J. about the tobacco memo and gives C.J. a prepared comment. C.J. is impressed with the statement, "like the fire we used to throw in early primaries." They need to put the memo away for a little while, because the scandal will dominate the news.

Sam takes a meeting with party strategists about who will run if Bartlet doesn't. Sam ends the meeting in frustration as the strategists talk about Hoynes running and imply Bartlet should resign so Hoynes will be the incumbent President.

The military junta in Haiti is laying siege to the embassy. McNally suggests sending Fitzwallace to Haiti.

We get a slow fade, with church bells, as a young Jed (Jason Widener) responds to a call from his father (Lawrence O'Donnell) and reprimand for his friends' smoking in the chapel. Jed's father introduces him to a young Mrs. Landingham (Kirsten Nelson), who will be working in his office.[537]

The President agrees to send Fitzwallace to Haiti. There is a tropical storm moving from Florida to South Carolina. President Bartlet asks Charlie to make sure there are pall bearers for Mrs. Landingham's funeral, at the National Cathedral.

C.J. briefs the press about Haiti; a reporter (Jane Lynch)[538] asks whether they have exhausted diplomatic options. Diplomatic options are still on the table, but military presence underlines the consequences for the military junta.

Sam says they need to move the press conference. Several reporters meet with C.J. under the pretext of talking about seating arrangements, but the purpose is to leak the President's multiple sclerosis. The President is briefed on the potential economic fallout before he goes to the funeral.

Flashback to young Jed and Mrs. Landingham arguing, with Jed pointing out the chapel service was supposed to be non-denominational. The service was Christian (and therefore not inclusive of non-Christians) and included the extended version of the Our Father prayer which is not used by Roman Catholics (like Jed). Mrs. Landingham asks why Jed works at the school when his family is wealthy; Jed gets free tuition and thinks it is appropriate to do some service. Jed calls his father, who is the headmaster, "Sir."

The motorcade drives to the National Cathedral. The President and First Lady talk about the drunk driver who killed Mrs. Landingham, who was released from the hospital but will be charged with manslaughter. President Bartlet's mind is far away. The First Lady mentions the President might consider stepping aside, emphasizing he hasn't decided whether he will run for reelection.

The staff attends the funeral service in the National Cathedral.

A young Mrs. Landingham and Bartlet argue about the pay disparity between women and men at the school faculty. Jed suggests she show him numbers.

Charlie reads from Wisdom 3:1.[539]

Mrs. Landingham provides numbers on the discrepancy in salary between members of the faculty to young Jed. Jed argues it may be based on the need to support a family; that is not how salaries work. This is intercut with the funeral. Mrs. Landingham asks Jed to take up the pay disparities with his father. Mrs. Landingham is sure Jed has made up his mind when he puts his hands in his pockets, looks away, and smiles.

Bartlet and Leo stand in the National Cathedral. Leo talks about how beautiful the service was. Bartlet asks to stay alone in the Cathedral for a moment. Bartlet gives a long monologue, cursing at God for killing Mrs. Landingham as he walks down the central aisle in the Cathedral. He resents that Josh was shot; Josh is like his son. He worries about the storm coming up from Florida and refers to the time that a storm resulted in the sinking of the tender ship (in "The State Dinner," 1.07). Bartlet has tried to be ethical.

BARTLET: You're a son of a bitch, you know that? She bought her first new car and you hit her with a drunk driver. What, is that supposed to be funny? "You can't conceive, nor can I, the appalling strangeness of the mercy of God," says Graham Greene.[540] I don't know whose ass he is kissing there, because I think you're just vindictive. What was Josh Lyman, a warning shot? That was my son. What did I ever do to Yours but Praise His glory, praise His name? There's a tropical storm that's gaining speed and power. They say we haven't a storm this bad since you took out that tender ship of mine in the North Atlantic last year. 68 crew—you know what a tender ship does? It fixes the other ships—doesn't even carry guns—it just goes around and fixes the other ships, delivers the mail—that's all it can do. *Gratias tibi ago, Domine.* ["Thank you, Sir," said sarcastically.] Yes, I lied. I committed many sits. Does that displease you, you feckless thug? Three point eight million new jobs—that wasn't good? Bailed out Mexico, increased foreign trade? Thirty million new acres for conservation? Put Mendoza on the bench? We're not fighting a war—I've raised three children— that's not enough to buy me out of the doghouse? *Haec credam a deo pio? A deo iusto, a deo scito? Cruciatus in crucem. Tuus in terra servus, nuntius fui. Officium perfeci. Cruciatus in crucem. Eas in crucem!* [Bartlet lights a cigarette and stamps it into the floor.] You get Hoynes!

The longer Latin passage is translated roughly, "I give thanks to you, O Lord. Am I really to believe that these are the acts of a Holy God? A Just God? A Wise God? To hell with your punishments. I was your servant here on Earth, your messenger. I did your work. To hell with your punishments. To hell with you." The "to hell with you" translation is a colloquialism; it is literally translated as "to the cross with your punishments. To the cross with you."

The motorcade returns to the White House. The staff discusses the possible answers on reelection, "yes" and "no." Sam wants to consider calling off the interview and press conference.

Toby meets with Greg Summerhayes (Don McManus), who wants to buy a media company[541] and start a 24-hour cable news channel. He offers Toby a job as the news director.

Donna is confused that the President and Leo are locked in the Oval Office deciding about reelection, without the senior staff. Toby is furious, because the meeting with Summerhayes was a way for Toby to get out. Leo set Toby up to leave the White House. Josh stops Toby and tells Toby that "it's answer B," the President is not running for reelection.

The President is on television, giving the sit-down interview ahead of the press conference. Toby tells Leo that he is not going to take the job with Summerhayes; Leo knew Toby wasn't going to take the job but wanted to show the President how loyal Toby is. Toby wonders if the President will change his mind on reelection.

Donna explains to the President that a tropical storm in May is rare.[542] C.J. wants to brief the President again; C.J. knows every reporter will ask about reelection, but one reporter will ask a medical question.

She suggests Bartlet call on that reporter first, to settle into the conference before answering on reelection.

Flashback to a young Jed meeting with his father, who is angry about a quote that Jed has in the paper. "If you hide your ignorance, no one will hit you and you'll never learn." The quote is Ray Bradbury. Jed used it in an article criticizing a professor for banning books, including *Fahrenheit 451*.[543] His father slaps him. Jed points out the religious service wasn't non-denominational.

The portico door blows open and Bartlet calls for Mrs. Landingham, forgetting for a moment that she is dead. Mrs. Landingham enters, a thought in his mind.[544] "God doesn't make cars crash and you know it," she tells him.

Mrs. Landingham points out Bartlet's father was an abusive jerk. She encourages Jed to run. She doesn't feel sorry for him. She knows how badly off people are. One-in-five children are in poverty; 44% of Americans don't have health insurance; the number one cause of death for Black men under 35 is homicide. Bartlet is having a difficult day, but the world is full of people worse off than he is. He has the means to help those people. Self-pity isn't acceptable.

Bartlet stands in the rain on the portico as Dire Straits's "Brothers in Arms" plays. Charlie comes out to take him to the press conference. C.J. takes questions from the press. The President will direct the appointment of a Special Prosecutor to investigate. The Presidential motorcade drives past the National Cathedral, where a janitor sweeps up a stray cigarette butt.

Bartlet takes a question from someone other than the reporter C.J. has designated. He puts his hands in his pockets, looks away, and smiles.

Bartlet's Multiple Sclerosis and the public's right to know

Bartlet's multiple sclerosis and his failure to disclose it seems novel, but it's not. Presidents refusing to disclose health conditions (minor and major) is common. For context, I've provided a short survey of the documented cases.

President Cleveland was diagnosed with cancerous lesions early in his second term. He refused to disclose this to the public. President Truman had a series of strokes when he was young and suffered from deteriorating health that left him unable to get out of bed, much less function as President. Even after recovering physically, his erratic behavior made acting as President impossible. President Taft had serious health issues, including sleep apnea and high blood pressure. While Taft's weight was well known, his further health issues were not.

President Franklin Roosevelt had two major health issues: the first was his history of polio and use of a wheelchair; the second was a serious heart condition discovered during his fourth reelection campaign, which made his death early in his fourth term easily foreseeable. Roosevelt was not forthcoming about either.

President Kennedy was ostensibly young and healthy, but suffered from Addison's disease, an adrenal insufficiency which causes serious problems with sleep, fatigue, diet, and even debilitating symptoms like low blood pressure. He was able to discharge his duties, but Addison's is a severe condition. It was known to White House physicians but was never disclosed to the public.

President Reagan's issues with mental health, the early stages of Alzheimer's disease, has been discussed extensively. The official story is that he was diagnosed with Alzheimer's in 1994 (five years after leaving office) but some suggests was noticeably symptomatic as early as 1984 (as controversially claimed by his son Ronald Prescott Reagan) or 1986 (as claimed by journalist Leslie Stahl).

Reagan publicly disclosed three successful treatments for cancer: colon and skin cancer surgeries in 1985 and a second skin cancer surgery in 1987, as well as several other surgeries throughout his presidency. For the most part, the publicly disclosed issues were regarded as a biproduct of Reagan's age (he was the oldest elected President at the time).

This provides some context on a range of Presidential health issues, though it is hardly comprehensive. I have left out discussion of Presidents George W. Bush's and Obama's histories of substance abuse. Both were disclosed and not public scandals.

In general, politicians should be forthcoming with the public about conditions which impact their ability to do the job. Politicians are public servants; they have obligations to the public, including candor, but health information is a delicate thing. It is deeply personal. *The West Wing* notes that public misinformation is a problem; sometimes the public isn't informed about health conditions.

In 1964, a group of psychiatrists gave interviews claiming Republican Presidential nominee Barry Goldwater (Senator from Arizona) was suffering from mental illness, resulting in an article published in *Fact Magazine*. Goldwater sued the magazine, winning $79,000 (~$745,000 adjusted to 2022) in damages. Years later, the American Psychiatric Association introduced the "Goldwater rule" in the code of ethics. Section 7.3 says, when asked for a professional opinion, "… it is unethical for a psychiatrist to offer a professional opinion unless he or she has conducted an examination and has been granted proper authorization for such a statement." Psychiatrists are obligated (under Section 7) to engage in public discussion but cannot offer professional opinions on the mental health of individuals without examination and authorization.

The Goldwater rule is controversial. Media companies still want to talk about the health of public officials, even if they don't have any information. Mental health professionals (and many, many non-experts) opined on the mental health of President Trump and President Biden. Is Donald Trump a pathological liar, a clinical narcissist, a sociopath? Does Joe Biden have Parkinson's disease? Speculate on the condition and it becomes a more sensational news story. Whether or not these things are pathological, what's concerning is the behavior.

Barry Goldwater's "mental health" wasn't the issue; the issue was Goldwater's incendiary rhetoric and erratic disposition at a time when nuclear war with the Soviet Union seemed like a real possibility. Fact magazine used psychiatrists to pathologize Goldwater, to portray him as unfit by reason of insanity. There wasn't anything pathological, but his behavior was a serious issue. In Goldwater's case, drawing attention to these issues was a good thing. Similarly, people critical of Presidents Trump or Biden might defend "diagnosing" them to start a conversation about their fitness for office, but sometimes the public "diagnosing" does harm, not just to the candidate but to the public.

Eight years after the Goldwater lawsuit, Democratic Presidential nominee George McGovern nominated Senator Thomas Eagleton as his Vice Presidential candidate. Following this nomination, some in the press discovered Eagleton had struggled with depression. He'd been hospitalized and treated with severe interventions including electro-convulsive therapy. The disclosure of his mental health issues was a major scandal and Eagleton withdrew from the ticket. The Goldwater rule was officially established the following year, 1973. Despite its name, Eagleton is probably more responsible for the rule than Goldwater. The public discussions of Eagleton's depression painted a bleak picture of mental health, stigmatizing the treatment of mental health and patients struggling with conditions.

Some health issues make a person unfit to serve as President. In the summer of 1952, President Truman's health was seriously ill;[545] he had a 103-degree fever and a potentially fatal pulmonary blockage. Truman wasn't able to act as President, but his administration covered up his failing health and continued to run the government under his auspices. Truman's press secretary lied to the press, representing it as a minor health condition.

Some medical conditions don't matter to one's ability to serve. Taft's weight and sleep apnea weren't relevant to the public interest; Roosevelt's polio had no impact on his ability to govern. The harder cases, though, are those where it's impossible to tell from the outside. I've never heard anyone raise Kennedy's health as an issue of fitness, but Addison's disease can be debilitating. Kennedy was heavily medicated, with a state-of-the-art treatment regimen that included inserting medicated pellets into his back and regular injections of cortisone. Should it have been disclosed? Probably. Kennedy's camp denied his Addison's diagnosis when it was raised by the press.[546] But would the public have understood Addison's disease at the time? Addison's can alter mood; would every statement by President Kennedy be interpreted through his diagnosis, to speculate on his level of pain?

The media isn't good at covering public health. Even after years of practice with the coronavirus pandemic, after decades of public discussion around a range of mental health conditions, even straightforward stories about mental health are reinforce public misperceptions. Allegations about Goldwater's mental health resulted in a legal victory, because they played on sensationalizing mental illness, characterizing those struggling with mental illness as erratic and dangerous. In Goldwater's case, one could argue the core issue that he was erratic and dangerous. There was an effort to raise a legitimate concern about his fitness for office.[547] But what about Tom Eagleton? There was no evidence his battles with depression influenced his fitness to serve.

Does the public have a right to know about the President's health?

Sometimes there are clear cases, where a President's likelihood of sudden death or inability to fulfill the duties of the office are compromised. There's a legitimate public interest in those cases. But the public and media often treat these issues as sensationalist, irresponsible partisan cudgels; it's hard to defend the public's right to know when media coverage of public health is a shambles.

This brings us back to President Bartlet. The multiple sclerosis and failure to disclose is a massive scandal; multiple sclerosis is a serious degenerative condition with symptoms that could impact his ability to serve. The decision not to disclose the multiple sclerosis may be defensible. Throughout the arc, many people point out preliminary polling indicates most Americans believe multiple sclerosis to be fatal (it is not) and otherwise misunderstand the disease; many people also believe it to be utterly debilitating, which (in the relapsing and remitting presentation of President Bartlet) it isn't. Public misunderstanding of multiple sclerosis can make a rapid public discussion dangerous to other patients, subject them to stigma and medical misinformation.

When I was studying the bioethics, we had a guest speaker who discussed challenges around patients' choice to disclose their diagnoses, especially for degenerative illness. Lots of patients are afraid to disclose diagnoses, especially for degenerative neurological or mental health conditions, because they are afraid of the way people around them will react. Bad public discussions can make that difficult situation worse.

One accomplishment of *The West Wing* is independent of its political messaging. The show provided a sympathetic, thoughtful look at addiction and multiple sclerosis. It humanized these conditions for millions of viewers, showing how these conditions impact our characters and create personal and moral struggles often invisible from the outside. One of the show's most powerful episodes, "The Long Goodbye" (4.13) shows C.J. struggling with her father's Alzheimer's diagnosis and the problems with providing care for that condition. There stories can help the public understand these conditions, and hopefully make them easier to discuss, for Presidents and for our own loved ones.

The West Wing, 25 Years Later

The West Wing is frequently criticized as liberal fantasy. The West Wing embraces a mythology about what politics can be; sometimes it ignores what politics are. "Mr. Willis of Ohio" is the story of an everyman taking over his wife's congressional seat; Sorkin periodically takes artistic license with the rules of government. While telling the Frank Capra-style morality tale, it fabricates a political process. To let the cast of characters (most of whom are communications staff) roam through different policy areas, Sorkin often takes artistic license. Sometimes that artistic license is necessary to tell a story; sometimes it gets in the way, taking us too far away from the real world.

The West Wing is aspirational fiction. In the world of *The West Wing*, reasonable people compromise, and find solutions. Some politicians are corrupt and self-interested, but moral people can build coalitions and make progress. Politicians consider the moral consequences of their actions, the harms to vulnerable people. *The West Wing* is a proposal for how the world ought to be; it's critique.

Some of Sorkin's critiques of the Clinton administration resonate today. Clinton should have taken gay rights seriously; his administration should have been candid about internal scandals, including President Clinton's own sex scandals. The characters in the show wrestle with similar issues, but in *The West Wing*, characters are rewarded and punished according to Sorkin's rules of drama. Sorkin provides us with characters who are trying to do their best; it asks us to expect (at least) similar effort from our leaders. The scandals of the Clinton years seem quaint; Bill Clinton and Newt Gingrich had salacious affairs and lied about them to the public. Politicians took money from companies in exchange for votes; some stole public money. These scandals seem quaint.[548] The political seriousness of *The West Wing* seems incompatible with our cartoonish, over-the-top political present.

"More and more, we've come to expect less and less of each other." Senator Marino's single scene gives us a line that resonates through the last 25 years.

Do we expect the President of the United States to behave with the moral decency we expect from our coworkers? Do we expect the President to show compassion for people in crisis, to treat their spouse and their employees with respect? Do we expect the President to tell the truth? One critique of *The West Wing* is that it expects too much of our politicians; that critique misses the point. The show wants us to expect more. It encourages us to expect more, to expect decency and compassion and intelligence and honesty. It encourages us to expect leadership from our leaders.

We expect politicians to act in their own interests. We expect less and less of political leaders; we don't expect politicians to forego even the chance to get or hold onto power. It's genuinely jarring when a politician steps away from an opportunity to build power, to get on television, to benefit themselves.

I am finishing this book in the later days of the 2024 Presidential campaign; as I rewrite this passage, President Biden just withdrew from the ticket after a month of criticism about his mental acuity. There was a public discussion about whether President Biden should remain on the ticket. Some people were concerned about his ability to maintain a campaign schedule, physically and mentally. He chose to withdraw from the ticket. He was praised for doing something outside of his immediate self-interest; he had a chance at a second term as President of the United States. Joe Biden had been working towards the oval office for his entire political life; his first presidential campaign was in 1988. He'd attained the Presidency and could've tried to hold it for another term. Some people expected him to withdraw; some didn't. Biden chose to step away from something he'd chased his entire life; that's an unusual thing for anyone to do, especially a politician.

Watching the 2024 election, we expect very little of the Republican candidate. Donald Trump frequently makes things up on the campaign trail. There are concerns about Trump's mental fitness, but no one expects him to forego his pursuit of political power. Everyone expects him to dispute the legitimacy of the election if he loses, regardless of the facts. These expectations are grounded in past behavior. Former President Donald Trump has been convicted of falsifying business records; he is under indictment for the wrongful possession of classified materials and a range of activities connected to overturn the 2020 election. We should expect more from a major party's presidential candidate, but we don't. Our expectations are low because Trump, and many other politicians, routinely limbo under even our lowest expectations.

Cynicism is an emotionally conservative strategy; cynicism protects us from disappointment. If we don't expect much, then we're not disappointed. If we expect nothing, getting anything is a pleasant surprise. Bad results suck less when we expect and prepare for them. The problem with expecting less is that it can make bad outcomes feel inevitable. We should set higher expectations because they give us something to pursue.

Realistic expectations are important. No reasonable person expects the guy with a long track record of lying to tell the truth; believing him is naïve. There's a crucial difference between expecting the proven liar to tell a lie and accepting lying as the default of political life. "Expect" is ambiguous between anticipating and accepting; we should anticipate lies from proven liars, but we shouldn't accept lies. We shouldn't tolerate lying from our political leaders.

Sorkin is a liberal fantasist. It's a major feature of his writing, from his fiction (*The American President; The West Wing; The Newsroom*) to his portrayals of American history. Sorkin's political histories, including *Charlie Wilson's War* (2007) and *The Trial of the Chicago Seven* (2020), take liberties to cohere with Sorkin's dramatic world. Villains have to be punished; heroes have to be rewarded. Sorkin's dramatic world has poetic and moral justice; the real world usually doesn't.

While drafting this section, Sorkin gave me the most prescient illustration of his writing's detachment from political reality. Following President Biden's withdrawal from the 2024 Presidential campaign, Sorkin wrote an editorial in *The New York Times*[549] which appealed directly to his writing at the end of Season Two.[550] His proposal: "The Democratic Party should pick a Republican. At their convention next month, the Democrats should nominate Mitt Romney… a clear and powerful demonstration that this election isn't about what our elections are usually about it [sic], but about stopping a deranged man from taking power."

When I first read the piece, I thought surely Sorkin understood this wasn't a real possibility. He acknowledges that Romney is out of touch with the majority of the Democratic Party on abortion, public education, LGBTQ+ rights, labor, and tax policy. "The writing staff would tell me I was about to jump the shark, that this is a "West Wing" fantasy that would never, ever happen…" but he then suggests, in a situation where winning is of utmost importance, that this is a visionary idea.

As someone steeped in Sorkin, the editorial made me sad. It made me sad because it misses what makes *The West Wing* optimistic. The political arena matters because its consequences resonate and reverberate through our lives. Politics can look like a team-based sport, red versus blue with eyes fixated on winning, but it's not. Toby says, "government can be a place where people come together and where no one gets left behind." What Sorkin suggests (by his own admission) is leaving behind reproductive rights, the LGBTQ+ community, the labor movement, and (though he doesn't mention them) racial, ethnic, and religious minority communities. He suggests focusing on winning the presidential election by abandoning the Democratic Party's core moral values and constituencies.

There are shortcomings throughout *The West Wing*; there's lots to criticize. The first two seasons of *The West Wing* are 44 episodes, at about 42 minutes a piece; 1,848 minutes of television will include a lot to criticize, especially when people talk as much and as quickly as Sorkin's characters. But I don't think there's anything as silly as that op-ed in the first two seasons of the show.[551]

Reasonable people can disagree about practical strategies of the 2024 presidential elections, especially those who see the election as democracy's last stand in America. But democracy is worth fighting for because democracy is a place where people can come together for the common good, where people's rights are respected and protected.

Some criticisms of Sorkin miss the point. Sorkin used the show to criticize President Clinton. The show asks us to imagine a President standing up for evidence-based policy on drugs and the equal protection of LGBTQ+ people, times when then-President Clinton didn't show moral courage. Was it unrealistic to expect more from political leaders given the political realities of the late-'90s? Sorkin expects more, against conventional cynicism.

Making cynical shows about politics is easy; most people are already cynical about politics. Schlamme notes part of the reason The West Wing got made was because of the scandals around then-President Clinton.[552] The West Wing criticized political cynicism at the time; it's prescient now, as our political cynicism deepens.

Most cynicism emerges from botched realism. Cynicism begins with observing a series of real constraints and problems. Cynicism about politics includes noting the realities of contemporary American politics. Money plays an enormous role, and the influence of money over lobbying, advertising, and litigating is enormous. Massive companies are insulated from accountability by battalions of lawyers; interest groups effectively lobby to edit laws which regulate them. Having the right connections and political capital often matters more than knowledge and ethics. It's easy to look at these things and assume politics is a game about pushing money and influence to accumulate more money and influence, and so on forever. The people who play the game well aggressively accumulate money and power. It seems impossible to extract control of the political machinery once it is captured by those interests.

The world isn't a just place, but at the end of the Cold War, there was a moment where it seemed like the universe was plodding in a good direction.

In 1992, the political economist Francis Fukuyama published *The End of History and The Last Man*. Fukuyama is Sorkin's philosophical sibling. They're both optimists about political disagreement and shared purpose, about liberal democracy as a way of resolving our differences and coming together as a society. *The End of History* examines the end of the Cold War and the revolutions in former Soviet states, the development of international liberal democracy as an end point in the transformative, often bloody revolutionary period of human history. Fukuyama surveys the crimes of the 19th and 20th century, but at the end of the first chapter, he ends on optimistic note. "... despite the powerful reasons for pessimism given us by our experience in the first half of this century, events in its second half have been pointing in a very different direction. As we reach the 1990s, the world as a whole has not revealed new evils, but has gotten *better* in certain distinct ways... Authoritarian dictatorships of all kinds, both on the Right and the Left, have been collapsing. In some cases, the collapse has led to the establishment of prosperous and stable liberal democracies."[553]

Fukuyama had a vision of the political future; in liberal democracies, peaceful discussion and democratic processes allow for social change without violent revolution. That vision turned out to be wrong; September 11, 2001 didn't threaten the stability of liberal democracies, but showed that reducing political history to states was a mistake, that non-state actors threatened violent disruption. More significantly, the global democratic backslide of the mid-to-late 2010s showed that Fukuyama's rosy picture of democracy ignored the wrinkles.[554]

Liberal democracy allows disagreements within a community to be resolved through discussion, rather than force.[555] Fukuyama distills Sorkin's politics in the West Wing. In *The West Wing,* the central figures share a commitment to democratic values; they discuss their differences, change their minds, and find compromise solutions. They see the political end in liberal democracy, where systems can be reformed and improved over time without constantly overthrowing them. Liberal democracy let us chart a way forward, together, discussing our values and our policies toward a shared end.

The last 25 years have disabused us of this idea. Fukuyama's thesis has become a punchline to a thousand different jokes. No one agrees what the jokes are about, or why they're funny, but history isn't over. Authoritarianism made major resurgences around the world; many liberal democracies lurched back towards authoritarianism. Fukuyama noted that many authoritarian states were overthrown and replaced by new authoritarian states, but Fukuyama saw liberal democracies as robust. Internal political shifts towards authoritarian politics in the United States, Europe, the democratic nations of South and Southeast Asia, show that liberal democracy still involves internal political struggles endemic throughout human history. It isn't self-sustaining; radical, violent revolutions and repressive authoritarianism can still happen in vibrant liberal democracies.

Fukuyama is writing political philosophy, a description of how he thinks the world is; Sorkin is writing fiction. If we read *The West Wing* as a description of what American politics *is*, then the show is painfully misguided. But it's not.

Sorkin wants to combat cynicism, wants people to find optimism about politics; it's an aspiration, not a description. Adopting unbridled cynicism can lead people to abandon guiding principles in favor of winning. In "Five Votes Down," Josh just wants to get his bill over the finish line; the use of political tactics to strong arm opponents into voting doesn't raise political objections until Leo meets with Rep Richardson. When Josh is beating up politicians who are just opposed to the bill for political reasons, there are no consequences. Richardson raises concerns that the bill is ineffectual posturing. They go around Richardson to get the votes, after insulting him. Josh and Leo are punished for their hubris, when Vice President Hoynes gets the credit. In the real world, away from Sorkin's laws of dramatic justice, strong arm tactics are rarely punished.

Sometimes, Sorkin's world makes no sense. Sorkin is out of touch with political realities; proposing Democrats nominate Mitt Romney at the 2024 convention is just silly. Sorkin fetishizes bipartisanship and radical compromise in decision making. As he acknowledges in that op-ed, *The West Wing* writers with actual experience in politics (Caddell, Myers, Attie, and others) would stop him before abject absurdity. In addition to his desire to "jump the shark," some of Sorkin's political views are questionable. When he's focusing on gay rights and drug decriminalization in the first two seasons, his positioning is strong; on foreign policy and economics, more complicated issues, he sometimes collapses into incoherence. His discussion of free trade focuses on geopolitics and ignores the human cost of exploited labor in other countries. His commentary on the pharmaceutical industry and price-gouging in Africa just collapse into a lamentation about how hard it is to be a political leader in a struggling country.

Politics makes good television because politics, like sports, neatly divides into internal conflicts and external opposition. Parties have team mentalities; winning drives dramatic conflict. The idea of winning drives the plot forward and sets up obstacles and a shared goal. In cynical political shows, winning is the focal point.

Thinking of politics in terms of winning is cynical; it ignores what makes politics different than sports. In sports, winning just is the whole goal. If the Yankees win the World Series, that's the end of their season. Then their focus turns to next season, to winning again. Politics shouldn't work like that, though it often does. Winning an election should be in service of policy and social goals; politicians want to win because winning allows them to work. Politics isn't baseball; winning isn't the end of the season.

Winning is necessary. If President Bartlet doesn't win, then our staff doesn't get to govern; that's a major point throughout Season Three. Winning is a necessary step towards other ends. When a politician wins, that's just the start. What's next?

Acknowledgements

I am grateful to so many mentors and friends through my life. I wrote this book while I was a doctoral student and postdoctoral fellow; I owe a great deal to my doctoral advisors John Baker and David Liebesman, senior faculty Mark Ereshefsky, Allen Habib, Mark Migotti, and Nicole Wyatt. I am grateful for extensive conversations with political philosophers who were excited to disagree with me when I was a postdoctoral fellow, especially Ryan Davis, John Hasnas, and Peter Jaworski. Among these, I am especially grateful for the late David G. Dick, who encouraged me to work on philosophy of political economy and whose personality was grounded in the optimism, kindness, and care that I hope to bring to this book.

This book owes enormous debts to scholars I studied with in college and graduate school. There are too many to name here, but I will do my best. As an undergraduate, I was especially influenced by professors Karen Bell, Andrew Fenton, Andrew Fiala, and Robert Maldonado. The work by Profs Fiala and Maldonado on religious understanding and pluralism was indispensable to this project, as was their sense of philosophy as a moral, social, and political (rather than solely intellectual) undertaking. In graduate school at NYU, I am grateful to the many brilliant philosophers with whom I interacted (and who probably don't remember me, one of several eager, excitable kids at the seminar table). I am grateful to S. Matthew Liao, Sharon Street, and Michael Strevens, who provided invaluable guidance and support as I dove into the big ocean.

I am also grateful to my amazing family, Micah McKechnie and Captain Steven Stein, and their lovely partners Forest and Morgan. I am grateful to C.J. Hirschfield, the C.J. Cregg of our family. My aunt Joan and uncle Dick, my cousins Emily, Paul, and Mary Willis all encouraged me and supported me through this process. Ridgley, who was an infant when this started and is now big, the reason for this is to make the world better for you and your friends.

Joshua Stein, Ph.D.

I also owe a great deal to my girlfriend Shelby Magid, who has taught me a lot about foreign policy and supported me through the grinding tail-end of this process.

About the Author

Joshua Stein is an academic who works on philosophy, politics, and economics. He has a Ph.D. from the University of Calgary in philosophy. He has written extensively on the ethics, social science, and politics of new technologies and government regulation. He writes across a range of platforms and has published in mainstream, academic, and think tank publications. His major focus is the ethics and economics of emerging technologies, especially digital and medical.

Endnotes

[1] "In Two Cathedrals" (2.22), Bartlet says that 44 million Americans don't have health insurance; on the United States Census in 2000, there were a little over 280 million people living in America, which would make the rate of uninsured 15.5-16%. As of 2020, the United States Census Bureau says about 28 million Americans are uninsured, 8.6% of the population. Most of this declined occurred following the implementation of insurance mandates and exchanges under the Affordable Care Act ("Obamacare") in 2014.
https://www.census.gov/library/publications/2021/demo/p60-274.html

[2] LGBTQ+ rights are one area where Sorkin is considerably more progressive than the Democratic Party of his time (led by Bill Clinton). California passed Proposition 8 in 2008, banning gay marriage, years after the show ended. Proposition 8 was among several laws challenged in the court system and struck down in Obergefell v. Hodges (2015) and United States v. Windsor (2013).

[3] This is hardly over, but the #MeToo movement helped create accountability for predators. Some scandals predate this, including the case of Dennis Hastert, the former Speaker of the House who had sexually assaulted and covered up the abuse of underaged boys. Some figures including Donald Trump and Jim Jordan remain influential despite their scandals; while writing the book, former President Trump was found liable in a civil proceeding for sexual abuse of writer E. Jean Carroll.

[4] This optimism contrasts with more cynical pieces of television that developed later, like the HBO comedy *Veep* (2012-2019) and the American version of the British drama *House of Cards* (2013-2018). The Shonda Rhimes epic *Scandal* (2012-2018) shows that some more cynical shows are themselves influenced by *The West Wing*.

[5] *The West Wing* Weekly podcast, which is a major influence on this project, has a strong sense of this. Much of the podcast aired during the 2016 Presidential campaign and the beginning of President Trump's administration, a time of crushing cynicism.

[6] This is an oversimplification, but illustrates one argument in Rawls' "Justice as Fairness" (1985).

[7] One major limit on reasonable disagreement is what I call "Baldwin's Razor," after the American writer James Baldwin. Baldwin wrote, "We can disagree and still love each other unless your disagreement is rooted in my oppression and denial of my humanity and right to exist." This is the best way I have found to distill a range of limits on reasonable disagreement in pluralist societies.

[8] *The West Wing Weekly.* September 28, 2016. "In The Shadow of Two Gunman," Part I (With Thomas Schlamme)."

[9] Sorkin wrestles with this in *The Newsroom*.

[10] *The American President* is the basis for the proportional response arc. Sorkin likes to borrow from himself.

[11] The lack of clear identification between Ed and Larry in the plot is a Sorkin homage to Stoppard's *Rosencrantz and Guildenstern are Dead*, where the two minor Hamlet characters are not clearly distinguished from one another.

[12] Butterfield's character is based on real-life Secret Service Agent Jerry Parr.

[13] The videos were created under fair use by YouTube user Kevin T. Porter.
The original is here: https://youtu.be/S78RzZr3IwI
The sequel is here: https://youtu.be/7jeuV3xXxUc

[14] The poker game motif appears in *The West Wing*'s "Evidence of Things Not Seen" (4.20) and *Sports Night*'s "Shoe Money" (1.10).

[15] The interview format is something Sorkin really likes; he uses it twice in the first season of *The West Wing* in "Celestial Navigation" (1.15) where Josh is interviewed and in "What Kind of Day Has it Been" (1.22) where President Bartlet is interviewed at a town hall.

[16] Regular Sorkin cast member and co-creator of *The West Wing Weekly* Josh Malina says he wanted the role of Sam Seaborn but was unable to take the role because the first season was shot simultaneously with the second season of *Sports Night*, on which he was a star. Malina would appear in *The West Wing* in Season Three and become a regular cast member in Season Four.
The West Wing Weekly, 1:01 "Pilot." March 2016. 4:00.

[17] Lisa Edelstein had previously appeared in several television series, including two episodes of Sorkin and Schlamme's *Sports Night* (episodes 1.13 and 1.19). She has since become famous for playing Lisa Cuddy on *House M.D.*

[18] Toby gives the flight attendant a series of specifications for the plane. Giving these technical descriptions is a tool Sorkin uses to establish a character's knowledge and seriousness, a Sorkin device.

[19] *The West Wing Weekly*, 1:01 "Pilot." March 2016. 8:20

[20] "The Day In History: May 23"
https://www.history.com/this-day-in-history/george-w-bush-recovers-from-bicycle-accident

[21] Schlamme takes some credit for establishing the aesthetic of the show, including the walk-and-talk. Schlamme also credits Steadicam operator David Chameides with helping to establish the style.
The West Wing Weekly, 2.01 "In The Shadow of Two Gunman, Part I (with Tommy Schlamme)." September 2016. 13:30.

[22] Leo's insistence that there is only one correct spelling of Gaddafi's name is wrong. Gaddafi's name was spelled in a wide range of ways. *The Christian Science Monitor* noted in 2011 that his official website used "Al-Gathafi," as well as the more conventional Al Qaddafi. They also note the alternative spellings "Kaddafi" and "Qadhafi."
Eoin O'Carroll. February 22, 2011. "Gaddafi? Kadafi? Qaddafi? What's the correct spelling?" *The Christian Science Monitor*. https://www.csmonitor.com/World/2011/0222/Gaddafi-Kadafi-Qaddafi-What-s-the-correct-spelling

[23] One may notice that I left C.J. out of the account of these roles. C.J.'s role in the show is complicated; she often hits stumbling blocks and creates small scandals in her time as Press Secretary. We see some instances of skill from her throughout the first season, but Lies, Damn Lies, and Statistics (1.21) establishes C.J.'s unique expertise and sets her apart from the rest of the staff.

[24] This is a not-especially-subtle reference to the tax prosecutions of right-wing Christian leaders during the 1980s, most famously Jim Bakker's conviction for wire fraud and Sun Myung Moon's conviction for tax evasion.

[25] Maloney is credited as a recurring character throughout the first season, despite appearing in every episode. She is credited as a full cast member at the start of the second season. Her chemistry with Whitford was recognized by the production staff of the show within the first few episodes.

Tyler Aquilina. August 27, 2020. "How The West Wing star Janel Maloney built her character Donna Moss 'from scratch.'" *Entertainment Weekly*. https://ew.com/tv/the-west-wing-reunion-janel-moloney-donna-moss/

[26] I barely remember pagers, personally; for those younger readers, pagers delivered a message from a phone

[27] Parker was a prolific character actor whose credits include *Good Times* (4.08), *The Jeffersons* (4.04), *Happy Days* (7.01), and *The Love Boat* (1.14).

[28] Sorkin makes clear from the start is that every group has good, sincere people and self-serving jerks. Leo's interactions with Caldwell help establish that Caldwell is a good and sincere person, even if he and Leo disagree politically.

[29] The use of euphemisms to talk about Jewishness and to use Jewishness to delegitimize certain liberal points of view is well ahead of its time, certainly beyond the sensibilities of network television in the late '90s. This rhetorical pattern is still common on the Christian right today.

[30] "The Lambs of God" are not a real group, however this probably evokes the militant anti-abortion group "The Lambs of Christ." (Boodman 1993) In episode 1.18, a Secret Service meeting refers to several real white supremacist groups, including the World Church of the Creator (also called "The Creativity Movement") that was active in the '90s. Sorkin sometimes uses real groups in his scripts, though the industry standard at the time was not to use real groups in negative portrayals.

Sandra G. Boodman. April 8, 1993. "A Protester's Story." *The Washington Post*. https://www.washingtonpost.com/archive/politics/1993/04/08/a-protesters-story/baa11ba2-19bd-4078-ad32-d0fb98c384a4/

[31] Alison Klein and Carol C. Leonnig. May 1, 2008. "DC Madam Commits Suicide in Florida." *The Washington Post*. http://voices.washingtonpost.com/dc/2008/05/dc_madam_believed_a_suicide_in.html

[32] Michelle Ye Hee Lee and Elise Viebeck. October 27, 2017. "How Congress plays by different rules on sexual harassment and misconduct." *The Washington Post*. https://www.washingtonpost.com/politics/how-congress-plays-by-different-rules-on-sexual-harassment-and-misconduct/2017/10/26/2b9a8412-b80c-11e7-9e58-e6288544af98_story.html

[33] Keli Goff. July 18, 2013. "Could a former stripper be elected President?" *The Washington Post*. https://www.washingtonpost.com/blogs/she-the-people/wp/2013/07/18/could-a-former-stripper-be-elected-president/

[34] Felicia Sonmez. August 31, 2011. "End of House Page Program is bittersweet for some lawmakers." *The Washington Post*. https://www.washingtonpost.com/politics/for-some-members-end-of-house-page-program-is-bittersweet/2011/08/30/gIQAWed9rJ_story.html

[35] I use the word "affair" here begrudgingly. Calling this an "affair" ignores the power dynamic between the President of the United States and an intern. "Affair" is probably too charitable to President Clinton.

[36] Annys Shin. June 21, 2018. "When Mark Sanford Apologized." *The Washington Post Magazine*. https://www.washingtonpost.com/lifestyle/magazine/when-mark-sanford-apologized/2018/06/18/68ac22dc-5e99-11e8-b2b8-08a538d9dbd6_story.html

[37] John Bedford Lloyd is a character actor probably best known for playing Victor Comstock in *Remembering WENN*. This scene is his only appearance in *The West Wing*.

[38] Two notes here. First, passing references to musical theater are a tool for Sorkin, though Sorkin prefers Gilbert and Sullivan to Puccini. Second, the representation of Mandy as a jilted woman who can sustain no life outside of her career is a major criticism of Sorkin. Some people criticize Moira Kelly for not being able to sustain Sorkin's dialogue, but (in my opinion) her work is strong outside of the relationship with Josh Lyman. The problem is that the flirtatious tension with Josh is her whole raison d'etre and without that, it's not clear Sorkin had a plan

for the character. Whitford's chemistry with Janel Maloney meant Kelly was boxed out of her principal role in the show.

[39] The character of Josh Lyman is loosely based on then-Clinton staffer Rahm Emanuel. This behavior is characteristic of Emanuel.

The West Wing Weekly, 1.02. "Post Hoc Ergo Propter Hoc." March 30, 2016. 11:30.

[40] Strictly speaking, the translation is wrong; hoc in Latin is the demonstrative, meaning the translation should be "this" instead of "it."

[41] The climactic scene of Season Two finale "Two Cathedrals" (2.22) features a monologue from Bartlet with whole passages in Latin. The fact that he was a theology minor at Notre Dame also brings out the use of Latin.

[42] Santiago-Hundson has a long television career, most notably as Captain Roy Montgomery on *Castle* and Raul Gomez on *Billions*.

[43] This episode is Dungey's only appearance in the series. Dungey has an extensive filmography, including *Once Upon a Time* (as Ursula) and *The Resident* (as Claire Thorpe).

[44] Matheson is best known for the role of Otter in *National Lampoon's Animal House*. He has a long list of credits as an actor, including recurring roles on *Burn Notice*, *The Good Fight*, and *Virgin River*.

[45] *The West Wing Weekly* co-host Hrishi Hirway notes this exchange gives him the idea that Vice President Hoynes might challenge Bartlet. It is unclear whether this potential conflict is something Sorkin intended; however, it would be inconsistent with later continuity. In Season Three (especially 3.14), we discover Hoynes has been operating under the assumption that President Bartlet will not seek reelection because of the President's concealed multiple sclerosis diagnosis. Hoynes was told about the President's MS and the decision not to seek reelection when Bartlet approached him about accepting the nomination for Vice President. Hoynes can't be thinking about challenging Bartlet because he thinks that Bartlet isn't going to run, but this is retroactive continuity.

[46] This is another point of criticism in the way Sorkin writes women. Laurie finds Sam's aggressive pursuit charming rather than creepy and dangerous.

[47] Buckland has worked mostly as a TV comedy director on *Scrubs*, *My Name is Earl*, and *Santa Clarita Diet*.

[48] The character of Josh Lyman is Jewish, as we learned in the pilot. Bradley Whitford is not. The strained pronunciation of the Yiddish word shiksa illustrates Whitford's gentile-ness.

[49] This scene feels different after the attack on the Capitol on January 6, 2021. Since the 2010s, there have been a range of incendiary claims from political figures and their supporters.

[50] Note that C.J.'s plot arc in 1.02 is concerned with being blindsided by a public statement made by the Vice President. Being blindsided by question is part of what makes C.J.'s job especially difficult throughout the series.

[51] Amos is most famous for Roots (for which he received an Emmy nomination) and *Good Times*, in his early career. His entire filmography is too long to list here.

[52] Hill's first appearance on television was *The Dick Cavett Show* in 1986, as a tap dancer. Hill is an accomplished dancer, in addition to his acting credits.

[53] Mrs. De La Guardia does not appear on screen until Season Three, when she is played by Lily Tomlin.

[54] Bartlet smoking comes up in "Celestial Navigation" (1.15), when Josh lies to the press. President Barack Obama smoking became a political issue.

[55] Sam is profoundly self-centered. Much of the staff is concerned with his potential scandal, but he is interrupting their work. Both Josh and Toby outrank Sam.

[56] I say "attempt" here because the scene gets rushed; the President doesn't apologize for yelling at Charlie.

[57] There are only two areas of contemporary conflict which involve two active nuclear powers. One area (India and Pakistan) is discussed extensively in *The West Wing*. The other (Russia and

NATO) is not but has become a flashpoint with the increased aggression of Russia under Vladimir Putin and Russia's invasion of neighboring countries including Georgia (2008) and Ukraine (2014, expanding in 2022).

[58] These actions still produced significant civilian casualties, but there are orders of magnitude difference between such drone strikes and (by contrast) dropping a city-leveling bomb.

[59] They don't wrestle with it well; they don't acknowledge that the United States itself has violated international law on many occasions during and after the Cold War. Sorkin does write about this more explicitly in *The Newsroom*, which includes arcs on drone strikes, domestic surveillance, and the use of chemical weapons.

[60] Thomas Nagel. 1972. "War and Massacre." *Philosophy and Public Affairs* 1.2: 123-144. Notably, Nagel's major point of engagement through the paper is Catholic absolutist moral theology, which is supposed to be a moral grounding position for Bartlet.

[61] Ibid. 128.

[62] Ibid. 142-143. Emphasis Nagel's.

[63] As a matter of fact, military conflicts today often involve crimes against humanity. There are extensively documented crimes against humanity committed by Russian forces during the invasion of Ukraine; the Israel-Hamas war included crimes against humanity in the attack by Hamas on October 7, 2023, and in indiscriminate strikes by Ibid. 142-143. Emphasis Nagel's. the Israeli Defense Forces. The ongoing wars and conflicts in Yemen, Sudan, west Africa, Haiti, Syria, and Central and South America all involve crimes against humanity committed by different belligerents. These are distinct from the kind of catastrophic response Bartlet contemplates, because the belligerents don't have access to the military resources of the United States.

[64] Both O'Donnell and Caddell were political operatives before joining the writing staff. O'Donnell was a staffer to Senator Daniel Patrick Moynihan (D-NY) and staff director of the Senate Finance Committee. Patrick Caddell worked on Presidential campaigns, including Carter's '76 and '80 campaigns.

[65] Gun control is still a prescient issue. Notably, this episode aired about six months after the Columbine High School shooting (April 20, 1999). The episode refers to an established assault weapons ban, which is meant to be a reference to the 1994 assault weapons ban passed by President Clinton. The assault weapons ban expired in 2004, and its lapse correlated with significant, annual increase in mass shootings and gun related deaths.

[66] Sorkin often introduces issues without explanation and gives exposition later. Here we get "five votes down" before we know the subject. This avoids dumping exposition when the characters don't need it. The reason we get exposition between Josh and Donna is because Donna doesn't always have the background knowledge; where our senior staff usually do.

[67] Schlamme mentions they had considered using this walk-and-talk sequence in the pilot. The scene was shot at the Biltmore Hotel, in Los Angeles.
The West Wing Weekly. September 2016. "The Shadow of Two Gunman Part I (with Thomas Schlamme)."

[68] The President is prescribed Oxycodone, which is the generic name for a family of opioids. Oxycodone (the generic) has been in use since 1916. The name brand drug OxyContin was approved by the FDA in 1995 for dosing every four to six hours (instead of the generic's standard 12-hour).

[69] This is Botsford's only appearance in the series.

[70] This is a running theme throughout many of Sorkin's shows. Many of his characters are stressed and have poor management of their personal lives.

[71] Toby is being accused of insider trading, that he received information not known to the public and used it to profit off trading. Rules regarding White House employees trading stocks are subject to executive orders and have changed over the years.

[72] This episode (late 1999) would have been towards the peak of the dot com boom (roughly 1995-2002, peaking in 2000).

[73] Josh Lyman is reportedly based on then-Clinton staffer Rahm Emanuel, these sorts of strong-arm tactics typify Emanuel's reputation.
Ewen MacAskill. November 6, 2008. "Economic rescue plan main priority as new chief of staff named." *The Guardian*.
https://www.theguardian.com/world/2008/nov/07/rahm-emmanuel-obama-white-house-economy

[74] Margaret says Leo made "$40,000 a pop" on the lecture circuit. Adjusted for inflation, this would be about $65,500 in 2021. President Obama made $400,000 a piece ($445,500 adjusted) for his first speeches after leaving office (Thrasher 2017); President Bill Clinton is estimated to have made around $750,000 ($824,000 adjusted) each for such speeches (Rucker, Hamburger, and Becker 2014); former Alaska Governor and Vice-Presidential candidate Sarah Palin's speaking fees were around $100,000 ($125,000, adjusted) (Smith 2010). All adjustments are from the date of publication of the pieces to 2021-dollar value.
Steven Thrasher. May 1, 2017. "Barack Obama's $400,000 speaking fees reveal what few want to admit." *The Guardian*.
https://www.theguardian.com/commentisfree/2017/may/01/barack-obama-speaking-fees-economic-racial-justice
Philip Rucker, Tom Hamburger, and Alexander Becker. June 26, 2014. "How the Clintons went from 'dead broke' to rich: Bill earned $104.9 million for speeches." *The Washington Post*.
https://www.washingtonpost.com/politics/how-the-clintons-went-from-dead-broke-to-rich-bill-earned-1049-million-for-speeches/2014/06/26/8fa0b372-fd3a-11e3-8176-f2c941cf35f1_story.html
Ben Smith. Jan 12, 2010. "Palin's Fee." Politico.com
https://www.politico.com/blogs/ben-smith/2010/01/palins-fee-024090

[75] Richardson is Chairman of the Congressional Black Caucus and a recurring character in the show. He appears in Ways and Means (3.04) and Angel Maintenance (4.19). In my opinion, Barry's performance as Rep. Richardson is far ahead of his time.

[76] They transition from talking about Oxycodone to using the name brands Percocet and Vicodin. Percocet is a form of Oxycodone (immediate release with paracetamol). Vicodin is not an Oxycodone, but rather Hydrocodone/Paracetamol.

[77] This is McGuire's only appearance on *The West Wing*.

[78] Justin Vogt. June 16, 2017. "How Washington Planned for a Cold War Apocalypse." *The New York Times*.
https://www.nytimes.com/2017/06/16/books/review/raven-rock-garrett-m-graff.html

[79] One can see archived pages discussing the Obama White House's "Big Block of Cheese Day" at this link: https://obamawhitehouse.archives.gov/blog/2015/01/16/big-block-cheese-day-back-and-its-feta-ever

[80] Grateful to Hrishi Hirway for this catch.
The West Wing Weekly. April 20, 2016. "The Crackpots and These Women (With Eli Ati)."

[81] This is Howard's only appearance in *The West Wing*. Howard played college basketball for the University of Michigan, was taken 5th overall in the 1994 NBA draft, and played 18 seasons in the NBA. When this episode aired, he was playing for the Washington Wizards (just renamed from the Washington Bullets).

[82] This is a sunny retelling of Jackson's legacy, as the "big block of cheese" would only have been available to white men. Jackson was a southern slave owner and responsible for the mass killing and deportation of Native Americans. Notably, Jackson's popularity has decreased precipitously over the 21st century. Jackson has decreased in Presidential historians survey from 13th in 2000 to 22nd in 2021.
https://www.c-span.org/presidentsurvey2021/

[83] Sam Lloyd is best known for playing Ted Buckland in *Scrubs* and *Cougar Town*. He was also a member of the acapella quartet The Blanks. Sam was the nephew of Christopher Lloyd, who appears in *The West Wing* (6.14).

[84] The Los Angeles fundraiser occurs in 20 House in LA (1.06).

[85] Sorkin wrestles with this issue again at length in *The Newsroom*, especially through Sloan Sabbith (Olivia Munn).

[86] *The West Wing* puts a lot of stock in getting facts right; given the pervasiveness of outright lying in contemporary politics, there's a different texture to seeing the President just make things up.

[87] The Endangered Species Protection Act was introduced in 1966, partly as a response to near extinction of the bald eagle. It was updated in 1969 and again to its modern form in 1973. The 1973 act established federal classifications and regulations for species, including the registries of critical habitats. These are managed by the United States Fish and Wildlife Service and the National Marine Fisheries Service.

[88] Josh Malina notes Shonda Rimes has confirmed the character David Rosen in *Scandal* (played by Malina) is named after this character.
The West Wing Weekly. April 20, 2016. "1.05: The Crackpots and These Women."

[89] Josh's therapist is named Stanley. The therapist played by Adam Arkin later in the series is also named Stanley. It's noteworthy here that Josh is seeing a therapist this early in the show, as he later resists receiving Many of Sorkin's major characters are Catholic. The President and First Lady are Catholic, as are C.J. and Leo.mental health treatment in season two.

[90] Many of Sorkin's major characters are Catholic. The President and First Lady are Catholic, as are C.J. and Leo.

[91] Moss is most famous for her roles in *Mad Men* and *The Handmaid's Tale*; she appears in 25 episodes of *The West Wing*.

[92] Mrs. Landingham tells Toby about the death of her two sons in "In Excelsis Deo "(1.10).

[93] Josh and Hrishi note the President uses the phrase "we touched the face of God" in talking about the space race. The line comes from Reagan's public address following the explosion of the Challenger shuttle, January 28, 1986.
The West Wing Weekly. April 20, 2016. "The Crackpots and These Women (With Eli Ati)."

[94] The biowarfare research programs in the United States were terminated by Nixon in 1969.

[95] Anthony Rimmington. 2021. *The Soviet Union's Invisible Weapons of Mass Destruction*. New York: Palgrave MacMillan.
_____. 2018. *Stalin's Secret Weapon: The Origins of Soviet Biological Warfare*. Oxford: Oxford University Press.

[96] Bacillus anthracis is a bacterium which can infect a person through inhalation, ingestion, or skin contact, depending on strain.

[97] During the Bush and Obama administrations, there were substantial efforts to bolster American biodefense strategy and especially public communications. As reporting at the time noted, there was a response plan developed for a contagious, high-mortality upper-respiratory illness, but this plan was ignored by the Trump administration. For discussion see:
Alejandro Camacho and Robert Glicksman. 2021. "Structured to Fail: Lessons from the Trump Administrations Faulty Pandemic Planning and Response." *Michigan Journal of Environment and Administrative Law* 10(2). https://scholarship.law.gwu.edu/cgi/viewcontent.cgi?article=2782&context=faculty_publications
Charles Parker and Eric Stern. 2022. "The Trump Administration and the COVID-19 crisis: Exploring the warning-response problems and missed opportunities of a public health emergency." *Public Administration*. https://www.ncbi.nlm.nih.gov/pmc/articles/PMC9115435/

[98] This is Christopher Misiano's first episode. He would direct 35 episodes of the show and become a figure in the production staff.

[99] Josh Malina notes there are several poker faux pas in this game. Toby engages in a string bet (calling and then raising, rather than raising in the initial declaration), players splash the pot (throwing money in, rather than putting forward discrete stacks), and C.J. seems to deal a card during a betting round.

The West Wing Weekly. April 27, 2016. "1.06: Mr. Willis of Ohio (with Janel Maloney)." 4:00

[100] Bartlet is wrong. The "seeds" on the outside of the strawberry are achenes (which are small fruits themselves) and the achenes have seeds on the inside.

[101] Bartlet's trivia in this seen is quite bad, it turns out. Bartlet says there are three words in the English language starting with "dw." He cites dwindle, dwarf, and dwell. Josh and Hrishi note he might have included "dweeb." He's also missing "dwine" (to waste, from old English).

[102] *The West Wing Weekly.* July 20, 2016. "1.15: Celestial Navigation (with Jay Carney)." 8:00.

[103] The last time that the federal government had a budget surplus was in the transition from the Clinton to Bush administrations in 2001. (See Monthly Treasury Statements at the link below.) Clinton had budget surpluses in fiscal years 1998 through 2001. Prior to Clinton, the last surplus year was under President Johnson in 1969.
https://datalab.usaspending.gov/americas-finance-guide/deficit/trends/

[104] The appropriations bill originates in the Appropriations Committee but has to pass through each committee with jurisdiction over those areas of the budget. The US Census Bureau is part of the Department of Commerce, so the Commerce Committee would be responsible for amendments related to the census. Sorkin (or whomever identified this) gets this obscure nuts-and-bolts bit right.

[105] Fann co-starred in *Bodies of Evidence* with a young George Clooney.

[106] The length of a bill does not say much about the amount it spends; rather, it speaks to the level of detail in the bill. Appropriating the Department of Defense a few trillion dollars can be a one sentence or it can be a very long bill, depending on how much detail is spelled out in terms of the constraints and targets of spending.

[107] Donna says the money she spends on a DVD player will go to employ people who make DVDs, but this is not how the market works. In economic theory, some hold increases in demand (Donna's buying) lead to increases in production, which would necessitate an increase in employment, but increases in demand and price are not necessarily passed on to workers.

[108] There is homophobia expressed by the White House staff throughout the entire show. Sorkin does seem aware of this, as he often criticizes homophobia in politics, but it doesn't age well.

[109] Statute currently prohibits sampling in the census for the purposes of representation and funding, but the Census Bureau uses sampling methods in other areas of their research.

[110] For those inclined to do a deep dive on this point, I recommend:
Howard Ohline. 1971. "Republicanism and Slavery: Origins of the Three-Fifths Clause in the United States Constitution." *The William and Mary Quarterly* 28.4: 563-584.

[111] This is the plot of Commencement (4.22) and Twenty Five (4.23)

[112] It's not an accident that Schlamme mentions the inspiration of Frank Capra, who directed *Mr. Smith Goes to Washington*, in interviews.
The West Wing Weekly. September 2016. "The Shadow of Two Gunman Part I (with Thomas Schlamme)."

[113] For introductory discussion, see Coady (2018). For Walzer's discussion, see Walzer (1973; 2004).
C.A.J. Cody. 2018. "The Problem of Dirty Hands." *The Stanford Encyclopedia of Philosophy.* https://plato.stanford.edu/entries/dirty-hands/
Michael Walzer. 1973. "Political Action: The Problem of Dirty Hands." *Philosophy and Public Affairs* 2.2: 160-180.
Michael Walzer, 2004. "Emergency Ethics." In *Arguing About War*. New Haven: Yale University Press.

[114] Costumer Lyn Paolo was nominated for an Emmy for this episode.

[115] The sourcing is unclear. The state of Indonesia executed 12 people between 1989 and 2000 (when this episode aired); half of those were executed for "subversion" related to being charged as communists, a capital offense during the 1965 mass killings of communists. Toby makes an off-hand reference to the fact that the United States supported the junta, confirmed by the International People's Tribunal in the Hague in 2015.

[116] YoYo Ma doesn't appear in this episode. He appears in "Noel" (2.10).

[117] Again, this situation reflects pre-9/11 attitudes. Violence isn't external; it's a domestic terrorist group. It evokes Randy Weaver (at Ruby Ridge) or David Koresh (at Waco), rather than Al Qaida.

[118] Busfield appears as Danny Concannon in 27 episodes of The West Wing. Busfield previously performed on Broadway in Sorkin's play *A Few Good Men*. He directed two episodes of Sports Night (2.16 and 2.21). He is probably best known for his Emmy-winning performance as Elliot Weston in *Thirtysomething*. He also appears as a recurring character in *Studio 60 on the Sunset Strip*.

[119] There is a vermeil display room in the White House, on the ground floor near the diplomatic reception area and the map room.

[120] After the Ruby Ridge standoff (August 21-31, 1992) and the Waco siege (February 28-April 19, 1993), the American militia movement drew attention throughout the '90s. This changed following 9/11, but shifted back following increased domestic terrorist activity from the early '10s to the present. The story in the episode seems to be based more on Ruby Ridge (in Idaho). For more information on the American militia movements, I recommend:
Kathleen Belew. 2018. *Bring the War Home*. Cambridge, MA: Harvard University Press.
Sam Jackson. 2020. *Oath Keepers*. New York, NY: Columbia University Press.

[121] As far as I know the President of Indonesia at the time, Abdurrahman Wahid, was never the target of a United States assassination attempt. But the CIA does have a record of assassinations.

[122] Abbey Bartlet is a recurring character throughout the series. Channing has an extensive filmography, including her Academy Award-winning performance as Ouisa Kittredge in *Six Degrees of Separation*.

[123] Portraits of the First Ladies are often displayed in the vermeil room of the White House.

[124] Lyn Paolo says the dress Channing wears in the episode has a lot of cleavage (partly because of a rushed fitting) and caused criticism from viewers. First Ladies are expected to dress conservatively. Paolo says Channing loved the dress.
The West Wing Weekly. May 4, 2016. "The State Dinner (with Lyn Paolo)."

[125] All guests at White House functions go through background checks performed by the Secret Service. Laurie would not be able to attend under an assumed name or as an escort.

[126] *The West Wing Weekly*. November 20, 2018. *"Parks and Recreation* (with Rob Lowe, Adam Scott and Michael Schur)."

[127] Presidential statements are tightly controlled because they often have far-reaching implications and influence. Bartlet addresses this directly in "20 Hours in LA" (1.16). It is a running theme throughout, because the show focuses on the communications staffers and had Dee Dee Myers and Eli Attie as consultants. This feels considerably different after the Trump administration, where the communications office was unprofessional, and President Trump routinely made wild personal statements.

[128] The President notes Truman did this during the steel strike in 1952. This was struck down by the Supreme Court in Youngstown Sheet & Tube Co. v. Sawyer.

[129] Bartlet refers to the destruction of this ship the Season Two finale "Two Cathedrals" (2.22).

[130] In some cases, the Chinese government has denied some abuses occur (like forced sterilization), but largely held the matter is one of internal affairs.
Madeline Roache. Dec 9, 2021. "China guilty of genocide in Xinjiang, tribunal rules." *Al Jazeera*.

[131] There is a reasonable debate about how Sorkin writes women, including women balancing their personal lives and their work. Perhaps the strongest point in defense of Sorkin's writing of women is this tension between relationship and work is true of many, even most, of Sorkin's characters, as we see with the collapse of Leo's marriage.

[132] Sam is consistently unprofessional in this interaction; by contrast, C.J. is trying to do her job.

[133] "The Internet is not a fad," as though this is a major discovery is a bit odd, since this was nearing the height of the dot com boom (in '00). One wonders whether Sorkin thought there was still widespread skepticism of the Internet; he does something similar on an episode of *Sports Night*.

[134] Among the staff, Josh is the most driven by "winning" rather than issues themselves. Josh is often the cynical political voice.

[135] Hoynes says that he "delivered the south" for the President, though we know (from 1.02) that the President lost Hoynes' home state of Texas. Which states Hoynes "delivered" is unclear.

[136] Whether Sorkin plans season-long arcs is often unclear, but this does build towards "Let Bartlet Be Bartlet" (1.19) and greater optimism at the end of the season.

[137] The Antiquities Act of 1906 gives the President the power to declare national monuments. The Supreme Court has upheld that this power includes the ability to designate large areas as monuments and thereby protect those areas. See Chief Justice Roberts' denial of *certiori* in Massachusetts Lobstermen's Association v. Raimondo for a recent, illustrative example.

[138] Josh and Hrishi express this. I agree.
The West Wing Weekly. May 11, 2016. "1.08: Enemies."

[139] Howard had a recurring role as Hank Hooper on 30 Rock and played Thomas Jefferson in Peter Hunt's film adaptation of 1776 (1972). Howard is a legend among actors for his role as a union leader. He was President of the Screen Actors Guild (SAG) and helped facilitate the merger with the American Federation of Television and Radio Artists (AFTRA) in 2012 and became the first President of SAG-AFTRA. Howard passed away March 23, 2016.

[140] Mason Adams is probably best known for his work as Charlie Hume in the series Lou Grant. He also worked extensively as a voice actor in radio during the '40s and '50s, including *The Adventures of Superman* and *The Adventures of Ellery Queen*.

[141] The discussion acknowledges that Supreme Court appointments are political. It follows the contentious appointment of Justice Clarence Thomas and failed appointment of Robert Bork. The politics of the Court have changed radically, with Bush v. Gore (in 2000), contentious nominations, and incendiary decisions on election law, abortion rights, and Presidential powers.

[142] This is Lillienfield's only on-screen appearance.

[143] The vague nature of Leo's instructions comes back to bite Josh when he is eventually deposed to testify about his investigation (episode 1.11), as Josh insists he didn't keep notes about the investigation.

[144] The politics of "short lists" and the role of identity in politics were established by the time the episode aired. President Biden made a campaign commitment to put a Black woman on the Supreme Court. President Biden would eventually follow through on that promise, appointing Justice Kentanji Brown Jackson.

[145] Many law schools (including the top tier programs; Harvard, Columbia, Berkeley, etc.) publish "notes" by their students. When publishing as students, these notes are often unsigned. *The Harvard Law Review* notes, for example, "All student writing is unsigned. This policy reflects the fact that many members of the *Review* besides the author make a contribution to each published piece." The publication of unsigned notes allows students to publish their views without concern about blowback early in their career.

[146] The House Government Oversight and Reform Committee is responsible for investigating everything in the legislative jurisdiction, the largest purview for investigative hearings in the House.

[147] For more discussion of the fishbowl, I recommend Ellen Totleben's interview on *The West Wing Weekly*. Totleben won an Emmy for Art Direction in 2000 and was nominated again in 2002, 2003, and 2004.
The West Wing Weekly. November 30, 2016. "2.10: Noel (with Bradley Whitford and Ellen Totleben)." http://thewestwingweekly.com/episodes/210

[148] Some scholars were critical of the use of a right to privacy (in the 4th and 5th amendment) as grounding abortion rights in Roe; some argue the right to abortion should apply on gender equity grounds and/or self-defense grounds. Among people critical of the judicial reasoning in Roe was the late Justice Ginsburg, who thought the decision centered physicians' rights to practice rather than privacy rights.

[149] Sam noting "who's gay and who's not" nods to worries about outing closeted LGBTQ+ people. However, the episode predates Lawrence v. Texas (2003), which struck down Texas's criminal punishments for sodomy because of a right to privacy. Lawrence was decided 6-3; Justice Kennedy wrote the majority opinion, while Justices Scalia and Thomas wrote dissents claiming there is no broad right to privacy.

[150] *The West Wing Weekly*. May 18, 2016. "1.09: The Short List (with Ronald Klain)."

[151] Justice Sotomayor was nominated to the District Court for the Southern District of New York in 1991 (by George H.W. Bush) and then to the Second Circuit Court of Appeals in 1997 (by Bill Clinton). Whether she influenced the character of Mendoza is unclear from the interviews, but (though Sotomayor was not a cop) there are many parallels in their backgrounds.

[152] Olmos's filmography includes *Stand and Deliver*, *Blade Runner*, and *Battlestar Galactica*.

[153] Harrison's relationship with Charlie seems to have been amicable, in contrast to Charlie's interaction with racist philanderer Ken Cochran (1.21). Also, "Sandy Hook" is likely intended to be a fake name, as the only Sandy Hook golf club is in Manitoba.

[154] Graves eventually jointed the production staff for the show, winning two Emmys for directing. He is also known for his work on *Game of Thrones*.

[155] Richard Schiff won an Emmy in part for his performance in this episode. He also noted in an interview the role of Toby was originally contested between him and Eugene Levy.
The West Wing Weekly. May 25, 2016. "In Excelsis Deo (with Richard Schiff)."

[156] The show has Al Roker playing Santa Claus without any controversy around Black men playing Santa. This is refreshing, and a reminder of my friend, the late Ron Zeno, who played Santa in Oakland for years.

[157] Given that C.J. Cregg is based on Dee Dee Myers. I wonder if this is based on one of Myers' codenames. There is a running list of publicly known Secret Service codenames on Wikipedia. https://en.wikipedia.org/wiki/Secret_Service_code_name

[158] The scene is shot at the memorial wall.

[159] Lowell Lydell is fictional but based on Matthew Shepherd. Shepherd was murdered in 1998.

[160] The core ideas of the bill developed following the murders of Shepherd and Byrd in 1998, but the bill itself was not passed until 2009 under President Obama.

[161] Both India and Pakistan encaged in nuclear testing in 1998. The episode responds to nuclear weapons tests on May 28-30 of 1998. Those tests marked Pakistan's establishment as a nuclear state; India became a nuclear state with the Smiling Buddha tests in 1974.

[162] Dee Dee Myers noted this experience is common for Press Secretaries. Myers has cited her own experience of a retaliatory strike against Iraq following a report that Iraq was involved in an attempt to assassinate George H.W. Bush.
David von Drehle and R. Jeffrey Smith. June 27, 1993. "U.S. Strikes Iraq for Plot to Kill Bush." *The Washington Post*.

[163] Citizen's Watch, the fictional group Claypool uses, is based on the right-wing group Judicial Watch, which frequently filed Freedom of Information Act (FOIA) requests. The founder of Judicial Watch is Larry Klayman.
Johnathan Mahler. October 12, 2016. "Group's Tactic on Hillary Clinton: Sue Her Again and Again." *The New York Times*. https://www.nytimes.com/2016/10/13/us/politics/judicial-watch-hillary-clinton.html

[164] Kashmir was a semi-autonomous state at the time this episode was made. India took control of most of the state and revoked its autonomy in 2019. Neither India nor Pakistan recognizes the other's claim to the region.

[165] Duffy was in the national tour of *A Few Good Men*, a Sorkin play.
The West Wing Weekly. June 8, 2016. "1.11: Lord John Marbury (with William Duffy and Peter James Smith)." 3:00.

[166] International law marks differentiates between acts of military aggression (which are criminal) and acts of self-defense (which are not). Both the Indian and Pakistani ambassadors argue they are acting in self-defense. Under international law, and given the scope of the episode, it's almost certain India is the aggressor under international law, but Kashmir (subject to disagreement about sovereignty) is complicated. We saw this in the Russian invasion of Ukraine; when Russia invaded the Donbas (2014), there was less international legal sanction than when it was uncontroversial that Russia was invading sovereign Ukrainian territory (2022). *The West Wing* aired after the Cold War and before the Russian imperialist push under Putin, including attacks on Georgia (2008), the invasion of the Donbas, and the full-scale invasion (2022).

[167] HIPAA (The Health Insurance Portability and Accountability Act of 1996) sets requirements on privacy of medical data, but it only applies to covered entities. Those covered entities include insurers and service providers.

[168] Comparing the situations of the United States and India is tacky. The United States was independent as of 1783 (the end of the American Revolutionary War) and India was not independent until 1947. Unlike India, the people who rule the United States were not indigenous to the country.

[169] Marbury is typically cast as a foil to Leo, with the notable exception of one argument with Toby (3.16).

[170] Sorkinism often uses credentials in introducing characters; he does this for comedic effect (when the credentials are silly) or to underscore seriousness. Marbury has both. The character is absurd and over-the-top, but he is discussing serious issues.

[171] Hrishi notes middle eastern and south Asian religious conflict was not well understood in mainstream American politics. Hrishi also notes it is very strange the show ends with a room full of white guys settling on how to dictate a solution for India and Pakistan.
The West Wing Weekly. June 8, 2016. "1.11: Lord John Marbury (with William Duffy and Peter James Smith)." 55:00.

[172] This is a harbinger of the eventual attempt to kill Charlie in 1.22, 2.01, and 2.02.

[173] Oppenheimer read the words on camera in the documentary *The Decision to Drop the Bomb* (1968).

[174] The idea of news breaking on the Internet wasn't new. Email lists like *The Drudge Report* (founded in 1995) broke stories like this, then picked up by mainstream websites. Drudge was the first group to publish the allegations Bill Clinton had sex with an intern.
January 25, 1998. "Scandalous Scoop Breaks Online." *BBC News*.
http://news.bbc.co.uk/2/hi/special_report/1998/clinton_scandal/50031.stm

[175] This process exists because many people in the line of succession are obligated to be at the State of the Union. In order: the Vice President, Speaker of the House, and President Pro Tempore of the Senate are all obligated to be present due to their roles in Congress; the Vice

President serves as President of the Senate. The Secretary of Agriculture is ninth in the presidential line of succession, behind Attorney General and Secretary of the Interior.

[176] Sorkin doesn't write healthy relationships often; the banter and supportive relationship between the President and First Lady is one of a few cases. They fight during the show (especially in Season 3), but are generally a supportive, loving couple.

[177] Josh takes this line to heart, though it is a mistake. Lots of exploding is expected, (e.g.) fireworks and demolitions.

[178] In this speech, which has become popular on YouTube in the years since it aired, Will McAvoy (Jeff Daniels) notes that the National Endowment for the Arts does not cost much money, but is wildly unpopular.

[179] This strains the Bechdel Test. The Bechdel Test was coined by cartoonist Alison Bechdel as a test for film. The canonical version of the test holds. "(1) The movie has two women in it (2) who talk to each other (3) about something other than a man." The central idea is that women should be characters capable of having independent interactions without being reducible to their relationship to men in the story.
Alison Bechdel. 1986. *Dykes to Watch Out For*. Firebrand Books.

[180] The show raised awareness of multiple sclerosis and that relapsing/remitting multiple sclerosis is manageable and not fatal. The show illustrates President Bartlet is capable of functioning normally during periods of relapse. The story also raises the concern that Presidents may not disclose their medical conditions, as Presidents Truman and Franklin Delano Roosevelt both failed to disclose their health issues; many have speculated both Presidents Kennedy and Reagan hid health issues from the public.
Lawrence K. Altman. October 9, 2001. "The Doctors World; Very Real Questions for Fictional President." *The New York Times*.
https://www.nytimes.com/2001/10/09/health/the-doctor-s-world-very-real-questions-for-fictional-president.html

[181] One of the Democratic Congressmen refers to the "Mapplethorpe Photographs," a series of subversive photographs taken by Robert Mapplethorpe.

[182] The line "the era of big government is over" is taken from Bill Clinton's 1996 State of the Union.

[183] This discussion felt like a relic at the time I wrote this, but sex education policies have come back into the public consciousness with conservative campaigns targeting school boards for LGBTQ+ inclusive education. Studies consistently demonstrate abstinence only sex education produces bad outcomes. See.
Mary A. Ott and John Santelli. 2007. "Abstinence and abstinence-only education." *Current Opinion in Obstetrics and Gynecology* 19(5): 446-452.
John Santelli, Mary A. Ott, Maureen Lyon, Jennifer Rogers, Daniel Summers, and Rebecca Schleifer. 2006. "Abstinence and abstinence-only education: a review of U.S. policy and programs." *Journal of Adolescent Health* 38(1): 72-81.

[184] Advance teams scout locations for politicians ahead of visits.

[185] The strategy no longer works in politics, given how social media scandals develop. The strategy is based partly on a debating technique called a gish gallop, where one debater presents a large volume of different arguments such that their opponent cannot appropriately respond to all arguments. The term was coined by science educator Eugenie Scott and named (pejoratively) after creationist Duane Gish.
Eugenie Scott. 2004. *Confronting Creationism*. Reports of the National Center for Science Education. p. 23.

[186] Professors tend to have a wide berth regarding what materials they teach in courses, because of academic freedom protections. Nothing here falls outside of academic freedom protection. Standards have shifted significantly since this episode; this would have been a bigger story if it happened in the contemporary university environment.

Joshua Stein, Ph.D.

[187] The support staff in the show are mostly women, while the senior White House staff (except C.J.) are men. While one can criticize the casting here, the White House staffing at the time did have these gender dynamics. Sorkin representing the younger women as incorrigible gossips is sexist.

[188] Matthews had recurring stints on *Gilmore Girls*, *The King of Queens*, and *Desperate Housewives*

[189] Both Barack Obama and Hillary Clinton, in 2008 appealed to their "evolution" on gay marriage. Both supported civil unions and leaving the issue to the states. Obama held, in 2008, "Personally, I do believe that marriage is between a man and a woman." (Wilson 2007, p. 114-115). Hillary Clinton defended her views during the '90s "not that many" people supported gay marriage in the '90s (Miller 2014). When this episode aired both supported some version of marriage discrimination and would not change their views until after the 2008 Presidential election.
Jake Miller. June 12, 2014. "Don't Twist My Position." CBS News. https://www.cbsnews.com/news/hillary-clinton-dont-twist-my-position-on-gay-marriage/
John Wilson. 2007. *Barack Obama: The Improbable Quest*. New York: Routledge.

[190] Weil is best known for playing Paris in *Gilmore Girls*.

[191] The criticism of *The West Wing* as pie-in-the-sky often focuses on moral positions, but the first season responds directly to political cynicism. C.J. is the major voice in this episode; Leo is in "Let Barlet Be Bartlet" (1.19) when the show shifts towards a more optimistic tone.

[192] The charitable interpretation is C.J. wants this out because she agrees with Mr. Lydell's criticism of the administration and thinks he should have a platform to raise his concerns.

[193] Failing to fire Larson, like failing to fire the stenographer in 1.08, is a departure from norms in political offices. Both are serious leaks; the employees would be fired. In Larson's case, she could be prosecuted.

[194] The inclusion of the ampersand is a policy within the Writers Guild of America which holds, for union credits, the two writers are to be treated as one person.
The West Wing Weekly. July 6, 2016. "1.14: Take This Sabbath Day." 1:00.

[195] Danielle Berrin. July 17, 2012. "A small glimpse into Aaron Sorkin's Jewish Story." *Jewish Journal*. https://jewishjournal.com/mobile_20111212/106205/a-small-glimpse-into-aaron-sorkins-jewish-story/

[196] Josh Malina notes Noah Emmerich was in the national tour of *A Few Good Men*, which is a link to Sorkin. I am grateful Malina mentions those who worked on the *A Few Good Men* stage productions.
The West Wing Weekly. July 6, 2016. "1.14: Take This Sabbath Day." 4:00.

[197] Andy Bowers. December 13, 2015. "Why executions happen at midnight?" Slate. https://slate.com/news-and-politics/2005/12/why-midnight-executions.html

[198] Proval is best known for his roles *Mean Streets* and *The Shawshank Redemption*. He also played Richie Aprile on *The Sopranos*.

[199] A Haggadah is a guide used for the Passover seder, the Jewish holiday celebrating the exodus from Egypt. It is unclear why Glassman is talking about the Haggadah, since the episode aired in February and Passover fell April 19-27, 2000.

[200] The California 46th congressional district is discussed by Sorkin as a swing district. This was accurate. The district was established in 1992 and represented Orange County. It was represented by a Republican from 1993-1997 and flipped in 1997. It was represented by a Democrat when the episode aired. The district was redrawn into a conservative district covering Orange County and parts of Los Angeles in 2003, before being shifted to a Democratic district when redrawn in 2013. It remained a solidly Democratic district during 2023 redistricting.

[201] Rabbi Glassman notes the rabbis put restrictions on the death penalty. Rabbis Tarfon and Akiva are credited as saying, "If we were in the Sanhedrin, no man would ever be executed."

224

(Makkot 7a) Shonkoff provides a primer on one of the relevant passages in the Torah (Deuteronomy 16:18-21:9) and "rabbinic hesitation" about capital punishment in the Talmud. Sam Shonkoff. "The Torah and Capital Punishment." *My Jewish Learning.* https://www.myjewishlearning.com/article/the-death-penalty/
[202] The Talmudic teachings in question are about 1800-1850 years old, not 2000. But he's rounding up.
[203] The President has broad constitutional discretion for the pardon power. as a constitutional matter, that President Bartlet can pardon the man. The issue of "following the law" is that his personal religious beliefs won't impact governance.
[204] "We're nowhere" and "we're absolutely nowhere" are Sorkinisms recycled across shows.
[205] Some criticize the show for focusing too heavily on C.J.'s failures. "Celestial Navigation" illustrates why: the job of Press Secretary is especially difficult. Dee Dee Myers (who wrote the story for this episode) also used her personal experience to inform C.J.'s storylines.
[206] Pounder is an accomplished actress best known for her stint on *E.R.* (produced by *West Wing* Executive Producer John Wells) and *The Shield*. She has been nominated for four Emmys for her acting work in *The X-Files* (1995), *E.R.* (1997), *The Shield* (2005), and *The No. 1 Ladies' Detective Agency* (2009). She was also among the finalists to play C.J. Cregg, at least according to *The West Wing* wiki.
https://westwing.fandom.com/wiki/CCH_Pounder
[207] American monetary policy is handled by two groups: the Treasury Department and the Federal Reserve. The Treasury Department issues and prints currency; the Federal Reserve manages supply. The Treasury Department is controlled by the President; the Federal Reserve is not and is supposed to stay apolitical. In my opinion, is especially weak is on economic policy. It overstates the powers of the President to manage inflation, unemployment, and the economy.
[208] In Birchfield v. North Dakota, the Supreme Court ruled breathalyzer tests of suspected drunk drivers do not violate a 4th Amendment right, but blood tests do. This is derived from the "search incident to a lawful arrest (SITA)" rule. This case was decided in 2016, long after the episode aired.
[209] Jorja Fox had recurring roles on *E.R.* (produced by *The West Wing* producer John Wells) and *CSI*.
[210] The tax credits expired in 2012. Their expiration was uncontested by farmers growing corn for ethanol.
Robert Pear. January 1, 2012. "After Three Decades, Tax Credit for Ethanol Expires." *The New York Times.* https://www.nytimes.com/2012/01/02/business/energy-environment/after-three-decades-federal-tax-credit-for-ethanol-expires.html
[211] Sorkin reuses "gather ye rosebuds" in *The Newsroom* (1.09).
[212] Balaban is an actor and director. His major film roles include *Close Encounters of the Third Kind* and *Gosford Park*.
[213] This storyline is based on the dispute between Bill Clinton and Democratic donor and Hollywood executive David Geffen over Don't Ask, Don't Tell. In more recent years, Geffen has discussed the issue publicly.
Stephen Braun and Dan Morain. March 4, 2007. "Famous allies were often at odds." *The Los Angeles Times.* https://www.latimes.com/la-na-geffen4mar04-story.html
[214] de Lancie is best known for his roles as Q in *Star Trek: The Next Generation* and Eugene Bradford in *Days of Our Lives*.
[215] Jeet Heer. October 23, 2017. "Liberals, Stop Applauding George W. Bush." *The New Republic.* https://newrepublic.com/article/145456/liberals-stop-applauding-george-w-bush
[216] The use of the ampersand indicates the O'Donnell and Redford worked as a team, while Sorkin was independent.

[217] Leo notes that the stock market could lose 300 points. In 2012, as part of reforms following the '08 market crash, the rules were changed to halt trading if the market had a large drop in a short period of time. This drop would trigger the halt under the current rules.

[218] Dajani also guest starred as Tina Lake on *Sports Night* (2.07).

[219] Adam Behsudi. April 16, 2015. "Democrats' civil war over free trade." *Politico.* https://www.politico.com/story/2015/04/democrats-free-trade-bill-117066

[220] Broad bipartisan consensus doesn't mean a view is right. In the case of free trade economic policy, relatively low unemployment during the Clinton years defused debate among economists and politicians, because it was clear free trade policy would not increase American unemployment and lowered prices of consumer goods.

[221] The discussion of trade policy and the automotive industry is extensive; trade policy does partly explain the '08 auto industry crash, though the economic consensus is the crash was a result of industry failures, rather than public policy.
Paul Ingrassia. 2009. *Crash Course: The American Auto-Industry's Road from Glory to Disaster*. New York: Random House.

[222] Again, this foreshadows. 2.01 sees an assassination attempt against Charlie result in other people (including the President and Josh) getting shot.

[223] Leo explains this issue to Margaret, that the Justice Department appointee supports monetary reparations for slavery. While reparations are now widely discussed, this is a recent development. This episode aired three months after the economist Richard America participated in a panel on reparations for slavery aired on CSPAN. Richard America was a major leader arguing for reparations; he is also a friend.
https://www.c-span.org/video/?154639-1/case-black-reparations

[224] Lumbly is an accomplished voice and character actor known for his work on Cagney and Lacey and as the voice of Martian Manhunter in the *Justice League Unlimited* and related DC series.

[225] This bit was written into the script by Sorkin following Janney doing the lip synch while Richard Schiff was smoking a cigar, during a late-night get-together on the lot at what was called "Café Flamingo." (Janney's trailer.)
The West Wing Weekly. August 10, 2016. "1.18: Six Meetings Before Lunch." 23:00

[226] Josh's father dying the night of the Illinois primary becomes a recurring and important story. We see this in 2.02, the impact of his father's death on Josh's relationship with Donna and the President.

[227] Breckenridge cites "Harold Washington" for his figure on reparations. As far as I can tell, there is no such historian or economist. Howard Washington was the name of the 51st Mayor of Chicago and member of the House of Representatives. Estimates of the cost of reparations have varied over the years, but Breckenridge's number is among the estimates.

[228] Special Field Order No. 15 was issued by General William Sherman on January 16, 1865. It instructed about 400,000 acres confiscated by the Union army to be divided into parcels no larger than 40 acres, and for those parcels to be given to formerly enslaved people. The order is the basis for the phrase "40 acres and a mule."

[229] This is a pivot back to the introduction of Agent Toscano in "20 Hours in LA", where the President makes clear that confidentiality and trust are important in making sure that Zoe is protected.

[230] The Sorkinism of "the silver bullet" appears here. This is a normal idiom, but Sorkin is especially fond of it.

[231] This discussion implies reparations were not paid to Holocaust survivors, but they were. Various states, especially then West Germany, paid billions in reparations to individual Holocaust survivors as well as organizations and the state of Israel. For further reading, one can look at the Conference on Jewish Material Claims Against Germany (1951) and other such

organized efforts on Holocaust reparations. Reparations and the repatriation of property taken by the Nazis were a major part of post-WWII international law and still an ongoing issue.

[232] Sorkin has some comedic range. This scene is one joke setup Sorkin likes: the cast describes something silly; give some time for the audience to get distracted by verbal jokes; end with the silly thing. Sorkin is often criticized for being excessively verbal; this is a bit unfair. Sorkin likes pratfalls, just not as much as he likes wordplay.

[233] Erica Chayes Wilda. December 3, 2018. "President George H.W. Bush never liked broccoli—and people still love him for it." *TODAY* Food Newsletter. https://www.today.com/food/president-george-h-w-bush-celebrated-never-liking-broccoli-t144284

[234] The FEC had more power when this episode aired, prior to Citizens United v. FEC (2010), which overruled Austin v. Michigan Chamber of Commerce (1990). Austin held that corporations could be restricted in political donations and electioneering; Citizens United ruled corporations could only have the same (much weaker) restrictions as private individuals.

[235] The CBO has a range of responsibilities, but its budget projections are the most significant. The CBO is a part of the legislative branch, though is independent. CBO projections have often been criticized (including on The West Wing) for inaccuracy, but the University of Chicago Initiative on Global Markets argues CBO budget projections are reasonably accurate, given high levels of uncertainty and legal restrictions on what the CBO can assume in modeling. https://www.igmchicago.org/surveys/the-cbo/

[236] These are White House events held every year.

[237] This error is indicative of an early problem in email and digital communications systems, namely the failure to predict errors by less tech-savvy users. Now most systems have design constraints which prevent this problem, for example: listservs function by blind copy (bcc) rather than regular copy (cc).

[238] Provenza is better known as a comic than an actor. He has an extensive filmography; I recommend his interview series *The Green Room* with Paul Provenza, which (although brief) was influential within comedy.

[239] For commentary on the more sophisticated elements of this, I recommend some scholarly articles.
Justin Levitt. 2010. "Confronting the impact of Citizens United." *Yale Law and Policy Review.*
Rick Hasen. 2011. "Citizens United and the illusion of coherence." *University of Michigan Law Review.*

[240] Major Tate is played by Ted Marcoux, who was in the original Broadway cast of A Few Good Men. Major Thompson is played by James DuMont. The Congressman (only referred to as "Ken") is played by David Brisbin. The Senate Aide is played by Aaron Lustig.

[241] Most countries have at least one national language. Canada has two, English and French. The reason the United States does not is partly political (pushing for English as the national language is arguably racist) and partly legal (languages on election ballots and official government documents would limit participation by non-English speakers).

[242] "John Amos is a great actor" is not a spicy take. There is a reason he's been a constant presence in film, television, and stage acting since the early '70s. Fitzwallace, as a character, plays two roles in the show: as a straight man (especially to President Bartlett and Secretary McNally, played by Anna Deavere Smith) and as the voice of the military establishment and military ethics. This commentary on gays in the military is different, because it illustrates a departure from both roles, and brings Fitzwallace's experience as a Black man who came up in military command as desegregation was still a serious issue.

[243] Don't Ask, Don't Tell was implemented in 1994 (under the Clinton administration) and fully repealed in 2011 (under the Obama administration). There were more than 13,500 known discharges under Don't Ask, Don't Tell (according to the Servicemembers Legal Defense Network), but the number is likely significantly higher.

[244] In later continuity, Bartlet is supposed to have agreed he would not seek reelection, causing friction when he decides to run through Season Three.

[245] Sorkin has openly discussed his issues with substance abuse, as have John Spencer and Martin Sheen. Sorkin received treatment for substance abuse issues throughout the 1990s; Sorkin was arrested in 2001 (after this episode aired) and enrolled in a drug diversion program. The characters of Leo and Vice President Hoynes illustrate the experiences Sorkin (and Spencer) had with substances.

[246] The United States Substance Abuse and Mental Health Services Administration (SAMHSA) was created in 1992 (under President George H.W. Bush), following the abolition of the Alcohol, Drug Abuse, and Mental Health Administration. SAMHSA shifted some of the research-oriented missions into the National Institute of Health and set up the Center for Substance Abuse Prevention (CSAP) and Center for Substance Abuse Treatment (CSAT) as major public initiatives. SAMHSA is still a primary source of data on mental health and includes the Center for Behavioral Health Statistics and Quality, which publishes statistics on mental health, including substance abuse.

[247] The American public often has views contradictory to experts, including medical experts. At the time, this was mostly a concern for substance abuse and mental health, where public opinion viewed substance abuse patients as "criminals" rather than patients. The idea of large swaths of the American public ignoring scientific consensus hits differently given climate change and the coronavirus pandemic.

[248] The character Andrea Wyatt is the result of an acting choice by Schiff. During the early episodes, Toby can be seen wearing a wedding ring. Sorkin confirms this was a decision that surprised him, but he and Schiff agreed Toby was not presently married, so Sorkin wrote the character of an ex-wife into later stories.

The West Wing Weekly. August 24, 2016. "1.20: Mandator Minimums (with Kathleen York and Mayor Karen Freeman-Wilson)." 25:30.

[249] York is an accomplished actress, as well as a singer-songwriter under the name Bird York. She won an Oscar for "In The Deep," which appeared in the film *Crash.* In discussing the role with *The West Wing Weekly*, York notes she was concerned playing a congresswoman would (and did) result in people thinking she was much older than she is. York would have been about 25 at the time of the episode (born 1975); she is about 20 years younger than Schiff (born 1955).

The West Wing Weekly. August 24, 2016. "1.20: Mandator Minimums (with Kathleen York and Mayor Karen Freeman-Wilson)." 58:00.

[250] There are extensive discussions of this issue available. For a useful introduction, I attach the following recommendations, which are accessible and thorough.

Michelle Alexander. 2020. *The New Jim Crow: Mass Incarceration in the age of Colorblindness.* The New Press.

Katherine Beckett. 2000. *Making Crime Pay: Law and Order in Contemporary American Politics.* Oxford: Oxford University Press.

Alexander Cockburn and Jeffrey St. Clair. 1998. *Whiteout: The CIA, Drugs, and the Press.* Verso.

[251] Sam says Onorato "played on my credulous simplicity," a line borrowed from Gilbert and Sullivan's Pirates of Penzance. Thanks to Josh Malina, again, for that catch. I have done my best to catalogue easter eggs from the podcast series.

The West Wing Weekly. August 24, 2016. "1.20: Mandator Minimums (with Kathleen York and Mayor Karen Freeman-Wilson)." 53:00.

[252] Scardino directed the original run of *A Few Good Men* on Broadway.

The West Wing Weekly. August 30, 2016. "1.21: Lies, Damn Lies, and Statistics." 2:00.

[253] Polling aggregators, including RealClearPolitics, track the results of the question over time.

[254] It's hard to tell why so much of C.J.'s story arc focuses on failure. Part of it may be the experience of Dee Dee Myers as Press Secretary. With that in mind, this is one of Janney's strongest performances in the season and was the second episode in her package (along with Celestial Navigation) for her Emmy win.

[255] There are increasing challenges in this. For discussion, see:
Gerald M. Kosicki. 2020. "Survey Methods, Traditional, and Public Opinion Polling." The International Encyclopedia of Media Psychology.

[256] Austin Pendleton is most famous for his work in theater, including originating the role of Motel in *Fiddler on the Roof* and the bumbling defense attorney in *My Cousin Vinny*. He is also an accomplished director, whose credits include *The Little Foxes* (1981) on Broadway.
The West Wing Weekly. August 30, 2016. "1.21: Lies, Damn Lies, and Statistics." 16:00.

[257] In 1.03, we are told that the Attorney General is Black, when Leo is commenting on potentially hiring Charlie as Bartlet's body man. In this scene, the AG is white.

[258] Typically, these minor ambassadorships are held by career foreign service officers or political operatives in foreign relations. The idea of appointing an FEC commissioner is unprofessional, though using appointments in political maneuvering is not unprecedented.

[259] This was a major source of concern for several decades, including during George W. Bush's campaign, where Bush was viewed as popular among Latino voters given his record as Governor of Texas. The issue of Latino support was central to Republican strategy memos prior to the nomination of Donald Trump. Particularly interesting is the study providing a post-mortem of the 2012 GOP election loss.
Mara Liasson. March 18, 2013. "RNC Report a Postmortem on Failed 2012 Election." All Things Considered. NPR. https://www.npr.org/2013/03/18/174665725/rnc-report-a-postmortem- on-failed-2012-election
David Siders. December 17, 2020. "'Everything's great': GOP ditches election post-mortems." *Politico*. https://www.politico.com/news/2020/12/17/gop-ditches-election-postmortem-447091

[260] Huddleston appeared in *The Big Lebowski*, *Blazing Saddles*, and *The Producers* during his almost 50-year career.

[261] *The West Wing Weekly*. September 6, 2016. "1.22: What Kind of Day Has It Been (with Tim Matheson)." 2:30.

[262] The Newseum was in Rosslyn at the time of the episode, but it was eventually moved to Washington, D.C. It closed in 2019.

[263] There have been some studies on generational political apathy. The generation President Bartlet discusses is Generation X, which had higher rates of political apathy, though both Millennials and (especially) Generation Z poll higher on levels of political understanding and engagement. Generation X's political engagement has also increased significantly in recent years.
Ted Rall. Feb 23, 2018. "Never Mind Millennial Apathy, Here's Generation Z." Rasmussen Reports.
Anthony Cilluffo and Richard Fry. May 29, 2019. "Gen Z, Millennials, and Gen X outvoted older generations in 2018 midterms." Pew Research Center.

[264] Sorkin likes to use references to "things" to show prior context; exposition about "the thing" then comes later and fills in our reader.

[265] The Columbia space shuttle disaster occurred in 2003 (after this episode), though Columbia had been in service since 1981. The real disaster was the result of the shuttle shedding polyurethane foam and damage to an external tank; the Columbia disintegrated during reentry, killing all seven crew members.

[266] This is a callback to Charlie's first appearance (1.03).

[267] Unlike many instances throughout the series, this episode refers to Iraq rather than a fictionalized country. This episode is after Operation Desert Storm but precedes the invasion of Baghdad by the United States in 2003.

268 According to the Congressional Budget Office, as of 2020, there are about 31 million uninsured Americans. The number of uninsured Americans decreased from around 17% of the total population to around 10% during the four-year period between 2012 and 2016, largely credited to the Patient Protection and Affordable Care Act.

269 This episode aired between two wars with Iraq, the first was the "Gulf War" under George H.W. Bush (1991) and the second was the invasion and occupation of Iraq under George W. Bush and later Barack Obama (2003-2011).

270 For a basic survey of the timeline and background resources, see the FDIC website: https://www.fdic.gov/bank/historical/sandl/

271 This is not a continuity error, but a tension in the scripts. Earlier in the season, it seems as though all members of our senior staff mistrust Hoynes, except Leo. The fact that Josh has an established, candid relationship with the Vice President does not jive with that.

272 This isn't true. The Seal of the President does not change based on whether the nation is at war. It was changed by President Truman in 1945 to face right (the talon with the olive branch).

273 President Bartlet is supposed to be related to Josiah Bartlett, a signer of the Declaration of Independence and representative to the Continental Congress from New Hampshire, later elected Governor of New Hampshire. Their surnames are spelled differently.

274 These facilitate discussion of disagreement on gun control (2.04), small business policy (2.06), and the Equal Rights Amendment (2.18).

275 In *The Newsroom*, Sorkin's protagonist Will McAvoy (Jeff Daniels) is a Republican who works for George H.W. Bush. The Newsroom spends a lot of time addressing the partisan divide in politics, especially the Tea Party and Occupy movements.

276 This is a Sorkinism. He uses it in his 2012 commencement address at Syracuse University.

277 Sorkin imposes his own moral rules on Bartlet. Sorkin himself says that hubris has to be punished; he chooses to punish Bartlet by hurting others. One might ask, "Why is Sorkin doing this to Bartlet?" rather than asking about God. Sorkin harms a character in the finale of all four seasons of *The West Wing* that he wrote.
The West Wing Weekly. September 19, 2017. "Posse Comitatus (Live with Aaron Sorkin, Allison Janney, and Melissa Fitzgerald)."

278 While dramatic, is point is also theologically thin. Bartlet treats the suffering of others as about him. Most approaches to Catholic theodicy would begin by pointing out that the harms to these people are (first and foremost) harms to them, rather than harms to Bartlet. Bartlet is making himself the center of the theological world.

279 O'Neill interviewed Jerry Parr, one of the agents responsible for getting Reagan into the car after the shooting. He walks through Parr's behavior, including procedure for checking for injuries.
The West Wing Weekly. September 28, 2016. "In The Shadow of Two Gunman, Part II (With Bradley Whitford and Michael O'Neill)."

280 There is a reference to the Munich Olympics, where the United States won a silver medal in basketball.

281 "x, don't x. It's entirely up to you," is a Sorkinism. It appears in *Sports Night*, from William H. Macy. Abigail Bartlet delivering this line doesn't make sense; telling the press would violate the American Medical Association code of ethics regarding confidentiality. There are a few exceptions to the AMA policy on confidentiality (imminent threat of harm to self or others; requirement by law or court order), but these don't apply. As a physician, Abigail Bartlet should know this.
See: AMA Journal of Ethics. 2012. "AMA Code of Medical Ethics' Opinion on Confidentiality of Patient Disclosure and Circumstances Under Which it May Be Breached." https://journalofethics.ama-assn.org/article/ama-code-medical-ethics-opinion-confidentiality-patient-disclosure-and-circumstances-under-which-it/2012-06

[282] *The West Wing Weekly*. September 28, 2016. "In The Shadow of Two Gunman, Part I (With Thomas Schlamme)." 2:30.

[283] Schlamme notes the flashbacks go into white in Part I and come out of white in Part II, rather than cuts to black used throughout the show.

[284] Sorkin, like many Democrats in the '90s, talks about prospective insolvency for Social Security and the need for reforms. Because Democrats opposed privatization (the proposal offered by many Republicans), these solutions required some combination of increasing funding, decreasing in benefits, or increasing the retirement age, all of which were politically unpopular. Sorkin is piggybacking here on the nomination of officials to the Social Security Administration throughout the '90s and a report on potential financing issues for Social Security produced by the Social Security Advisory Council in 1997.
For more information, see the history page on the Social Security Administration website: https://www.ssa.gov/history/1990.html

[285] This exposition dump is a standard feature of Sorkin's writing; the technical details (like the exact amount of money) are rarely salient to the story, but underline the expertise of the speaker and evoke attitudes.

[286] We learned in 1.18 that Josh's father died the night of the Illinois primary.

[287] One of these oil tankers does crash into the United States in "Bad Moon Rising (2.19)". Sam is an environmentalist, also raised in "The Drop In (2.12)."

[288] Butterfield is based) thought the President hadn't been shot. Parr noticed during an exam in the car that President Reagan was coughing up oxygenated blood. Like Bartlet, Reagan was reportedly in good spirits when entering George Washington University hospital; the hospital didn't initially believe the President was being admitted. The major concern was blood loss.

[289] Dr. Abigail Bartlet has a specialty in thoracic surgery; she is an expert in the procedures.

[290] McNally becomes a recurring character through the rest of the series. Deavere Smith is also known for her work in Nurse Jackie and extensive theater career.

[291] It is unclear whether this policy is intended to reference concerns from when President Truman was incapacitated in 1952. There were concerns about who was running the executive branch when Truman was seriously ill and unable to perform his duties, and potential failure to disclose these matters to the press.
Samuel W. Rushay, Jr. 2012. "The President is Very Acutely Ill." *Prologue Magazine* 44(2). https://www.archives.gov/publications/prologue/2012/fall/truman-ill.html

[292] Lynch has an extensive filmography, though is best known for her Emmy-winning performance as Sue Sylvester in *Glee*. She appears again in "Two Cathedrals (2.22)."

[293] McNally cites Section 202 of the National Security Act of 1947. The passage creates and specifies the position of Secretary of Defense. McNally (accurately) quotes the passage as saying, "The Secretary of Defense shall be the principal assistant to the President in all matters relating to the national security." However, McNally then claims the scope of those duties is unclear; this is wrong. The passage establishes four responsibilities of the Secretary of Defense, summarized in order of the subheading: (1) establishing general policies for the military, (2) exercising "general direction" over the military, (3) eliminating "unnecessary duplication" in military responsibilities and procurement, and (4) preparing reports on the budget for the branches of the armed forces. As a matter of fact, this passage establishes responsibility for command of the military absent the presence of the President fall to the Secretary of Defense under subheadings (1) and (2); there is some vagueness to "general direction" in (2).

[294] The show refers to the "New England Dairy Farming Compact," probably a stand-in for the real Northeast Interstate Dairy Compact of 1997, which set the price of milk purchased by processors in the region. Because of the commerce clause of the United States Constitution (Article I, Section 8, Clause 3), interstate compacts are subject to congressional approval. The Northeast Interstate Dairy Compact was replaced under the 2002 farm bill.

[295] The compact Bartlet voted on seems to restrict the pricing without subsidizing farmers for potential losses. The actual Northeast Interstate Dairy Compact actually benefited farmers, by setting a higher price for processors purchasing milk from the farm, so

[296] This feels different given the ongoing 2024 election between Joe Biden and Donald Trump, where age and mental acuity is a major issue.

[297] Leo points out Bartlet getting elected to Congress and Governor is not a political feat given his family's extensive history in New Hampshire. We have seen similar critiques directed at (for example) the Bush and Kennedy families.

[298] Sam references the (real life) crash of the Exxon Valdez (1989) and damage to Exxon sales. The company treats this solely as a public relations issue.

[299] The studio is called "Atlantis." *The Newsroom* focuses on Atlantis World Media and Atlantis Cable News as the fictional company.

[300] Emily's List is a real organization dedicated to raising money for women running for office and advancing gender equality issues.

[301] References to a coup fee difference, after the attempt to circumvent the electoral college through false filings following the 2020 election.

[302] The scene is shot in LAX.

[303] The episode alternates between talking about the Grand Unified Theory and the Theory of Everything, almost interchangeably. These are different things. The Grand Unified Theory is a label for a set of proposed theories which hold, at high energy levels, certain basic natural forces (electromagnetic, strong, and weak nuclear forces) are all a single force. The Theory of Everything is a broader theoretical class of theories which would combine a Grand Unified Theory (or some other theory covering the electromagnetic, strong, and weak forces) with other basic theories, like theories of subatomic particles. The White House staff does not understand the basics here, which is realistic.

[304] The contemporary CPI is calculated in several different ways. The Bureau of Labor Statistics keeps a separate CPI for urban consumers, because costs in urban areas (especially rent) are much higher. During the early 2010s, there was consideration of shifting to revised CPI system, but those changes were never adopted. The changes discussed in this episode are focused on weighting; those changes have been implemented.

[305] Both Denton and Creskoff appeared in *Desperate Housewives*. Kathryn Joosten (who plays Mrs. Landingham) is the narrator of *Desperate Housewives*. Denton appeared in 180 episodes of the show as Mike Delfino.

[306] This episode hits differently after September 11, 2001. After 9/11, the FBI engaged in intelligence gathering operations targeting groups in violation of civil liberties, especially targeting Muslim religious communities.

[307] Federal election law prohibits the use of government resources for campaigning. There are clear cases of government resources, like the use of public funds. The Bartlet White House arguably does violate electioneering law at some points in the series, but the President's phone calls are not an issue.

[308] Election Night (4.07)

[309] My fourth-grade teacher, Mrs. Melton, insisted words like "stuff," "thing," and "whatever" as stand-in nouns was bad writing. This is a good lesson for fourth graders, but that stuff works sometimes.

[310] Sam understates the severity of constitutional violations during the civil rights movement. We find in 2.16 that civil rights and law enforcement action is an area of expertise for Sam (which ties into his focus on civil liberties and privacy in 1.09). For longer discussion of the civil rights violations by the FBI during the movement for Black civil rights during the '50s and '60s, see:

David Garrow. 2015. *The FBI and Martin Luther King, Jr.: from "Solo" to Memphis*. Open Road Media.

Tim Weiner. 2012. *Enemies: A History of the FBI.* New York: Random House.

[311] It is convention to stand when the President enters or exits the room.

[312] Jenna Jacobs is a fictionalization of Laura Schlessinger. Schlessinger had a Ph.D. in physiology.

[313] The White House staff seems frustrated with this outcome, but perhaps they shouldn't be. Historically, midterm elections are advantageous to the party out of the White House. Congress staying even is a good outcome, when usually the Republicans would significantly improve.

[314] Hayes' treatment throughout the episode is transparently sexist, starting with Sam. Much of the White House staff fixates on Ainsley being a woman. Even at the time, this seems regressive and "boys club" from the supposed protagonists.

[315] Zades Mokae was an accomplished actor, especially on stage. He won a Tony award for his performance in "Master Harold"... and the Boys and was nominated for Song of Jacob Zulu. He also appeared in anti-apartheid films *Cry Freedom and A Dry White Season.*

[316] Among the pharmaceutical executives are Len Cariou (*Blue Bloods* and the original *Sweeny Todd*) and soap opera actor Michael Cavanaugh.

[317] The two common fictionalized countries Sorkin uses are Kumar (in the middle east) and Kundu (in Africa).

[318] There were extensive US and international sanctions on Iraq during the 1990s; selling drilling equipment would have violated those sanctions. The sanctions were controversial, some analysts argued sanctions contributed to the deaths of Iraqis, especially prior to the creation of the Oil-for-Food Program in 1995.

[319] Cecelia Dugger. November 25, 2008. "Study Cites Toll of AIDS Policy in South Africa." *The New York Times.* https://www.nytimes.com/2008/11/26/world/africa/26aids.html?pagewanted=all&_r=0

[320] Pride Chigwedere, et al. 2008. "Estimating the Lost Benefit of Antiretroviral Drug Use in South Africa." *JAIDS* 49(4): 410-415.

[321] Nimbala's translator is played by Michael Chinyamurindi. Chinyamurindi has a long filmography, though I remember him for his role in the live action version of *George of the Jungle.*

[322] Borlaug's work focused on the genetic modification of drought- and pest-resistant varieties of dwarf-wheat that had higher yield. Bartlet gets this account more-or-less right when talking to Leo in the following scene. Borlaug was eulogized as "the Father of the Green Revolution" when he died in 2009.

[323] Charlie makes fun of the President with a reference to Puccini. This is the second Puccini reference, after Post Hoc, Ergo Propter Hoc (1.02).

[324] There is some conflicting discussion about whether the character of Hayes is based on Ann Coulter (who was not yet famous for her more incendiary, racist views at the time); the claim she's "going to be a star" does seem to be a reference to a career trajectory like Coulter's.

[325] The economics of pricing pharmaceuticals is complicated, because of the need to compensate companies for their up-front investment in research, but often the pricing does reflect questionable market dynamics. This has increasingly affected the United States domestic market in recent years.
Lisa D. Ellis. March 14, 2019. "The Need to Treat the Ailing U.S. Pharmaceutical Pricing System." *Inside Health.* https://www.hsph.harvard.edu/ecpe/united-states-pharmaceutical-pricing/

[326] This includes the Trans-African Highway network, a massive construction effort started in 2007 to build about 35,000 miles of highway around the continent. Much of its major corridors are already substantially complete (TAH 1; TAH 2; TAH 4).

[327] In 7.21, this proposal is considered directly when C.J. is offered a job by a billionaire (Xander Berkeley). She cites the failure of aid projects based on the lack of highways. However, at the point that episode aired, the TAH project was already being discussed and funding put together by the African Union.

328 Global Health Observatory. "Number of People Dying from HIV-related causes." https://www.who.int/data/gho/data/indicators/indicator-details/GHO/number-of-deaths-due-to-hiv-aids

329 Given the sexism Hayes encounters during the preceding episode, C.J. is right.

330 Larroquette is an established actor with a tendency for playing lawyers (*Night Court*; *The Practice*; *Boston Legal*).

331 Sam mentions the Southern Poverty Law Center, a real organization dedicated to combatting extremism.

332 Tribbey is an abrasive character through most of this episode. Ainsley showing admiration is noteworthy, especially before Tribbey has Ainsley's back in firing Brookline and Joyce.

333 Sam mentions *Hunter* by William Pierce. Hunter is white supremacist propaganda, a novel in which the "protagonist" murders interracial couples. It is dedicated to Joseph Paul Franklin, a white supremacist serial killer who targeted interracial couples, those he believed promoted interracial relationships, and synagogues. Franklin was motivated by the desire to start a race war. Franklin was executed by lethal injection in 2013.

334 In 2006, congress passed the Stolen Valor Act, which made stolen valor a misdemeanor. In 2012, in United States v. Alvarez, the Supreme Court struck down the Stolen Valor Act for violating free speech rights.

335 Bly was an American journalist who investigated brutality in mental institutions. Her exposé of the Women's Lunatic Asylum was responsible for major reforms and is a precursor to modern investigative journalism. The reports were republished in her book *Ten Days in a Mad-House*.

336 The SPLC has an extensive and ongoing record of such litigation. One can view their case docket on their website: https://www.splcenter.org/seeking-justice/case-docket

337 Corroborating this point has been difficult, but Emily Procter says this with confidence in her interview with *The West Wing Weekly*; that's authoritative.
The West Wing Weekly. October 11, 2016. "2.04: In This White House (with Emily Procter and Ambassador Deborah Birx)."

338 These are not the most scholarly resources on the subject, but provide extensive links to the instances of homophobia, racism, and antisemitism.
Anti-Defamation League. September 17, 2015. "ADL Calls Ann Coulter's Tweets "Ugly, Spiteful and Anti-Semitic."" https://www.adl.org/news/press-releases/adl-calls-ann-coulters-tweets-ugly-spiteful-and-anti-semitic
Karl Frisch. August 7, 2010. "Homophobe Ann Coulter—"The Right Wing Judy Garland"—to headline party for gay GOP group." *Media Matters*. https://www.mediamatters.org/ann-coulter/homophobe-ann-coulter-right-wing-judy-garland-headline-party-gay-gop-group
Roque Planas. November 14, 2013. "Ann Coulter: Still Racist." *Huffington Post*. https://www.huffpost.com/entry/ann-coulter-immigrants-criminals_n_4273401

339 There are several major political philosophers who argue this point, prominent among them Jeremy Waldron.
Jeremy Waldron. 1999. *Law and Disagreement*. Oxford University Press.

340 I owe a great deal to my former teacher Jeremy Fantl.
Jeremy Fantl. 2018. *The Limitations of the Open Mind*. Oxford University Press.

341 This isn't true. There is money around foreign relations.

342 This storyline is probably inspired by the 1996 Comprehensive Nuclear-Test-Ban Treaty (CTBT) passed by the United Nations in 1996. The US signed the treaty, but the treaty was never ratified. Of the active nuclear powers, only two (the United Kingdom and France) have ratified the CTBT.

343 During the Trump administration, a White House staffer leaked a schedule showing that 60% of President Trump's scheduled time was listed unstructured "executive time."

Eliana Johnson and Daniel Lippman. Oct 29, 2018. "9 Hours of Executive Time: Trump's unstructured days define his presidency." *Politico*. https://www.politico.com/story/2018/10/29/trump-daily-schedule-executive-time-944996

[344] Most major media outlets separate editorial content from news content, though practices vary. This became relevant in lawsuits concerning Fox News Channel, which maintained its news and editorial side are separate entities for the purpose of defamation lawsuits.
David Folkenflik. "You Literally Can't Believe the Facts Tucker Carlson Tells You. So Say Fox's Lawyers." *NPR*. https://www.npr.org/2020/09/29/917747123/you-literally-cant-believe-the-facts-tucker-carlson-tells-you-so-say-fox-s-lawye

[345] Lazarev is an accomplished Belarussian actor. His major American appearances include *The Sum of All Fears* and *Lord of War*.

[346] Ukraine was in government tumult during the late 1990s. Ukraine became an independent country in 1991. The country was run by President Leonid Kravchuk from 1991-1994, until he lost reelection to Leonid Kuchma. Kuchma was President until 2005. It's unclear whether Konanov is a general reformer or draws from real-life reformer Victor Yuschenko; who became President following a tumultuous election, the Orange Revolution, and an assassination attempt by poisoning.

[347] A page discussing this episode at the workplace safety site MySafetySign directly points out that the scope of coverage of OSHA has changed significantly over time.
https://www.mysafetysign.com/blog/osha-exemption-coverage-record-keeping/

[348] Throughout this episode, they refer to "the Ukraine." This was common at the time but is presently regarded as somewhat offensive. "The Ukraine" refers to a region; "Ukraine" refers to a nation. Referring to the region is often taken to imply denying the nationhood, which has been an issue since the Russian occupation of the Donbas region (2014) and the Russian war of aggression (2022) against Ukraine. Much appreciation to my partner Shelby Magid (an expert on Eurasian foreign policy) for catching this during our rewatch.

[349] This is another questionable case of sexist writing. Ainsley (a White House lawyer) is encouraging C.J. to ignore professional responsibilities in favor of romantic interest.

[350] Starr has appeared in a range of films, including *Miller's Crossing*, *Ed Wood*, and *Dumb and Dumber*. He only appears in this scene of *The West Wing*.

[351] The current keyboard layout, the QWERTY formulation (named for the ordering of keys on the top left) is ergonomically problematic. It was designed for typewriters, to keep keys from crashing into each other by distancing commonly used letters (note the positioning of vowels). The more ergonomic design is the DVORAK keyboard, though it has never seen significant uptake, because we are all trained on QWERTY.

[352] The President says "it's not a democracy" which is not correct. America is a representative democracy, but this is still a form of democracy.

[353] For wide-ranging discussion on the JCPOA, see the Brookings Institute's page on the subject. https://www.brookings.edu/series/debating-the-iran-deal/

[354] There are many gulfs in the Middle East; presumably this is the Persian Gulf.

[355] Josh giving romantic advice to Donna is the pot calling the kettle black.

[356] Iraq was ruled by Saddam Hussein. The sanctions in place were implemented in 1990 following Operation Desert Storm. Oil exports from Iraq were legal in some circumstances under the Oil For Food Program (OFFP) starting in 1996, but payments were held in escrow and could only be used to purchase and import certain goods approved by the Security Council committee. Sanctions enforcement was technically multinational but run by the United States.

[357] Iraqi sanctions were approved by the United Nations Security Council; the United States couldn't alter the fine.

[358] Ainsley's relationship with food is a running joke throughout the show.

[359] President Clinton signed the Defense of Marriage Act (generally "DOMA") into law in 1996. Section 3 of DOMA held, for the purposes of federal definition including spousal

benefits, marriage was between one man and one woman. Section 3 of DOMA was struck down by the Supreme Court in Obergefell v. Hodges (2015).

360 This was the position adopted by the Clinton administration in defense of signing DOMA. Until at least 2008, this was the standard position within the Democratic Party, including both Hillary Clinton and Barack Obama during the 2008 Presidential primary.

361 This hits differently after the Trump administration, because the notion of vetting and evaluating policy proposals wasn't really a thing for that administration. The Trump administration was full of policy proposals because of their political impacts; many of those proposals were never fully implemented because they were logistically impossible. The most notable being the "build the wall" position, because there are logistical issues which make building a full wall along the southern border impossible (e.g., erosion makes large parts of the border unsuitable for construction, costs and labor, etc.).

362 This was true of DOMA in '96. In the House, DOMA passed 342-67 (about 84%); 224 Republican votes and 118 Democratic votes in favor and only one Republican and 65 Democratic (and one independent) vote against, with 22 abstentions. In the Senate, it passed with 85 votes; 53 Republicans and 32 Democrats voted for it and 14 Democrats (and no Republicans) voted against it, with one abstention.

363 Again, Sorkin writes a "devil's advocate" argument that sucks. Lots of people opposed to interracial marriage argued "racial purity" and "heritage" are values incompatible with interracial marriage, and that interracial marriage, school integration, etc. was "legislating values." The distinction Skinner makes is just false.

364 In 2004, John Kerry supported a Missouri law banning gay marriage and said, had he been a resident of Missouri, he would have voted with the 71% of voters who voted for the ban on gay marriage.
Steven Thomma. August 5, 2004. "Missouri approves measure to ban gay marriages." *Knight Ridder Tribune News.*

365 The phrase "Judeo-Christian morality" is subject to derision among many Jewish people. The phrase exclusively picks out right-wing Christian priorities, in contrast to the broadly liberal orientation of the majority of American Jews. It also ignores traditional Jewish ethics and scholarship, where Jewish religious teaching is radically different from Christian teaching.

366 The "we can't pay out those extra social security benefits" line is nonsense, but the line is a throwaway for Sorkin.

367 In this note, Josh mentions Lawrence Tribe's critique of DOMA. Tribe is a real person, a Harvard law professor. Skinner points out that Tribe is not a Supreme Court Justice.

368 Perhaps the most famous outing campaign occurred during the reelection campaign of George W. Bush during 2004, when Michael Rogers and several others outed Bush campaign officials Karl Rove, Ralph Reed, and Ken Melhman, as well as Rep. Ed Schrock (R-VA). Rogers discussed the ethics of this practice at Politico.
Michael Rogers. June 26, 2014. "Why I Outed Gay Republicans." *Politico.* https://www.politico.com/magazine/story/2014/06/mike-rogers-outed-gay-republicans-108368/

369 Signorile outed David Geffen, Andrew Dice Clay, and gossip columnist Liz Smith.

370 Exodus International was a "pray-away-the-gay" ministry. Paulk was a major fixture in the movement, an "ex-gay" man married to an "ex-lesbian" woman. Paulk has since come out against conversion therapy practices. For longer discussion, I recommend the documentary Pray Away (2021), in which Paulk and others involved in Exodus are extensively interviewed.

371 They refer to "Fujin" in the opener. Presumably, this refers to the province of Fujian (which is coastal) and not the city of Fujin (which is not).

372 Some discussions note Ed and Larry are a stand-in for Rosencrantz and Guildenstern, the interchangeable Shakespeare characters from Hamlet about whom Stoppard wrote Rosencrantz and Guildenstern are Dead. The coin continues coming up heads in the Stoppard play.

373 The Turkey Pardoning tradition is extensive. President Clinton once (incorrectly) claimed the tradition came from President Truman, but Truman never issued a "pardon." President Lincoln issued a pardon at the request of his son Tad; President Kennedy associated the tradition with Thanksgiving after returning a live turkey in 1963; President Nixon arranged to send turkeys to a petting zoo; the first instance of the Thanksgiving pardon as practiced today was by President Reagan in 1987 and formalized by President George H.W. Bush in 1989. Thanks to PBS for their video on the history: https://youtu.be/id69ZdHyEOM
374 Josh routinely deals with immigration and refugee crises throughout the series.
375 Sorkin likes the phrase "all about Eve." The President says Leo's sister is "all about Eve."
376 During the last several years, the international community has focused on Chinese oppression of the Muslim Uyghur minority in Xinxiang, in concentration camps. China still persecutes Christians, including protestant pastors, though details on severity and extent of such persecution are difficult to assess based on limited information coming out of China. Human Rights Watch. December 13, 2018. "China: Repression of Christian Church Intensifies." https://www.hrw.org/news/2018/12/13/china-repression-christian-church-intensifies
377 This is F. William Parker's second appearance, after the pilot (1.01). These are his only two appearances.
378 The song is "We Gather Together," and we hear the children singing it at the end of the episode. It is a 16th century Dutch hymn by Adrianus Valerius. The song celebrates a Dutch military victory over the Spanish at Turnhout.
379 Like F William Parker, this is Annie Corlie's second (after the pilot) and final appearance in the show.
380 Caldwell is right. Religious freedom was explicitly added to the Chinese constitution in 1982 and a handful of denominations and churches are recognized by the Chinese Communist Party. The rest are pushed underground. In Catholicism, for example, there is the so-called "Catholic Patriotic Association" which allows for some forms of Catholic but denies many Catholic doctrines; the CPA was not in communion with the Vatican until 2018 when Pope Francis recognized some bishops. This decision was controversial, with Cardinal Joseph Zen Ze-kiun (formerly Bishop of Hong Kong) criticizing the decision to work with the CPA and the CCP. Rev. Caldwell refers to Catholics being imprisoned and tortured for recognizing the authority of the Pope, which is well documented. Wen, Joseph. 2018, October 24. "The Pope Doesn't Understand China." *The New York Times*. Archived: https://archive.ph/3P9YR
381 As a convention, I use Evangelical (upper case) to refer to the movement of protestant organizations and churches based on political alignment; this is like the convention for Conservative (upper case) to recognize that some people may be conservative (ideologically, lower case) or evangelical without being a part of those movements.
382 Daniel Schorr. May 15, 2006. "Bush Loses Evangelical Trail on the Way to the Border." *NPR: All Things Considered*. https://www.npr.org/templates/story/story.php?storyId=5406153
383 The most vivid illustration is the International Day of Prayer for the Persecuted Church, which is spearheaded by major Christian denominations: the United States Conference of Catholic Bishops, the World Evangelical Alliance, and the Southern Baptist Conventions. These institutions also operate organizations which advocate only on behalf of persecuted Christians.
384 The viewer never sees the photo, only Toby's reaction to it.
385 This is Hedwell's only appearance on *The West Wing*. She also appeared in two episodes of *Homeland* and three episodes of *Mare of Easttown*.
386 Sorkin connects religious persecution in two places through this episode: the violent, state-sanctioned religious persecution of Christians by the People's Republic of China and the individualized bullying of religious minorities in the United States. The United States government does not actively engage in religious persecution (at least, not to the degree of

China or Saudi Arabia), but it also does not protect its citizens from religious persecution effectively, even in public spaces like schools.

[387] Henry O was born in Shanghai in 1927. He immigrated to the United States to pursue work as an actor. He appears in *The Last Emperor* (1987) and *The Sopranos*, among many other places.

[388] This creates a second logistical problem, not addressed in the episode. If the refugees escape the INS detention facility, then they will not be documented in the United States, which creates problems when it comes to getting jobs and the like.

[389] There is a Galileo space probe, though it studied Jupiter and its moons, rather than Mars. The Galileo probe was launched October 18, 1989, entered service December 8, 1995, and ended its mission September 21, 2003.

[390] Aquino is fictional.

[391] Statehood for Puerto Rico isn't taboo anymore, after several votes in the 2010s. In 1998, shortly before this episode, there was a plebiscite (popular vote) which rejected the status quo. There was another in 2012. The 2012 plebiscite was inconclusion, but spurred several subsequent votes, including another plebiscite in 2017 (where statehood received 97% of the vote) and 2020 (where it received 52%).

[392] The International Whaling Commission instituted a ban on commercial whaling in 1982 (implemented in 1985), which bans all whaling except when conducted by indigenous peoples on a subsistence basis. Several countries, including Iceland, don't abide by the ban. The United States allows commercial whaling of beluga whales in Alaska.

[393] This storyline is loosely inspired by George H.W. Bush's express dislike of broccoli.

[394] The theme of C.J. being less intelligent than other staffers runs throughout the first two seasons, most notably the census arc in "Mr. Willis of Ohio (1.06)." This is one point area for criticizing sexism in Sorkin's writing.

[395] Putting someone on a stamp doesn't indicate endorsement. The United States has recognized Simón Bolívar on a stamp in 1958; no one thought that was an endorsement of Bolívar. Declaration of Independence signer Josiah Bartlett (one of President Bartlet's ancestors, despite the difference in spelling) was honored in 1976.

[396] This is Cornwell's only appearance in *The West Wing*. Cornwell was a British actress who worked with the Royal Shakespeare Company and National Theater.

[397] The President bounces off a major criticism, that "classical music" refers to a formal style, rather than music of a particular era. "It is not classical music if the guy finished writing it this afternoon." Bartlet says, "anything written after 1960 sucks," to Charlie. He then disparages a series of real pieces of modern classical music.

[398] Richard Andreychuk is a fictional hockey player. Dave Andreychuck was a Canadian hockey player active when the episode aired (playing for the Buffalo Sabres) and won the Stanley Cup with the Tampa Bay Lightning in '03-'04. Dave was inducted into the Hockey Hall of Fame in 2017 and is 15th among goal scorers all time with 640.

[399] The assessment of what counts as a "real scandal" changed during the Trump administration, but *The West Wing* wrestles with this, especially during the tail end of season two and through Season Three with the fallout of President Bartlet's multiple sclerosis cover-up.

[400] United States missile security has also come under scrutiny in recent years.
CBS News/Associated Press. May 24, 2018. "US Troops Guarding Nuclear Missiles Took LSD, Air Force records show." https://www.cbsnews.com/news/us-air-force-airment-lsd-cocaine-warren-air-force-base-wyoming-nuclear-missile-sites-records-show/
Joe Pappalardo. January 16, 2014. "The Nuke Silo Cheating Scandal, Explained." *Popular Mechanics*. https://www.popularmechanics.com/military/a12003/the-nuke-silo-cheating-scandal-explained-16388244/

[401] Arkin appears as Keyworth in three other episodes of *The West Wing*: "Night Five" (3.14), "Posse Comitatus" (3.22), and "Holy Night" (4.11).

[402] This is Bedi's only appearance on *The West Wing*. She had previously appeared on the John Wells show *E.R.* (7.01).

[403] The organization is fictional. The relevant organization would be the American Trauma Society.

[404] This is an odd practice for an outpatient setting, where the ability to follow a patient is limited, but there is precedent for having a second health care worker monitor patients with psychiatric conditions. I cannot find out whether this was standard practice for ATS.

[405] Slips in therapeutic context are a Sorkinism. There are several in this episode. There is the instance of talking about Josh's sister in "The Crackpots and These Women" (1.05) and in "Night Five" (3.13). There are similar instances in *The Newsroom* (1.08 and 1.09).

[406] Zaharian never appears on screen.

[407] The SPR is an oil stockpile created following the energy crisis in 1973; there are laws governing the levels of SPR and the rate oil can be withdrawn. The SPR is filled through direct purchases (by the Department of Energy) and royalties for contracts. The size of the SPR was significantly increased following the September 11, 2001, attack. Since the mid-2010s, filling and withdrawing from the SPR has become increasingly political, as the Government Accountability Office recommended lowering the size of the SPR. In 2020, President Trump attempted to use purchasing by the SPR to create a windfall for oil companies when oil prices dropped (from low demand during the coronavirus pandemic). In 2022, President Biden released oil from the reserve to decrease oil prices when prices spiked (partly due to Russia's invasion of Ukraine and energy-related sanctions).
Department of Energy. Mar 19, 2020. "Department of Energy Executes on Direction of President Trump, Announces Solicitation to Purchase Crude Oil for the SPR to Provide Relief to the American Energy Industry."
Jacob Fischler. Mar 5, 2022. "Biden OKs Release of 30 million barrels of oil from the Strategic Petroleum Reserve." NBC 12 Richmond, VA.

[408] Whitehead appears again in "A Change Is Gonna Come" (6.07).

[409] Cailloux is fictional, though perhaps based on successful impressionist Gustave Caillebotte, as Thatch compares Cailloux to Corbet, "who was considerably more gifted." The Cailloux painting is called "The Cliffs at Etretat." There are several paintings called "The Cliffs of Etretat," including Corbet (1869) and Claude Monet (1885).

[410] Etyl Leder is not an actress. She was a Holocaust survivor and the wife of director and writer Paul Leder. Paul and Etyl had three children, including Mimi and Reuben Leder, who would direct and write (respectively) the short "Sentimental Journey" based on Paul and Etyl's story following the liberation of Auschwitz. (Paul was an American soldier in WWII.)
Army Archerd. September 25, 1998. "Leders to film parents' WWII love story." Variety Magazine. https://variety.com/1998/voices/columns/leders-to-film-parents-wwii-love-story-1117480750/

[411] Repatriation of art taken during the Holocaust has been a major issue since the war, since identifying provenance can be complicated. Many auction houses and museums ignore provenance research when it is expedient to do so. This issue reemerged in May, 2023, with Christie's auction house selling the collection of jewelry belonging to Heidi Horten, whose husband Helmut was a Nazi collaborator and used Nazi property laws to build his wealth.

[412] This episode predates public discussion of post-traumatic stress disorder, especially following 9/11 and widespread post-traumatic stress disorder induced over entire cities (including New York).

[413] A very common Sorkinism throughout *The West Wing* and other Sorkin shows.

[414] Scott Winant is a director and producer whose work includes *Breaking Bad* and *True Blood*. He won an Emmy for work on *Thirtysomething* in 1990.

[415] Sam notes it the patient's bill of rights doesn't matter without the ability to sue; there's no way for patients to hold providers legally accountable. The Senate and House passed a version

of the patient's bill of rights in 2001, but the reconciled version of the bill failed after President Bush threatened a veto unless the Senate removed a passage allowing patients to sue.

[416] Karen Cahill is based on columnist Maureen Dowd, known for her work on the Bill Clinton sex scandals (she won a Pulitzer prize in 1999) and later for accidentally taking too much of a marijuana edible.

[417] Huffman is best known for her roles on *Desperate Housewives* and *Transamerica*, as well as being convicted of mail and honest services frauds in the 2019 Varsity Blues college admissions scandal. She starred in Sorkin's series *Sports Night.*

[418] Kazakhstan declared independence from the Soviet Union on December 16, 1991; the Soviet Union disintegrated on December 26th. Kazakhstan inherited about 1,400 nuclear warheads. Kazakhstan signed the Treaty on the Non-Proliferation of Nuclear Weapons. By the time this episode aired, Kazakhstan no longer possessed nuclear weapons; their stockpile had been destroyed in 1995. They remain a major producer of low-enrichment uranium. Kyrgyzstan did not inherit nuclear weapons and is also a party to the Central Asian Nuclear-Weapons-Free-Zone.

Putz, Catherine. 2022. "How Did Kazakhstan Give Up the Bomb?" The Diplomat. https://thediplomat.com/2022/02/how-did-kazakhstan-give-up-the-bomb/

[419] This is a Sorkinism he carries over from *Sports Night* (2.02), where Dan (Josh Charles) makes a similar gaffe during a breakfast with then-First Lady Hillary Clinton (who does not appear on camera either) over "secular" and "non-secular"/"sectarian" programs.

[420] Stark mentions small businesses suffer, and unemployment goes up with increases in the minimum wage. This was a Republican talking point going back to at least the Reagan administration; this is not what the contemporary economic data indicates. The effect of minimum wage shifts is more complicated. Jeff Chapman noted in 2004 that raising the minimum wage does not correlate with appreciable job loss at a state or federal level; Jeffrey Clemens more recently notes (Yoe 2021) companies may use other measures to save costs and compensate for wage increases.

Chapman, Jeff. 2004. "Employment and the Minimum Wage—Evidence from Recent State Labor Market Trends." Economic Policy Institute. https://www.epi.org/publication/briefing papers_bp150/

Yoe, Jonathan. 2021. "A $15 minimum wage changes more than just take home pay." *Bureau of Labor Statistics.* https://www.bls.gov/opub/mlr/2021/beyond-bls/a-15-minimum-wage-changes-more-than-just-take-home-pay.htm

[421] This seems to have come to Sorkin by way of Emily Procter (who plays Ainsley Hayes). Procter says this happened to her during a lunch meeting with Sorkin.

The West Wing Weekly. October 11, 2017. "2.04: In This White House (with Emily Procter and Ambassador Deborah Birx)."

[422] They refer to the event simply as "The Will Rogers Dinner." This may be a reference to the fundraiser by the Will Rogers Memorial Fund, which merged with the Foundation of Motion Picture Pioneers in 2002 (a year after the episode). Will Rogers was a Cherokee humorist and early pioneer in film (first in silent and then "talkies"). Rogers mounted a mock presidential campaign in 1928 as the "Anti-Bunk Party."

[423] The missile defense system is a direct criticism of the Reagan era Strategic Defense Initiative (commonly called Star Wars) to shoot down missiles in anticipation of a Soviet nuclear strike. The program cost trillions and never produced an effective defense system.

[424] The Global Defense Council is a fictitious organization based on the environmentalist group the Natural Resource Defense Council, which is a legal organization that advocates environmental issues. The NRDC was founded in 1970. It is primarily a litigation organization, but also maintains lobbying and educational wings.

[425] In the late '90s, there was significant environmental terrorism. These include the 1992 sabotage of Japanese whaling vessels by the Sea Shepherd Conservation Society and "tree

spiking" (inserting metal rods into trees to prevent removal) by Earth First! Some of these cases are controversial, as the FBI and local police were found to have violated the civil rights of Earth First! leaders during investigations.
Zamora, Jim Herron. Jun 12, 2002. "After 11 Years, Jury Vindicates Earth First Pair." *San Francisco Chronicle.* https://web.archive.org/web/20100209025943/http://www.sfgate.com/cgi-bin/article.cgi?file=%2Fc%2Fa%2F2002%2F06%2F12%2FMN87302.DTL
[426] "Cap and trade" is an environmental regulation that caps pollution but allows companies to sell their allowance to other companies. If a company has a one-ton CO^2 cap, but the company comes in at 0.5-tons, they can sell the remaining 0.5-ton allowance to another company. The proposal is supposed to restrict pollution while also providing a business incentive (a "cash incentive") to decrease their use, meeting environmental benchmarks.
[427] It's unclear whether this is a stand-in for the White House Correspondent's Dinner, which involves roasting the President. There is a dinner fundraiser for the Will Rogers Pioneer Fund, but the President doesn't attend.
[428] The episode refers to "environmental terrorism" when the appropriate term is "eco-terrorism." (When this episode aired, that terminology wasn't established.) Eco-terrorism generally, though not exclusively, focuses on property damage and disrupting projects. This use of eco-terrorism, like survivalists in "The State Dinner" (1.07) and anti-abortion terrorists in the pilot (1.01), illustrates a difference in discussions of terrorism prior to 9/11.
James F. Jarboe. February 12, 2002. "The Threat of Eco-Terrorism." Testimony Before the House Resources Committee, Subcommittee on Forests and Forest Health. https://archives.fbi.gov/archives/news/testimony/the-threat-of-eco-terrorism
[429] Marbury is played for laughs. This ages badly, as many of his remarks are sexist, including referring to Margaret as "buxom."
[430] The Anti-Ballistic Missile Treaty was an arms control treaty signed by Nixon and Brezehnev in 1972. The treated limited both the United States and Soviet Union to only two missile research complexes with 100 missiles each. The United States withdrew from the Treaty in 2001, under President George W. Bush, citing nuclear threats from countries other than Russia and a need to increase the United States' arsenal.
[431] This episode aired before the political polarization and media attention on the White House Correspondent's Dinner. The first high-profile instance at the dinner was Colbert's roast of George W. Bush, after which the dinner got increased national attention.
[432] Sorkin has worked as a ghostwriter for speeches in the years since *The West Wing*, though it's hard to know how extensively, because ghostwriting is typically anonymous.
[433] The "friends are honest with each other" line is also used in The State Dinner (1.07).
[434] Marbury says, "we're both signatories to the '72 ABM treaty." This isn't true. The only two signatories were the United States and Soviet Union. The United Kingdom was not a signatory.
[435] Toby yells at the President in 2.18. Both he and Josh have moments of unprofessional comportment in the oval office this season.
[436] This is a variation on a line from late 19th century Speaker of the House Thomas Brackett Reed, "A statesman is a successful politician who is dead," and adapted by President Truman (after leaving the White House, from remarks in 1958).
[437] Sorkin likes giving viewers an already developed environment. Using shorthand terms without exposition is a way to establish what's going on, set pacing, and draw attention to something (in this case, the commission) even if the viewer doesn't know what it is yet. This is a sharp contrast to Sorkin's sometimes wordy expository style.
[438] *Capitol Beat* is a program throughout *The West Wing*. It is structured like *State of the Union*.
[439] Scandals around invitations to the *State of the Union* are common.
[440] Charlie uses the code to get Leo's attention in "Bad Moon Rising" (2.19).
[441] Dr. Bartlet uses the line, "don't talk to me like I'm other people." This is a Sorkinism.

442 After protests about police brutality and the Black Lives Matter movement, this discussion feels different. The situation doesn't have any footage associated with it, as it almost certainly would today.

443 The VAWA expands federal investment into the investigation and prosecution of crimes against women, especially domestic violence, and setting up civil litigation for victims of such crimes. It was signed by Clinton in 1994, reauthorized by Clinton in 2000 and then by Bush in 2005. Further reauthorization was disrupted and (following a short extension in 2018) the bill lapse in 2019. A reauthorization was passed by the house in both 2019 and 2021 and it was fully reauthorized as part of the 2022 appropriations bill through 2027.
Ashley Killough. April 4, 2019. "House Passes Reauthorization of Violence Against Women Act." *CNN Politics*. https://www.cnn.com/2019/04/04/politics/house-passes-violence-against-women-act-reauthorization/index.html
Caroline Vakil. December 16, 2021. "Senators reach deal on framework for reauthorizing Violence Against Women Act." *The Hill*. https://thehill.com/homenews/senate/586217-senators-reach-deal-on-framework-for-reauthorizing-violence-against-women-act

444 This came up during the Obama administration, as Obama was public about quitting smoking and had a policy agenda opposed to the tobacco industry.

445 One feature of C.J.'s character consistent throughout the show is her aptitude for presentation. She is clear and gets details like advising the officer to wear a suit rather than his uniform.

446 The photographs and video of caskets arriving from Vietnam were important to news coverage of the war. In 2003, just before declaring the war in Iraq, the Department of Defense issued a directive that the arrival of caskets would not be ceremonial and would be closed to the press.
Millbank, Dana. Oct 21, 2003. "Curtains Ordered for Media Coverage of Returning Coffins." *Washington Post*. https://www.washingtonpost.com/archive/politics/2003/10/21/curtains-ordered-for-media-coverage-of-returning-coffins/13375c81-187e-4f91-a565-2ce8f3bf3549/

447 This issue was also discussed in "Mandatory Minimums" (1.20) and through the end of the first season.

448 Begley only appears in this scene *The West Wing*. He is famous for *St. Elsewhere*; he was nominated for an Emmy in six consecutive years.

449 "I'm going to own your ass" is a Sorkinism used throughout *The West Wing* and *The Newsroom*.

450 Most governments have an explicit policy against negotiating with terrorists, especially in kidnappings. These policies are based on the theory that allowing negotiation incentivizes terrorists to engage in kidnapping. However, most governments do not stand by this policy universally and do engage in ransom payments under some conditions. This includes the United States.
Office of the Coordinator for Counterterrorism. November 2001. "Fact Sheet: International Terrorism: American Hostages." *US Foreign Policy Agenda* 6(3): 32-33. https://www.google.com/books/edition/Terrorism_Threat_Assessment_countermeasu/pMGWdTJEtiIC?hl=en&gbpv=1&pg=PA32&printsec=frontcover
Rukmini Callimachi. July 29, 2014. "Paying Ransoms, Europe Bankrolls Al Quaeda Terror." *The New York Times*. https://www.nytimes.com/2014/07/30/world/africa/ransoming-citizens-europe-becomes-al-qaedas-patron.html

451 This agreement is a source of tensions in continuity throughout season one. Many of the President's decisions seem motivated by reelection. Leo and the President make this explicit in "Let Bartlet Be Bartlet" (1.19), when Bartlet says it's "more important than reelection."

452 The show received praise for its discussion of multiple sclerosis. At the time, there was public misunderstanding of MS and degenerative illnesses.

453 Bartlet considers sending the CIA in with a blanket mission to destroy the drug cartel. While this option is treated as a clear ethical line, the scene doesn't mention that covert operations have been used to overthrow cartels and even governments in Central and South America; most famously Nicaragua under the Reagan administration.

Robert Parry and Peter Kornbluh. 1988. "Iran-Contra's Untold Story." *Foreign Policy* 72: 3-30.

Gary Webb. 2014. *Dark Alliance: The CIA, the contras, and the crack cocaine explosion.* Seven Stories Press.

454 This is Place's first appearance in *The West Wing*. She returns in "In The Room" (6.08) and "Impact Winter" (6.09).

455 The scheduling system does not associate classification with harm; rather, a drug is Schedule I if it has "no currently accepted medical use and a high potential for abuse" under DEA criterion. Since this episode, marijuana has seen widespread medical use and recreational legalization in many states. Federally, it is still a Schedule I narcotic, but the Department of Justice is in the process of changing marijuana to Schedule III.

456 The Family Values Leadership Council is not a real organization. The name is a hodgepodge names adopted by right-wing groups, including the Family Research Council.

457 Richard Schiff is responsible for the pink rubber ball, known to New Yorkers of a certain age as a Spalding. He explains how getting the ball was a logistical challenge.

The West Wing Weekly. February 14, 2017. "2.18: 17 People (with Richard Schiff, Emily Procter, Rebecca Walker, and More)." 7:00.

458 Superficially, this may seem reasonable; however, classification refers to legitimate medical use and potential for abuse. Calling classification a political and legal claim, but not a medical claim, is false.

459 This is a reference to Don Imus. Imus is mentioned at the radio event in "The Midterms" (2.03).

460 This is Knepper's only appearance in *The West Wing*.

461 This is a reference to C.J.'s time working in Hollywood, established in 2.02.

462 They also refer to "Liz," the President's oldest daughter. Liz does not appear until Season Five; she is Annie's mother, who President Bartlet refers to receiving the Raggedy Anne doll in the pilot.

463 It is a short soliloquy to Charlie, but gets the economics of protectionist tariffs right. Dropping prices on exported goods results in other countries increasing tariffs to protect domestic production. Japan drops the prices of the steel they're exporting; the United States imposes retaliatory tariffs to protect the American steel industry, so American companies don't just buy exclusively from Japanese importers.

464 This is established in "Six Meetings Before Lunch" (1.18).

465 Siemaszko appears as Ellie Bartlet in nine episodes, though this is her only appearance in the Sorkin-run era. She would not appear again until 7A WF 83429 (5.01).

466 Many mice used in laboratory testing are genetically modified to be susceptible to cancer. Oncomouse was modified to have an active oncogene that increases the mouse's susceptibility to cancer. Oncomouse was patented in 1988 (the patent lapsed into the public domain in 2005). Mice used in cancer testing are more susceptible to cancer.

467 One principal responsibility of the Surgeon General is to issue public health warnings. Maintaining medical accuracy and impartiality is important. This episode evokes Surgeon General Jocelyn Elders, who was fired by President Clinton in 1994 after suggesting masturbation "is part of human sexuality, and perhaps it should be taught," favoring marijuana legalization, and criticizing political emphasis on abortion.

468 Ellie says that endocrinology concerns disorders of the thyroid, which is only partly true. The thyroid is one organ in the endocrine system. Endocrinology involves the study of hormones and the organs that produce them, including the thyroid.

[469] At the time of writing, the IMDB synopsis says that Sam's father has been having an affair for 27 years. Perhaps this is a crossed wire; when Sorkin uses this as a plot device in *Sports Night* for Jeremy Goodwin (played by Joshua Malina), Goodwin says his father had the affair for 27 years. This plotline is recycled by Sorkin.

[470] Leo's reason for forgiving and reinstating Karen Larson in "Take Out The Trash Day "(1.13) includes their shared experiences with alcoholic fathers. This is another glimpse, though brief, into Leo's family.

[471] It's not clear why Sam is working on pardon recommendations; he may be evaluating recommendations made by the Office of the Pardon Attorney (within the Department of Justice), but taking a meeting on Daniel Gault and making direct recommendations is inappropriate.

[472] When this episode aired, the WTO was still relatively new; the WTO was established in 1995 as an independent agency to negotiate trade agreements and provide dispute resolution between countries. The principal criticism is, while putatively independent, the WTO is mostly led by people from wealthy countries. Negotiations and dispute resolutions favor those countries.

[473] The name "Daniel Gault" evokes the Ayn Rand character John Galt (in *Atlas Shrugged*). It is unclear if Daniel Gault is a reference to a particular person persecuted as a part of the Red Scare, but Sorkin does reference Whittaker Chambers and Alger Hiss (in the very first scene of the pilot, where Sam jokes about the "secret pumpkin").

[474] The Maxwell School is the graduate school focused on politics and public policy at Syracuse University.

[475] This is Maffia's only appearance in *The West Wing*; her chemistry with Schiff is great.

[476] Gregg is a frequent Sorkin player, cast in the stage shows for *A Few Good Men* and the sitcom *Sports Night*. Gregg appears as Agent Casper in eight episodes of *The West Wing*. He is also known for playing Agent Phil Coulson in the Marvel Cinematic Universe.

[477] Africa is larger than Greenland and South America is much larger than Europe, but the Mercator Projection represents those pairs as similar in size. Land masses towards the north and south poles appear larger (hence Greenland and northern Europe appearing large) while areas on and near the equator (including much of Africa and South America) appear smaller.

[478] They not Germany is much further north than it appears in the Mercator Projection. "Nothing's where you think it is."

[479] The Gall-Peters Projection is widely used, though there are other alternative models. The projection was created by Arno Peters (for whom it is named) to capture the relative size, based on the mathematics and description of James Gall. The issue discussed by Sorkin was widespread among cartographers at the time, though Sorkin influenced political uptake.
Jeremy Crampton. 1994. "Cartography's defining moment: The Peters projection controversy, 1974-1990." *Cartographica* 31(4): 16-32.
Mark Monmonier. 2004. *Rhumb Lines and Map Wars: A Social History of the Mercator Projection*. University of Chicago Press.

[480] The United States and the Soviet Union both ran decryption projects during the Cold War. The Venona Project was carried out from 1943 to 1980 by the Signal Intelligence Service (eventually the National Security Agency). This included discovering Soviet espionage at the Manhattan Project and other major operations.
Robert Louis Benson. 2001. *The Venona Story*. National Security Agency, Center for Cryptologic History.
John Earl Haynes and Harvey Klehr. 1999. *Venona: Decoding Soviet Espionage in America*. Yale Nota Bene.

[481] This view makes questionable assumptions but was widely advocated by the Democratic and Republican parties at the time. It also illustrates the Bartlet White House is similar to the Clinton White House on trade.

[482] At this point, we know (a) Toby and Leo have decided to set up the reelection campaign and (b) President Bartlet and his wife are arguing about his promise not to seek reelection, as a result of his multiple sclerosis.

[483] We eventually meet C.J.'s father in *The Long Goodbye* (4.13).

[484] Coe is an accomplished character actor. He appears in three episodes of *The West Wing* as Senator Stackhouse; his other two appearances are 4.04 (where he is a central character) and 4.06 (where he is uncredited).

[485] There are two sets of rules on the filibuster. One set of rules requires Senators who filibuster legislation speak the entire time to keep debate ongoing; this is "the talking filibuster" or "the standing filibuster" because it requires the Senator to speak to hold the floor. Another set of rules allows for a filibuster simply by refusing to pass a cloture motion closing debate. The latter has been effect in recent years.

[486] Josh refers to Mike Piazza, a 12-time All Star who spent most of his career with the New York Mets (where he was playing when this episode aired). Piazza was elected to the Baseball Hall of Fame in 2016. There are several points of sports fandom throughout *The West Wing*. The President is a die-hard fan of Notre Dame (his alma mater); Toby is a New York Yankees fan (and his ex-wife, the Congresswoman from Maryland, is an Orioles fan); Josh Lyman is a Mets fan.

[487] The most famous talking filibusters since *The West Wing* are the filibuster of TARP by Senator Bernie Sanders (I-VT) and of the Patient Protection and Affordable Care Act by Senator Ted Cruz (R-TX). Sanders' filibuster was a long speech against the bailout of the financial sector; Cruz's filibuster included Dr. Seuss's *Green Eggs and Ham*.

[488] Having given many lectures during my academic career, speaking without pause for longer than an hour is grueling.

[489] It's not plausible to read a whole book by Dickens as a part of a filibuster. The audiobook of *David Copperfield* (recorded by Richard Armitage) is 36.5 hours, but we see him reading other books.

[490] The intern, Winifred Hooper, is right, but given what we know about Sam's intellectual character, he should know better.

[491] The awareness of autism at the time this episode aired was low. This changed with increased diagnosis in the years since. Stackhouse mentions the "staggeringly high number of cases in which autism is misdiagnosed" and (at the time this aired) misdiagnosed autism posed a serious problem in pediatrics.

[492] The exchange is homophobic, though Leo notes this homophobia in his rejoinder, illustrating some self-awareness.

[493] Ainsley mentions Rebecca Walker, Gloria Steinem, Ann Coulter, and Naomi Wolf are going to be on the panel. All are real people. Walker is interviewed by *The West Wing Weekly* about the Equal Rights Amendment.
The West Wing Weekly. Feb 14, 2017. "2.18: 17 People (with Richard Schiff, Emily Procter, Rebecca Walker, and more)."

[494] It isn't plausible *The West Wing* staff would write this speech without comedians contracted to help.

[495] Maher has never hosted the White House Correspondents Dinner.

[496] This comes up throughout the show. Doctor-patient confidentiality and attorney-client privilege are standard. *The West Wing* illustrates similar privileges more specific to the White House. The Secret Service cannot comment on the behavior of the protectee, as we see with Gina Toscano (1.16 and 1.18). The analogous case is between Charlie and the President, though Charlie would be bound by a Non-Disclosure Agreement, not a professional obligation.

[497] Sam mentions Phyllis Schlafly, a famous opponent of the Equal Rights Amendment.

[498] Hrishi Hirway notes when Bartlet starts yelling here, it's because his rationalizations for concealing his illness have collapsed.

The West Wing Weekly. Feb 14, 2017. "2.18: 17 People (with Richard Schiff, Emily Procter, Rebecca Walker, and more."

[499] The Pay Equity Act was passed in 1963 but had problems with enforceability as non-disclosure of pay rates make filing a suit difficult. The law was reinforced in 2009 with the Lilly Ledbetter Fair Pay Act, which allowed for recourse under federal non-discrimination law.

[500] It's possible the anesthesiologist could leak this information, but it would breach doctor-patient confidentiality. It would expose the anesthesiologist to a lawsuit from Bartlet and disciplinary action from the licensing board. Sorkin pays a lot of attention to attorney-client privilege but overlooks doctor-patient confidentiality throughout this arc.

[501] This is an odd position and would indicate opposition to the Civil Rights Act and the Voting Rights Act.

[502] Lots of people (including Joey Lucas) note the romantic tension between Josh and Donna. This is an important moment of Josh and Donna themselves acknowledging it.

[503] Schiff notes in *The West Wing Weekly* episode that the last shot, with Leo closing the door as the President and Charlie are in the background, is borrowed from *The Godfather*.

[504] This is a remarkable pace unmatched in American history. The Office of White House Counsel was created in 1943 (under President Franklin Roosevelt). There are some cases where a President went through three or four White House Counsels in a short period. Lyndon Johnson had four over a period from 1964-66, though slightly more than two years. Ford had four from 1974-75, but Philip Buchen served the entire time. Multiple people can hold the office of White House Counsel at the same time.

[505] This is the second instance where the White House Counsel gets suddenly violent, as Tribbey is constantly explosive and belligerent, including bursting into Leo's office with a cricket bat.

[506] This plotline is almost certainly a direct reference to the Mexican peso crisis of 1994, because Josh invokes the Mexican government's refusal to slowly devalue the peso. The details of that crisis are complicated (and involve the Mexican government creating economic instruments denominated in pesos but paid out in US dollars, as well as domestic political unrest and other factors), but the United States did intervene with a bailout of around $50B (about $98.7B, adjusted to 2022 dollars).

[507] Babish is not a medical expert, so it makes sense he does not use the technical terminology. What he's referring to here could include either absence seizures (historically "Petit mal seizures") or focal onset impaired awareness seizures (historically "complex partial seizures"). Both can occur in multiple sclerosis patients and do occur at higher rates than in the general population; however, they are not symptomatic of multiple sclerosis.

[508] There is a question as to whether the White House Counsel exchanges are covered by executive privilege, rather than attorney client privilege, but the scope of executive privilege is vague.

[509] This has come up several times during the various criminal investigations into Donald Trump. Trump's legal team has attempted to bar testimony from White House council Pat Cipollone and others. Attorney-client privilege does not apply, and Trump's legal team has instead invoked executive privilege. This defense has not been successful.

Katherine Faulder, Olivia Rubin, and Josh Santucci. Mar 6, 2023. "Trump fighting to bar use of White House council's grand jury testimony in special prosecutor probe." *ABC News*.

[510] Josh goes the optimistic route, talking about Lend-Lease and support for allied powers against the Nazis, but the issue is simpler. The United States lends money to countries and industries because maintaining economic stability is necessary both to prevent spiraling economic conditions (in our self-interest) and serious harm to the most vulnerable people (the morally right thing to do).

511 One serious deficiency is that "tough love" means massive suffering for people in the country and has minimal consequence for those in power. Showing "tough love" to Mexico harms Mexican people, not the Mexican government.

512 Donna mentions "Whittaker Chambers and the secret pumpkin," the second reference to the secret pumpkin story regarding exchange of documents and Soviet espionage. The first reference is in the pilot.

513 C.J. invokes *Spartacus*. "I am Spartacus."

514 The Office of the Special Counsel is a separate office for politically sensitive investigations handled independently of the Department of Justice (because, while it is supposed to be independent, the Attorney General is a political appointee). The OSC has independent powers and protections laid out by statute, including specific requirements for fighting the Special Counsel. The OSC was first used to investigate a President in the Watergate scandal and many of the modern OSC reforms developed following Watergate. The OSC investigated the Iran-Contra affair (under Reagan) and the Whitewater and eventual sex scandal (under Clinton); more recently, the OSC has been used to handle a range of investigations into President Trump, including the allegations of Russian influence in the 2016 election (by Robert Mueller) and the January 6, 2021, Capitol attack and classified documents (by Jack Smith). A recent finding by the district court Judge Aileen Cannon found Smith's appointment to be illegal; we are waiting on appeals of that ruling.

515 Americans for Tax Justice is fictional, but based on Citizens for Tax Justice, a political advocacy organization founded in 1979.

516 The Progressive Caucus is within the Democratic Caucus. It was created in 1991 and is usually considered the left-most wing of congressional Democrats.

517 This is an odd thing for Leo to say, because (when the episode was written) there was a master settlement with tobacco companies and 46 states (as well as Puerto Rico, D.C., and four other territories), including funding and directing the Tobacco Center, the 1998 Master Settlement Agreement. These arcs proceed as though civil litigation against the tobacco companies was unwinnable, but both public and private civil lawsuits were well-established by 2000. Notably, many of the public lawsuits came from state Attorneys General, not the federal government. It's possible that Sorkin modeled parts of this discussion over the proposed 1997 settlement legislation prior to the MSA, but most of this discussion is not factually or legally well-grounded.
https://www.naag.org/our-work/naag-center-for-tobacco-and-public-health/

518 "I pay more in taxes" is a specious argument; extremely wealthy people can pay far more in taxes (as a total figure) while paying less as a percentage of income. Tax policy is one area where *The West Wing* is frequently fast-and-loose.

519 I am skeptical of this line, though it motivates Babish's interactions with the First Lady. Her medical background creates a special legal exposure in the scandal. Medical forms signed for college admissions aren't subject to penalty in the event of omission, unless that omission turns out to be relevant to the purpose of the document. Unlike lying about one's health in a deposition or on an insurance form, such forms aren't subject to perjury. However, Babish (correctly) notes that Dr. Bartlet has violated rules of medical ethics by treating her husband. AMA Code of Ethics prohibits doctors from treating family members except in (a) an emergency or (b) for acute, short term conditions. Bartlet's relapsing/remitting multiple sclerosis doesn't meet those exceptions.

520 The show refers to Betaseron, a brand name for interferon beta 1b. It is standard treatment for multiple sclerosis, modulating immune response and especially effective in relapsing/remitting cases like President Bartlet's.

521 This isn't true. There have been a handful of instances of injury due to space debris, including an incident where a Japanese boat was struck by a satellite, injuring several sailors. In 2002, a six-year-old Chinese boy was struck by a satellite; he suffered a minor head injury and a broken toe.

[522] The intersection of 18th St. SE and Potomac Ave. SE is next to the congressional cemetery. It is an odd place for Mrs. Landingham to be driving back to the White House, since the major road is Pennsylvania Ave. (several blocks over).

[523] The National MS Society and doctors who work on the illness praised the show for informing the public about the disease. Many patients do not disclose a multiple sclerosis diagnosis because of widespread public misunderstanding of the illness.
Barbara Vancheri. May 16, 2001. "*The West Wing* lauded for accurately portraying MS story line." *The Pittsburgh Post-Gazette.* https://old.post-gazette.com/tv/20010516westwing2.asp
Randy Dotinga. November 26, 2001. "MS Goes 'West'." *HealthScoutNews.* http://mult-sclerosis.org/news/Nov2001/WestWingDepictionOfMSUnrealistic.html

[524] The political figures cited here are fictional, though the name Dessalines is the surname of Emperor Jacques I, the first leader of Haiti following the revolution and independence from France.

[525] C.J. points out "Ted Baxter" (as an example of a dumb reporter) would ask about reelection; Baxter is the fictional television personality from *The Mary Tyler Moore Show.*

[526] Williams appears as Robbie Mosley in eight episodes of *The West Wing*; this is the first time he is a major source of dialogue with Leo and the President.

[527] In 1991, the Haitian military staged a coup to depose President Aristide (the first democratically elected President); the United States was involved in restoring Aristide to power in '94. The CIA also contributed to the funding of the anti-Aristide movement. Aristide was forced into exile in 2004 following another coup and returned in 2011. He was put under house arrest in 2014. United States history in Haiti is complicated, to put it mildly.

[528] Attacks on diplomatic missions occur periodically; however, such attacks are typically conducted by non-state actors (terrorists; drug cartels; etc.) rather than the official military of a government.

[529] "Hackett" is a name Sorkin uses frequently. Rear Admiral Hackett (Madison Mason) takes over as physician to the President after the death of Morris Tolliver, appearing only in "He Shall From Time to Time..." (1.12).

[530] Rubinstein, Walden, and McGonagle only appear in this episode.

[531] See the extensive history at the CDC website.
https://www.cdc.gov/tobacco/data_statistics/sgr/history/index.htm

[532] Mrs. Landingham argues "Caesar's wife must be above repute" and the importance of avoiding even the appearance of impropriety.

[533] The official AMA guidance regarding treatment of family members prohibits Dr. Bartlet's conduct. Family members are generally prohibited from treating family members except in emergencies and for minor problems. Further, physicians who do treat family members are required to document extensively and consider the reluctance of patients to act against medical advice, especially when they have a close relationship (e.g., marriage).

[534] The American Medical Association code of ethics generally prohibits doctors treating family members, but many doctors do not adhere to the AMA code. Dr. Bartlet is an especially severe case because she's not a specialist in neurological conditions and because the treatment was complex and ongoing.
Mary Click. May 11, 2018. "Should Doctors Treat Family Members?" *The Hastings Center.* https://www.thehastingscenter.org/doctors-treat-family-members/

[535] The last two episodes of Season Two include climactic moments with virtually no dialogue. This final scene of 18th and Potomac is entirely without dialogue as Leo tells with the President that Mrs. Landingham is dead. In "Two Cathedrals," the extended sequence of the President driving to the press conference is without dialogue, as Dire Straits' "Brothers in Arms" plays. Some may think this is rare for Sorkin, but not as much as one might think. He does this in the climactic sequence of the season three finale Posse Comitatus (3.22), as well.

[536] Perry appears only in this episode. Ornstein appears again in *A Good Day* (6.17).

[537] Mr. Bartlet mentions she "will be taking over for Mrs. Tillinghouse." Tillinghouse is a name that Sorkin uses often, including as the name of a Southern Democratic member of Congress in "Five Votes Down" (1.04).

[538] This is Lynch's second and final appearance in *The West Wing*.

[539] The reading is taken from the King James Version.

[540] Greene was an English novelist whose work deals heavily with his Catholicism and theological questions. His most prominent religious works includes *Brighton Rock* (1938), *The Power and The Glory* (1940), and *The Heart of the Matter* (1948). I cannot locate the quote to figure out if it is sarcastic; given the arc of Greene's work, which is critical of this sort of devotion, he probably is sarcastic just as Bartlet is.

[541] The company is called "Atlantic," a common Sorkin name.

[542] I don't understand why Donna, Josh's assistant, is giving this briefing; it should be given by an expert from the NOAA or the National Weather Service.

[543] Bartlet points out the professor "banned *Fahrenheit 451*, which is about banning books."

[544] Sorkin is clear in interviews that this is in Bartlet's mind; Mrs. Landingham is not a ghost.

[545] Samuel W. Rushay, Jr. 2012. "The President is Very Acutely Ill." *Prologue Magazine* 44(2).

[546] Kenneth R. Crispell and Carlos F. Gomez. 1988. *Hidden Illness in the White House*. Duke University Press.

[547] This defense has come up in many public commentaries on the mental health of both Presidents Trump and Biden. In both cases, concerns about fitness don't require speculating on pathology. As with Goldwater, the issue is behavior. Whether the behavior is the result of underlying pathology doesn't matter.

[548] The most striking illustration here is the idea that Sam's friendship with Laurie would be a political scandal. Set that in contrast to former-President Trump's actual affairs with adult performers (Stormy Daniels and Karen McDougal) or the court-proven allegations of sexual assault; political gravity is different.

[549] Aaron Sorkin. Jul 21, 2024. "How I Would Script This Moment for Biden and the Democrats." *The New York Times*.

[550] Whether Sorkin wrote the op-ed before Biden withdrew is unclear, but since the whole predicate for the piece is Biden's withdrawal, it's irrelevant.

[551] There are "jump the shark" moments later in the show, and in other parts of Sorkin's world.

[552] Schlamme's interview on the "In the Shadow of Two Gunman, Part One" episode of *The West Wing Weekly*.

[553] Page 12, emphasis Fukuyama's.

[554] Timothy Snyder's On Tyranny (2017) revisits the historiography of the 20th century in terms of this democratic backsliding. Snyder and Fukuyama have engaged in interesting and (in my opinion) illuminating conversation on the topic; Fukuyama is still optimistic, as in his 2022 piece, "More Proof That This Really Is the End of History" in *The Atlantic*.

[555] Arguably, popularity is power in liberal democracy. But this is a longer, more complicated point about how to build safeguards in a liberal democratic society to protect minority communities.

Other Riverdale Avenue Books Binge Watcher's Guides You Might Like

The Binge Watcher's Guide to Doctor Who:
A History of the Doctor Who and the First Female Doctor
By Mackenzie Flohr

The Binge Watcher's Guide to the Films of Harry Potter
An Unauthorized Guide
By Cecilia Tan

The Binge Watcher's Guide to The Handmaid's Tale
An Unofficial Companion
By Jamie K. Schmidt

The Binge Watcher's Guide to Black Mirror:
An Unofficial Companion
By Marc W. Polite

The Binge Watcher's Guide to The Twilight Zone:
An Unofficial Journey
By Jason Trussell

The Binge Watcher's Guide to Riverdale
By Melissa Ford Luken

The Binge Watcher's Guide to Supernatural
By Jessica Mason

The Binge Watcher's Guide to The Golden Girls
By Marissa DeAngelis

The Binge Watcher's Guide to The Marvel Universe
By Jessica Mason

www.ingramcontent.com/pod-product-compliance
Lightning Source LLC
Chambersburg PA
CBHW071017280326
41935CB00011B/1386